Who Gets In?

REBECCA ZWICK

# Who Gets In?

*Strategies for Fair and Effective College Admissions*

 Harvard University Press

Cambridge, Massachusetts, and London, England

2017

First printing

*Library of Congress Cataloging-in-Publication Data*

Names: Zwick, Rebecca, author.
Title: Who gets in? : strategies for fair and effective college admissions /
    Rebecca Zwick.
Description: Cambridge, Massachusetts : Harvard University Press, 2017. |
    Includes bibliographical references and indexes.
Identifiers: LCCN 2016041943 | ISBN 9780674971912 (alk. paper)
Subjects: LCSH: Universities and colleges—Admission. | Universities and colleges—
    United States—Administration. | College choice—United States.
Classification: LCC LB2351.2 .Z95 2017 | DDC 378.1/610973—dc23
    LC record available at https://lccn.loc.gov/2016041943

*To Gregg*

# Contents

# Preface

Getting into college in America is remarkably easy. We have over a thousand community colleges, most of which take all comers, and more than half of our four-year institutions have admission rates of 75 percent or higher. But in our consumer-oriented society, we are obsessed with the best. And it's assumed that the best are those with the lowest acceptance rates. Along with reports on the best cars and the best toasters, we can find ratings and rankings of American educational institutions. A quick Web search reveals that Harvard and Yale have granted degrees to the largest number of U.S. presidents and that Harvard and Stanford have hatched the largest number of Fortune 500 executives. The ubiquitous *US News & World Report* ranking (simultaneously deplored and worshipped by universities) currently tells us that Princeton and Harvard are the best national universities. In 2015, Princeton, Harvard, Yale, and Stanford all had admission rates below 7.5 percent. As applications to the top-rated schools increase, the admission rates plunge, which boosts the demand even more, producing the competitive frenzy we see today. More than ever before, admission to the most prestigious colleges is a treasured good.

I have thought about college and university admissions from many angles. Like countless others, I've been on the receiving end of admissions decisions. And in a dozen years as a faculty member at the Gevirtz Graduate School of Education at the University of California, Santa Barbara, I participated in making admissions decisions. During this time, I also conducted research on admissions and served on advisory committees for the College Board, where some of my fellow committee members were admissions directors and high school counselors, providing yet another perspective. Finally, in more than 20 years as a researcher at ETS, I have studied college, graduate school, and professional school admissions tests.

In *Who Gets In? Strategies for Fair and Effective College Admissions,* I consider the equitability and effectiveness of college admissions systems. (I use "college" and "university" interchangeably in most cases.) I explore the missions and admissions policies of today's colleges and examine various definitions of fairness. I use analyses of nationally representative survey data from applicants to the nations' top schools to study the impact of college admissions procedures based on ranking, lotteries, and techniques borrowed from operations research. I examine an array of admissions criteria, including high school grades, admissions test scores, race, socioeconomic status, and students' academic aspirations.

In discussing the degree to which various groups have access to higher education, there are many important applicant characteristics that I do not explicitly consider. For example, I do not discuss issues that are unique to applicants who have disabilities, lack fluency in English, or are the first in their families to attend college, and I address gender issues only briefly. Instead, I have chosen to focus on the representation of historically excluded ethnic and socioeconomic groups, which I consider the most pressing issue in college admissions today.

Inevitably, this book contains many discussions and analyses based on admissions tests. And because I have spent the last three decades either working for Educational Testing Service or teaching about testing and educational research at the University of California, Santa Barbara, readers may wonder about my position on standardized tests. I'm not an unabashed proponent, nor do I fit the definition of a testing expert proposed by Chester Finn, president emeritus of the Thomas B. Fordham Foundation—"a person with a PhD who has the reputation of knowing something about testing but who has never met any test that he thinks should actually be used for any real purpose." Unlike these alleged experts, I am not dismissive of the potential value of tests. In the absence of comprehensive evidence about a test's value, I am neither a believer nor a disbeliever.

Although the public conversation about testing tends to be polarized—commentators are expected to be unambiguously pro or con—there's no logical reason this should be so. Asking whether standardized tests are good is much like asking whether cars are good. If they're constructed well and used intelligently, they can be very valuable. Some are just plain bad. Even good ones can be harmful if misused. None are perfectly reliable. The decision to use a particular admissions criterion, whether it be tests, grades, income, or grit, can be evaluated in terms of its fairness and effectiveness, and that is the territory explored in *Who Gets In?*

## A Note about Racial and Ethnic Designations

I have not drawn a sharp distinction between the terms "race" and "ethnicity," though this distinction is considered important by some scholars. I often use the term "ethnic groups" as a shorthand for "groups defined on the basis of race and ethnic background." Publications and data sources differ widely in their treatment of racial and ethnic designations, not only in terms of labels, but in terms of how each group should be defined, and how refined the classification should be. In referring to racial and ethnic groups in this book, I have generally maintained the group labels used in the original sources of data. (This results in some inconsistencies; for example, I use both "Asian" and "Asian-American.") Because of U.S. Department of Education data security regulations, which prohibit reporting results for very small groups, I was required to combine certain groups in reporting my analyses of data from the Education Longitudinal Study of 2002 (ELS:2002). Therefore, in most cases I combined results for American Indian, Hispanic, and Black students under the label "underrepresented minorities" (a common practice in educational research). The scarcity of students in these three groups among the applicants to competitive colleges—and even more so among the enrollees in these schools—is a finding in itself.

## Analysis Details

I have created an online appendix that contains technical information that may be of interest to some readers. The appendix includes detail about the ELS dataset and lists all the ELS variables that were used in my analyses. Computational details are provided, along with information about sampling weights, standard errors, and sample sizes. In particular, for all tables in this book, further details, including sample sizes, standard deviations, and information on missing data, can be found in this online appendix. The appendix is available at the *Who Gets In?* page on the Harvard University Press website, http://www.hup.harvard.edu.

The opinions I have expressed in this book are my own and not necessarily those of Educational Testing Service.

Who Gets In?

# Introduction

> The first question to ask about selective admissions is why it should be
> selective at all. Most people feel ambivalent about selectivity. On one
> side, we laud excellence . . . and endorse admissions on the basis of
> merit rather than ascriptive characteristics. On the other, we worry
> that a merit system and educational stratification may breed a
> privileged caste.
>
> —*Robert Klitgaard*

On a public radio show some time ago, the featured guest lamented that debates about college admissions are often cast as a question of who should be
allowed to occupy the places around the table. Instead, she said, we should
think about adding more chairs. But what if there are no more chairs? This
is the reality of college admissions at selective institutions. When there are
limits on a resource—in this case, places in a school—it's a zero-sum game:
Including one person means excluding another.

Controversies about college admissions are never far from the public eye.
The use of racial preferences in admissions, for example, has been an incendiary topic for the last five decades. In late 2015 the Supreme Court
reconsidered the case of *Fisher v. University of Texas at Austin,* a challenge to
the university's affirmative action admissions policy that was originally
heard in 2013 and then remanded to a lower court. To the surprise of many,
the Court ruled in favor of the university, permitting its affirmative action
efforts to continue. In its opinion, issued in 2016, the Court systematically
rejected Fisher's arguments, including her claim that race-neutral methods
could have been used to meet the university's diversity goals.[1]

Another ongoing source of conflict in admissions policy is the role of
standardized admissions tests—the SAT and its Iowa cousin, the ACT. Do
these tests measure anything useful? Are they fair? The editor of a 2012 book,

*SAT Wars,* called the SAT "a more reliable proxy for privilege than for college performance" and claimed that the use of standardized admissions tests "transmits social biases [and] is a type of social Darwinism."[2] Lending a British perspective, *The Economist* recently suggested that to increase the fairness of college admissions policy in the United States, "intelligence tests should be more widely used,"[3] a proposal that is unlikely to win much enthusiasm this side of the Atlantic, where the aversion to IQ tests far outweighs criticism of admissions tests. A supposedly less contentious approach to admissions, rediscovered with astonishing regularity, is the lottery. According to one proponent, lottery admissions would take the pressure off potential applicants: They wouldn't need to excel—they'd just need to be lucky."[4]

From today's vantage point, it is interesting to consider that, until the late 1800s, American postsecondary institutions were passive participants in the admissions process. According to Harold Wechsler, a historian of education, colleges typically "waited for students to present themselves for examination by the faculty."[5] Initially these exams were oral, but by the late nineteenth century, many schools had switched to written tests. Each school had its own unique examination process, which made life difficult for students who applied to more than one institution. A turning point in college admissions occurred in 1870 when the University of Michigan initiated a policy of inspecting feeder high schools and waiving entrance exams for graduates of approved schools. (Interestingly, this transition took place at the same time as another monumental change: the admission of women to the university.) These students were granted certificates and automatically admitted to the freshman class. This certificate system spread to other institutions, eventually becoming the most prevalent method of college admission in the United States.[6]

On the face of it, the certificate system would seem to be far less stressful for students than today's high-pressure admissions competition. Apparently, however, the system was not well liked by Michigan students, who feared that "without entrance examinations, teachers and students had become more lax in their preparation," degrading the quality of the student body—an intriguing contrast with today's widespread opposition to admissions tests.[7] Students also regarded the policy as unfair because it allowed deficient students from good high schools to be automatically admitted to the university, while accomplished students from poor high schools were still required to take entrance exams. Nevertheless, the certificate system thrived and spread to most American colleges by 1915. The holdouts tended to be elite schools like Harvard and Yale, which continued to require entrance exams.

Another milestone occurred in 1900, when the leaders of 12 colleges and universities formed the College Entrance Examination Board, which was to create a common system of admissions tests. (Apparently the negotiations did not go smoothly: Nicholas Murray Butler, who was soon to become the president of Columbia, described it as trench warfare without the poison gas.)[8] The Board's essay examinations were to be administered by the member institutions and scored centrally by the Board. A sample botany question: "Give an account of the life-history of a fern. (Illustrate by sketches.)"[9] A geography question asked the candidate to "contrast, as to several important features, a young with an old river valley."[10]

Complex admissions systems involving both academic and nonacademic criteria did not evolve until after World War I.[11] Another postwar development was the first administration of the Scholastic Aptitude Test, given in 1926 to about 8,000 candidates. The ACT, a latecomer to the admissions scene, was first administered in 1959 to about 75,000 students.

Today's admissions climate is vastly different from that of the mid-twentieth century. Of the members of the high school class of 2015, about 1.7 million took the SAT and 1.9 million took the ACT.[12] (Some took both tests.) Aided by the Common Application, which allows access to more than 600 colleges and universities with a single application, American students submitted 9.2 million applications to undergraduate institutions in the 2013–2014 academic year.[13] More than one-third of 2015 college freshman had applied to seven or more schools.[14] Words like "frenzy and "rat race" often crop up in discussions of college admissions, and a recent opinion piece referred to the current process as "a mutant version of the 'Hunger Games'"—a fictitious dystopian event in which teens must fight to the death.[15]

Just how hard is it to get into college in America today? The answer may be surprising to families caught up in the college admissions whirlwind. There are about 4,300 degree-granting postsecondary institutions in the United States that enroll first-year undergraduates, about 2,600 of which are four-year schools. As of 2014, 29% of the four-year institutions were "open admissions"—that is, they accepted all applicants. Another 26% accepted three-quarters or more of their applicants. Only 13% of four-year institutions accepted fewer than half of those who applied. The results for two-year schools are even more striking. Nearly all public two-year institutions (98%) had a policy of accepting every applicant.[16]

As these statistics show, academic obstacles to a college education are far less significant than is often believed. However, many applicants are aiming for more than a "store brand" college education—they hope to get into a top "name brand" college. And these institutions do indeed have daunting admissions statistics. In 2016, Harvard's admission rate dropped to an all-time low of 5.2%, still a bit more generous than Stanford's 4.7% acceptance rate.[17]

And of course, the cost of a college education can be a serious impediment to access. According to U.S. Department of Education figures for the 2014–2015 academic year (which do not take financial aid into account), the annual tuition and fees for an in-state student at a four-year public institution averaged about $7,900. For private nonprofit four-year institutions, the average cost was about $25,500. Two-year public and private institutions cost roughly half as much per year as their four-year counterparts. For public and private nonprofit schools, tuition and fees have increased about 3% since 2012–2013 (taking inflation into account). In addition, room and board, books, and supplies cost nearly $10,500, on average.[18] Although many elite colleges offer generous financial aid packages, low-income students are greatly underrepresented in these schools, as we will discuss in later chapters.[19]

## The College Selection Process

When we consider college admissions, we tend to focus on the screening practices that take place at the institutional level. But some of the most significant selection processes occur before the candidate even decides to apply. One of these is self-selection: If a student feels uncomfortable in big classes, she won't apply to schools in which large lectures are common. If a student wishes to be close to—or far from—his family, he'll pick a school accordingly. While these kinds of decisions may be entirely benign, some prior selection processes are more insidious. In his landmark monograph *College Admissions and the Public Interest*, first published in 1966, B. Alden Thresher, a former MIT admissions director, argued that "most of the real screening" occurs through "accidents of socioeconomic origins, early environment, and the various levels of aspiration habitually characterizing particular groups and subcultures. . . . The determining factors that control entry into higher education are rooted in the home and school environment of children from infancy on."[20] A succinct description of this phenomenon comes from Mitchell Stevens, who conducted a sociological study of admissions in 2000. As he describes it, candidates are "delivered to the point of application by social systems that send children from different groups to this particular destination at different rates."[21]

Stevens vividly describes the way these social forces play out at a small liberal arts college (not identified by Stevens but subsequently "outed" as Hamilton College).[22] The classic privileged student has typically benefited from consistently good housing, nutrition, and medical care. She has parents who actively cultivated her abilities and knew how to wield influence with school system officials. She has attended academically rigorous schools with a wide range of honors courses and extracurricular activities—including athletic programs, which can be particularly relevant to college admission.[23] She also has a savvy high school guidance counselor who "has a thing going" with the college admissions office. Students with fewer advantages may not consider applying to college or may even be actively discouraged from doing so.

Clearly, race, as well as socioeconomic status, plays a role in determining whether students are "delivered" to academia—and to which gates. One piece of evidence is the ethnic and socioeconomic disparity in high school graduation rates. In 2014 the public high school graduation rate was only about 70% for American Indian students, 73% for Black students, and 76% for Hispanic students, compared to 87% for Whites and 89% for Asian Americans. Among "economically disadvantaged" students, the graduation rate was about 75%.[24]

Despite the substantial impact of these prior selection processes, single-digit admission rates are testimony to the fact that demand far exceeds supply at some colleges and universities. What criteria are most often used in determining who gets admitted? One source of information is the *State of College Admission* report issued by the National Association for College Admission Counseling (NACAC). Each year, NACAC surveys institutions to gather information on college applications, admissions decisions, enrollment, and admissions office operations. (Results need to be interpreted cautiously because response rates are low.)

The *2015 State of College Admission* report includes results from surveys conducted in 2014 and 2015. In 2014, 1,253 four-year postsecondary institutions that were NACAC members were asked to participate in the survey; 27% did so. In 2015, 1,380 institutions were invited; 50% responded. In both years, larger institutions were more likely to respond.[25] Institutions were asked to rate potential admissions criteria as being of considerable, moderate, limited, or no importance. In terms of the percentage answering "considerable importance," the top four criteria were "grades in college prep courses" (79%), "grades in all courses" (60%), "strength of curriculum" (60%), and "admission test scores (SAT, ACT)" (56%). The factors most likely to be rated as being of no importance were scores on the SAT Subject Tests, state graduation exam scores, and "portfolio," which refers to supplementary materials submitted by applicants.[26] Academic performance in college preparatory courses has been consistently rated as the top factor in admission decisions since 1993, with about 80 percent of colleges rating it as considerably important. Class rank, however, has declined in importance over the years; in the most recent report, only 14% of schools rating it as considerably important.[27] So while students' grades are viewed as highly important, their relative position in their graduating class is not.

In theory, academic criteria need not be involved at all in allocating scarce higher education opportunities. A possible, but highly unpalatable, solution would be to raise the cost of attending these institutions to the point where supply and demand were equal. In his 1985 treatise on admission to selective institutions, Harvard economist Robert Klitgaard presents an amusing "fable" in which admission to Harvard is accomplished through an auction. The auction solves the problem of excess demand but, needless to say, creates a few problems of its own.[28] At the other extreme, a "first come, first served" policy or a lottery could be used to select the entering class. What, then, is the justification for using academic accomplishments as a basis for college admission? From an institutional perspective, one commonsense reason for considering such factors as grades and test scores is to attempt to identify candidates who are likely to be able to do the academic work required of them. In this era of rising costs, the strategy of admitting marginally qualified students and then flunking them out as necessary—referred to by one admissions director as the "Darwinian, sink or swim" approach—is not in favor at selective institutions.[29] Picking academically qualified students can be viewed as simply a matter of efficient resource utilization.

The explanation offered by Thresher for selectivity in admissions is far less benign: "Some professors . . . can never quite reconcile themselves to the fact that some students are better than others. If we could only chloroform all but the top 1 percent, how ideal the world would be!" Thresher goes on to describe how exclusivity simplifies the professor's job: "It is easy for selection to become, to a degree, a substitute for education. A student body so outstanding in its talents that it shines under any kind of educational process may have the effect of reducing the motivation for improving that process.... If a good supply of [students], able and eager, is deposited annually at [the professor's] door, he need give little thought to improving the quality of the educational process."[30] Because low admission rates and high average SAT scores have come to be seen as measures of institutional quality, the very exclusivity of a college can then become a major drawing card as well.

## Allocating Educational Opportunity

The question of how to distribute opportunities for a college education has generated innumerable academic treatises, court cases, and political screeds. A policy that is compatible with a particular zeitgeist may meet with rejection at a later time, and a process that seems fair in the abstract may seem less so in practice. A further complicating factor is that diversity and fairness goals are often seen as antithetical to the maintenance of academic excellence. For example, UCLA law professor and vocal affirmative action opponent Richard Sander concluded in a 2012 report that the "only significant, tangible effect" of UCLA's attempts to increase the representation of African American students through "holistic admissions" was a "reduction in the proportion of academically gifted students—of all races—admitted by the university."[31] And in a piece called "The Performance-Diversity Tradeoff in Admission Testing," psychologist Paul Sackett noted that while emphasizing test scores is disadvantageous to African Americans and Hispanics, "decreasing emphasis on the use of tests in the interest of achieving a diverse group of selectees often results in a substantial reduction in the performance gains that can be recognized through test use."[32]

In evaluating the fairness and effectiveness of a selection procedure, it is important to consider the components of the entire admissions system. At the core is an *admissions policy*, which embodies a particular philosophy and, in many cases, a particular set of institutional objectives. For example, does the institution seek primarily to nurture talent, or does it also strive to foster social mobility? Does it hope to attract students with a wide variety of academic goals, or does it focus on specific fields of study? Another characteristic of an admissions system is the type of *student data* that is gathered for purposes of making an admissions decision. Some institutions require no more than evidence of high school graduation (if that); others request extensive evidence of student accomplishments, including portfolios, auditions, or interviews. Students' demographic characteristics, personal attributes, family connections, and finances may be considered as well. Finally, what *procedures and decision criteria* are used to consider the student data and determine who gets admitted? The applicant data may be processed in a largely mechanical fashion at some universities, perhaps yielding a predicted first-year grade-point average (FGPA), or it may be the subject of intensive deliberations by an admissions committee. Decisions might be based on numerical cutoffs or might involve a consensus vote by a committee. Each of these components of the admissions system raises two key questions: Does it ultimately produce the desired entering class? Is it fair to individuals and groups?

Standardized admissions tests, of course, have featured prominently in the debate about what kind of data to consider in admissions. Opinions tend to be polarized. According to one proponent who has spent his career in the testing industry, "To argue against good testing . . . one needs to dismiss the idea that relevant information can lead to better decisions. This is a fundamentally weak position, no matter how often or how stridently it is stated."[33] Presenting an entirely opposite view is a letter to *Science* magazine that pronounced reliance on graduate admissions tests to be "scientifically unsound and socially reprehensible" and added that even if standardized testing could help identify promising candidates, "only a crude, backward society would actively seek to limit opportunity in this manner."[34] Occupying a middle ground, psychologist and intelligence theorist Robert Sternberg states that although they are not "horrible and evil," the standardized admissions tests used today are mired in the early twentieth century.[35]

Members of the public often consider standardized tests to be unfair because of the differences in average scores between White students and students of color and between students from high- and low-income families. The SAT in particular has been maligned as a wealth test, a crooked yardstick, and an obstacle to success for low-income students and people of color.[36] The existence of racial score gaps on the SAT has even been invoked as a raison d'être for affirmative action.[37] However, in the early to mid twentieth century, the SAT served as a gateway to elite colleges for applicants who didn't fit the Ivy League profile, and many today consider it to be an impartial gauge of student skills that improves the quality of admissions decisions. The ACT, though it also reflects racial and socioeconomic disparities, tends to draw much less controversy than the SAT, probably because it does not carry the same historical baggage. A key aspect of fairness in higher education admissions involves a determination of what role, if any, standardized tests should play in the process.

Some test critics, including Richard Atkinson, the former president of the University of California, have claimed that high school grades are less tied to socioeconomic status than are admissions test scores and that selecting students based on grades is therefore more equitable than test-based admissions. According to UC researchers, "high-school grades provide a fairer, more equitable and ultimately more meaningful basis for admissions decision-making."[38] My own research, however, has shown that high school grades reveal patterns of socioeconomic and ethnic-group differences that are fairly similar to those found in standardized test scores.[39] Other studies have shown that grades do not have equivalent meanings across schools (or even within them), are subject to inflation over time, and may be influenced by students' gender, personality, and behavior.[40]

Even among those who accept the legitimacy of admissions tests, the content that can appropriately be included in them continues to be a topic of debate: Should these exams be more like achievement tests, closely linked to the high school curriculum, as argued in 2001 by Richard Atkinson, or is fairness to minorities enhanced by using "aptitude tests that go beyond prior achievement," as claimed by cognitive psychologist David Lohman?[41] Although testing only school-based material may lend an appearance of fairness, scores on achievement-based tests often reflect large socioeconomic differences in educational quality, putting students from inferior schools at a disadvantage. As a recent report of the Programme for International Student Assessment (PISA) notes, "many countries . . . show a strong relationship between the socio-economic background of students and their success at school and, in some of these countries, the disparities are magnified by large variations in the schools' socio-economic backgrounds."[42]

Policy debates about test content can become quite specific. Consider the issue of whether to include writing skills in admissions tests. Back in 1996, a writing section was added to the Preliminary Scholastic Assessment Test / National Merit Scholarship Qualifying Test (PSAT / NMSQT), an exam typically taken by high school juniors as a practice test for the SAT and an opportunity to qualify as finalists for college scholarships. The writing component was added to settle a federal civil rights complaint by the American Civil Liberties Union and the National Center for Fair and Open Testing (FairTest). According to the 1994 complaint, the use of the test as part of the process for awarding National Merit Scholarships discriminated against girls.[43] This claim emerged from the finding that fewer girls than boys won National Merit Scholarships even though girls outnumbered boys among test takers and, on average, earned higher grades than boys in both high school and college. The addition of the writing section was intended to boost overall PSAT scores for girls, who generally perform better than boys on writing tests. Writing tests were also championed by former UC president Atkinson in the same 2001 speech in which he called for admissions tests to be more achievement-based.[44]

Ironically, however, the University of California had a role in nixing a plan to add a writing component to the SAT back in 1990. At that time a blue-ribbon panel, commissioned by the College Board and chaired by Harvard president Derek Bok and UC president David Gardner, was considering an overhaul of the SAT and other tests. Patrick Hayashi, a commission member from UC Berkeley, raised serious concerns that adding a writing component to the SAT would be unfair to Asian Americans and other minority groups.[45] In a memo to Gardner, Hayashi complained that the College Board had done "an abysmally poor job in examining the possible effects on non-native speakers."[46] These concerns, which were echoed by other California legislative and education officials, played a role in the College Board's decision against adding a writing component to the main part of the SAT at that time. It was not until 2005 that a writing test was added. Ironically, Asian Americans have scored higher than Whites, on average.[47] In yet another twist to the story, the SAT writing test became optional beginning in 2016.

What about abandoning standardized test scores entirely and using high school class rank to select an entering class? Admissions policies that embody this idea, called percent plans, mandate that students whose grades put them in the top ranks of their high schools be granted admission to an institution. (Other requirements, such as the completion of certain courses, may be included.) The plans are intended to foster diversity by requiring that a fixed percentage of students—those with the top high school grade-point averages, or GPAs—be admitted from each high school, regardless of its quality.

However, the percent plans, now operating in Texas, California, and Florida, have drawn fire not only from conservatives, who claim that these programs promote lower educational standards,[48] but from the civil rights community. In 2000, Mary Frances Berry, then the chair of the U.S. Commission on Civil Rights, wrote an opinion piece, "How Percentage Plans Keep Minority Students Out of College," in which she described the plans as public relations ploys that were ineffective substitutes for race-based affirmative action. The plans, she said, were also "pernicious" in that their success was "contingent upon the continued segregation of our public-school system."[49] That is, percent plans are advantageous to students of color only if these students are attending lower-quality high schools, where it is easier to make it into the top ranks. Percent plans have also been denounced for removing incentives for students and high schools to improve. And indeed, investigators at the National Bureau of Economic Research recently claimed that some Texas students are choosing to attend lower-achieving high schools to improve their chances of college admission, a behavior the researchers called "opportunistic downgrading." Although they conceded that the phenomenon was not widespread, the researchers concluded that "strategic high school choice tends to undermine the racial diversity goal of the top ten percent plan."[50]

Following the civil rights era, researchers in the fields of psychology and education proposed various statistical approaches for determining whether a given admissions process is fair. These attempts to invoke statistically based fairness criteria have not produced any breakthroughs, however. Each proposed fairness definition embodies its own particular set of values, and each has led to conflict. For example, as defined in some approaches, fairness can be achieved only through the use of admissions criteria that vary by group—say, one rule for women, one for men. This in turn violates a well-ingrained principle of fairness—that the rules of the game should be the same for all players.

This uniformity principle, of course, is also violated by various types of admissions preferences, including special admissions policies for athletes and children of prominent alumni or donors, as well as race-based affirmative action. Each of these departures from uniform admissions rules has been a chronic source of discord. Although race tends to be the more central issue in the United States, gender preferences have been used to counter the growing male-female imbalance on campus. (In 2014, 57% of U.S. undergraduates were women.)[51] About 15 years ago, the University of Georgia, where women constituted a sizable majority, gave a preference to men in making admissions decisions about borderline candidates.[52] The practice was ended in 1999, after a female applicant filed a lawsuit. The gender imbalance at American universities prompted some debate about the possibility of nationwide admissions preferences for men. One presenter at the 2000 annual NACAC meeting referred to affirmative action for men as "the issue that dare not speak its name."[53] Explicit gender preferences have been invoked outside the United States. A recent fairness controversy in China arose from the fact that women "have become victims of their own success" on the *gaokao,* the university admissions test that is administered nationwide. Because women tend to score higher, universities that want to equalize gender enrollment are apparently using more stringent cutoff scores for women than for men, leading, predictably, to protests from women's rights groups and their sympathizers.[54]

At the core of these many ongoing controversies is the fact that an admissions policy cannot be evaluated in a vacuum—it must be judged with reference to the mission of the institution and, more broadly, the ideals of the society at large. What is the purpose of a college education, and who should be eligible to receive one? Until these questions are addressed, no meaningful evaluation of an admissions system can take place. Clearly, no statistical rule can provide a satisfactory resolution to the complex task of defining fairness and effectiveness in admissions decisions. Although evaluating selection procedures may involve technical analyses, it will inevitably require value judgments as well. In this book, I will identify key dimensions of fairness and effectiveness in college admissions and will explore alternative perspectives on these issues.

Throughout the book, I will use analyses of actual student data from the Education Longitudinal Study of 2002 (ELS:2002), a survey conducted under the direction of the National Center for Education Statistics, to illustrate the implementation and outcomes of various admissions processes. This survey was "designed to monitor the transition of a national sample of young people as they progress from tenth grade through high school and on to postsecondary education and / or the world of work." The database includes records for more than 13,000 high school students who graduated in 2004.[55]

What makes this survey well suited to the present purpose is that it links students to colleges to which they applied, not merely colleges at which they were accepted. The database includes the applicants' admissions test scores, high school grades, socioeconomic status, race, and gender, along with information on their aspirations and plans for the future. Information about students' college grades, graduation rates, and postbaccalaureate attainment is also available. I used this unique database to try out competing admissions models. For example, what happens if you use test scores alone to select students? What if race or socioeconomic status is taken into account? What about a lottery? I then compared the resulting "entering classes" in terms of their demographic makeup and their academic accomplishments.

Some basic information about the ELS senior cohort appears in Tables I-1 through I-3. The results are weighted so as to represent the 2.5 million members of the nation's high school class of 2004 who ultimately attended at least one postsecondary institution.[56] The tables show the mean high school grade-point average (GPA) for academic courses and admissions test score for groups defined by gender, race, and socioeconomic status (SES). The ELS database includes various kinds of admissions test scores. The one I used in my analyses is the student's highest admissions test score, reported on the SAT scale. To obtain this value, ELS data analysts started with the student's most recent ACT or SAT score. ACT scores were converted to the approximately equivalent score on the SAT scale, which, in 2004, ranged from 400 to 1600 (for the sum of verbal and math scores). Then, for students who took both the SAT and the ACT, the higher score was selected. For example, if a student scored 1300 on the SAT and also took the ACT, receiving a score that converted to 1350, he would receive a value of 1350. Table I-1 shows GPA and admission test results for women and men. Women had an advantage on grades, while men had slightly higher test scores.

Tables I-2 and I-3 show that grades and test scores varied widely over ethnic and socioeconomic groups. The socioeconomic categories provided in the database were obtained by forming a composite of mother's and father's education, mother's and father's occupation, and family income, and then dividing the original ELS participants into four equal groups, called SES quartiles, based on these composite values. The highest socioeconomic group had an average GPA of 3.0 and an average test score of 1092, compared to 2.5 and 887 for the lowest group. The gaps between the highest- and lowest-performing ethnic groups (Asian and Black students) were even larger. One way to put the GPA and test-score differences onto the same scale is to translate them into standard deviation units. The standard deviation (SD) is a measure of how spread out a set of values is—in this case, GPAs or test scores. The SD for GPA was about 0.7 and the SD for test scores was about 187. Roughly speaking, this means that the average distance of a GPA value from its mean was 0.7 and the average distance of an admissions test score from its mean was 187. For GPA, the difference between the highest and lowest SES groups was three-quarters of an SD unit (0.75); for test score, it was 1.09 units. The largest ethnic-group difference was 0.96 for GPA and 1.28 for test score. Using well-recognized guidelines, differences of 0.8 standard deviation units or more are considered large in behavioral science research.[57] Although these ELS results are more than 10 years old, the patterns of achievement differences are very typical of those that have been found in the United States in recent years. We will explore these patterns in later chapters.

My analyses of admissions scenarios, which appear throughout the book, are based on a portion of the high school seniors of 2004—those who applied to one or more of the nation's selective colleges and universities. These 174 institutions were categorized as "most competitive" or "highly competitive" in the Barron's rating system, which classifies schools into six competitiveness levels. (I used the Barron's codes that were assigned in 2004 to match the senior year of the ELS cohort.) The schools in these top two levels had admission rates of 50% or less—sometimes much less—and accepted applicants with at least a B average in high school.[58] The schools in these categories include elite private schools (Harvard, Princeton, Yale), prestigious public universities (UC Berkeley, University of Michigan, University of Virginia), and top liberal arts schools (Amherst, Bowdoin, Swarthmore).

In Tables I-4 through I-6, I have provided summary information for the ELS senior cohort, the applicants to the top schools (who constitute roughly 20% of the cohort), and the students who actually enrolled in one of these schools, who represent 41% of those who applied. Table I-4 shows that the percentage of women fluctuates only slightly as we move from the senior cohort to the applicants and then the enrollees. As shown in Table I-5, the change in the ethnic composition of these groups is much more striking. Whereas 28% of the ELS senior cohort are American Indian, Black, or Hispanic— groups considered to be underrepresented in academia—only about 21% of the applicants and 12% of the enrollees are in these ethnic groups. Eighty-four percent of the enrollees are White or Asian. Even more noteworthy is the change in socioeconomic characteristics, shown in Table I-6. In the senior cohort, 31% of students were in the highest SES quartile and 19% were in the lowest.[59] But 54% of the applicants to the selective schools come from the top level, and only 8% from the lowest level. Among the enrollees, about 64% are from the highest level and only 4% are from the lowest level.

Using the information in Tables I-1 through I-6 as a backdrop, we can explore the demographic and academic results of applying various admissions rules to the applicant data. Of most interest are rules that match the actual enrollment rate of 41%. For example, suppose we rank-ordered the applicants by high school GPA and kept accepting them until the admission rate was 41%.[60] What would the resulting "class" look like? A variety of other criteria can be used to rank applicants. We will also consider results for a set of rules that admit only 10% of applicants and will examine rules that are not based on ranking at all.

A limitation that my ELS analyses share with most admissions research is that the distinction between admission and enrollment is not explicitly addressed: The characteristics of the ELS enrollees reflect not only the outcome of institutional decisions, but also the accepted applicants' own decisions about whether to attend. In the case of the hypothetical admissions scenarios, however, we can't know which of the "accepted" students would actually choose to attend. How do high school students decide whether to attend a college that has accepted them? According to a theoretical model proposed by economists Robert K. Toutkoushian and Michael B. Paulsen, students' ultimate enrollment decisions are based on essentially the same factors that contribute to their initial determinations about whether and where to apply to college.[61] Under this model, students evaluate the increased earnings potential that is expected to result from college attendance, along with the nonfinancial rewards, which include learning itself, as well as extracurricular activities and campus amenities. To evaluate each school they wish to consider, prospective applicants weigh these benefits against the cost of attendance, taking into account the available financial resources. They then apply to schools that exceed some desirability threshold, possibly limiting the number based on the cost of application and the perceived chance of acceptance. When applicants find out which schools accepted them, they choose to attend the most desirable one, using the same criteria invoked earlier. I don't explicitly consider the enrollment decision in my admissions scenarios, so when I refer to the selected students as an "entering class," I'm using the term as a convenient shorthand.

Of course, the ELS analyses are artificial in other respects as well. A large group of schools is being treated as though it were a single school. In reality, the applicants applied to 170 different schools and the enrolled students actually attended 160 different schools. Similarly, the "entering classes" selected in the admissions scenarios will have actually earned their college grades and degrees at a variety of schools. Finally, the admissions rules applied in this book are obviously much simpler than the typical admissions process. The selection models used here can be implemented in seconds by a computer. There are no applications, interviews, review committees, exceptions, appeals, or waiting lists. In fact, the analyses are not meant to mimic the complexities of actual admissions processes. The intention is to apply each rule in "pure" form to gain a better understanding of the undiluted impact of the admissions policy in question.

The nine chapters of this book are described below.

*Chapter 1: Evaluating the Fairness and Effectiveness of an Admissions System.* What does it mean to say that a set of admissions policies and procedures is fair, and what role does the institutional mission play in this determination? The admissions policies of institutions of higher education collectively embody a wide range of objectives. While expanding access or promoting socioeconomic mobility may be a priority for some schools, others seek to reward and nurture applicants who are especially academically talented or unusually dedicated. And while some goals seem quite sweeping and noble (maximizing the benefit to society as a whole), others are plainly practical (finding a trombonist for the band or a quarterback for the football team). What can be said about the legitimacy and fairness of these goals? Similarly, what does it mean for an admissions policy to be effective? What can statistical analysis contribute to the analysis of fairness and effectiveness?

*Chapter 2: Admissions Tests and High School Grades: What Do They Measure?* A College Board publication on admissions notes that every admissions philosophy "suggests an attribute on which prospective students may be evaluated or compared."[62] A corollary is that every student attribute or accomplishment that could potentially be considered in the admissions process is associated with a fairness debate. High school grades and admissions tests scores are repeatedly found to be the main factors considered in undergraduate admissions. Some educators have advocated placing greater emphasis on grades or eliminating tests entirely, claiming that high school grades are less highly correlated with socioeconomic status than are admissions test scores and are therefore more appropriate for use in the admissions process.[63] What do admissions tests and high school grades measure, and why do they sometimes tell a different story?

*Chapter 3: Performance Predictions and Academic Indexes.* Predictions of college performance are a feature of some admissions systems. Performance may be forecast through the use of statistical models or through more informal "clinical" approaches. Predictors typically include admissions test scores and high school grades, which are sometimes combined into an index score. Candidates whose predicted performance is high are more likely to be admitted. But some policymakers find any kind of statistical prediction to be objectionable on principle. And incorporating data that improves prediction accuracy—say, family income—can lead to decisions that are contrary to social goals. Are performance predictions a legitimate component of the admissions process, and if they are, what features should be included as predictors?

*Chapter 4: Admissions Preferences: Who Deserves a Boost?*    Race-based affirmative action admissions programs have been a lightning rod for controversy since they were first initiated in the civil rights era. Opponents argue that affirmative action is antithetical to the maintenance of academic excellence; proponents maintain that it is necessary to compensate for our nation's history of racial discrimination and to promote a more diverse educational environment. Those who favor affirmative action also point out that admissions preferences that are not academic in nature are routinely used by many institutions, such as preferences for athletes, veterans, legacies (children of alumni), and children of potential donors. Because the future of race-based affirmative action is viewed by many as hanging by a thread, proposals to give preference to applicants from lower-income families have attracted increasing attention. Can these socioeconomic affirmative action programs promote racial diversity as well?

*Chapter 5: Percent Plans and Other Test-Optional Admissions Programs.*    Admissions systems based on class rank, or percent plans, are now in effect in some form in Texas, Florida, and California. The primary goal of these plans is to facilitate ethnic and socioeconomic diversity. Students from impoverished schools who otherwise would not have a chance to attend a flagship institution are automatically admitted if they have completed course requirements and are in the top ranks of their graduating class. These plans are controversial, however, because of their exclusive focus on grades and because their success depends on the existence of racially and socioeconomically segregated schools. An overlapping development in college admissions has been the adoption of "test-optional" programs, which reduce or eliminate the use of standardized test scores as admissions criteria but may otherwise operate in fairly traditional ways. The test-optional admissions policies have also been promoted as a way to increase campus diversity. What are the pros and cons of deemphasizing or eliminating test scores in making admissions decisions?

*Chapter 6: Noncognitive Attributes: A New Frontier in College Admissions?*    Some researchers and university officials view "noncognitive measures"—personal attributes and talents outside the traditional cognitive domain—as a key innovation in college admissions, paving the way for a broader assessment of candidates and a concomitant increase in campus diversity. The factors designated as noncognitive range from run-of-the mill biographical data to student performance on tasks like creating an advertisement, designing a house, or building a Lego model. Certain noncognitive factors such as perseverance, motivation, and study skills appear to hold promise in the admissions context and may help to attract a more diverse student body. But there is historical precedent for using noncognitive measures in less benign ways. What is the current status of noncognitive factors in college admissions?

*Chapter 7: Casting Lots for College.* The idea of admitting students to college via lottery recurs with astonishing regularity. Within a single four-month period in 2012, it resurfaced twice—in the *Chronicle of Higher Education* and in the *Atlantic.*[64] At each of its rebirths, the lottery is proposed as a solution to the perplexing problem of how to equitably select students when places are limited. Is admission by lottery the ultimate in fairness because it does not distinguish among applicants, or is it unfair precisely because it doesn't reward excellence? What would be the impact of lottery admission? And why does the lottery seem so much more appealing in theory than in practice? Might a lottery with a threshold—a set of minimum qualifications— be the ideal compromise?

*Chapter 8: Crafting a Class.* Most admissions systems involve implicit or explicit rankings of applicants, but this need not be the case. An institution could choose to focus instead on the properties of the entering class as a whole. A group-based approach, developed nearly 20 years ago for possible application to law school admissions, is based on established optimization techniques from the field of operations research.[65] In theory, an admissions officer could say, "I want to admit 500 students, of which at least 20% should be ethnic minorities, at least 25% should be low-income, and at least 35% should be from within the state. Given those conditions, I want the students with the highest possible combination of test scores and grades."[66] What are the advantages and disadvantages of group-based approaches to admissions decisions?

*Chapter 9: Conclusions.* What are the most promising strategies for enhancing and evaluating the fairness and effectiveness of higher education admissions decisions? This chapter summarizes the content of the book and proposes future directions for admissions policy and research.

Table I-1. Average High School GPA and Test Score for Women and Men in the ELS
Senior Cohort

|  | GPA | Test Score |
|---|---|---|
| Women | 2.9 | 997 |
| Men | 2.7 | 1025 |
| **Total Group** | 2.8 | 1010 |

Table I-2. Average High School GPA for Socioeconomic and Ethnic Groups
in the ELS Senior Cohort

| | Socioeconomic Status (SES) | | | | |
|---|---|---|---|---|---|
| Ethnic Group | Lowest | Second Lowest | Second Highest | Highest | Total Group |
| American Indian | — | — | — | — | 2.4 |
| Asian | 2.7 | 3.0 | 2.9 | 3.2 | 3.0 |
| Black | 2.2 | 2.2 | 2.4 | 2.5 | 2.3 |
| Hispanic | 2.4 | 2.4 | 2.6 | 2.8 | 2.5 |
| More than one race | 2.5 | 2.5 | 2.7 | 2.9 | 2.7 |
| White | 2.7 | 2.8 | 2.9 | 3.1 | 2.9 |
| **Total Group** | 2.5 | 2.6 | 2.8 | 3.0 | 2.8 |

Note: Some results on American Indians were suppressed because of small sample size,
and results for two Hispanic groups ("no race specified" and "race specified") were combined.

Table I-3. Average Test Score for Socioeconomic and Ethnic Groups in the ELS
Senior Cohort

| | Socioeconomic Status (SES) | | | | |
|---|---|---|---|---|---|
| Ethnic Group | Lowest | Second Lowest | Second Highest | Highest | Total Group |
| American Indian | — | — | — | — | 911 |
| Asian | 949 | 1015 | 1084 | 1177 | 1080 |
| Black | 793 | 806 | 846 | 930 | 840 |
| Hispanic | 844 | 887 | 916 | 1033 | 907 |
| More than one race | 885 | 929 | 1032 | 1065 | 996 |
| White | 949 | 993 | 1045 | 1106 | 1052 |
| **Total Group** | 887 | 947 | 1014 | 1092 | 1010 |

Note: Some results on American Indians were suppressed because of small sample size,
and results for two Hispanic groups ("no race specified" and "race specified") were combined.

*Table I-4.* Percentages of Women and Men

| Gender | Senior Cohort | Applicants | Enrollees |
|---|---|---|---|
| Women (%) | 53.3 | 51.8 | 53.4 |
| Men (%) | 46.7 | 48.2 | 46.6 |

*Table I-5.* Percentages of Students in Each Ethnic Group

| Ethnic Group | Senior Cohort | Applicants | Enrollees |
|---|---|---|---|
| Asian (%) | 4.7 | 9.8 | 12.1 |
| Underrepresented minority (%) | 28.2 | 20.5 | 12.4 |
| More than one race (%) | 3.7 | 3.8 | 3.8 |
| White (%) | 63.5 | 66.0 | 71.7 |

*Note:* Results for Black, Hispanic, and American Indian students were combined to conform with Institute of Education Sciences data security requirements. Some column totals are not exactly 100% because of rounding.

*Table I-6.* Percentages of Students in Each of Four Socioeconomic Categories

| Socioeconomic Status (SES) | Senior Cohort | Applicants | Enrollees |
|---|---|---|---|
| Highest (%) | 31.1 | 53.6 | 63.6 |
| Second highest (%) | 26.5 | 24.2 | 20.8 |
| Second lowest (%) | 23.4 | 14.0 | 11.4 |
| Lowest (%) | 19.0 | 8.3 | 4.2 |

*Note:* Some column totals are not exactly 100% because of rounding.

# CHAPTER ONE

# Evaluating the Fairness and Effectiveness of an Admissions System

*The grounds on which [an admissions] decision is based may seem arbitrary and capricious to one observer, while to another they may seem natural reflections of values deeply and sincerely held. In any case there are few guidelines, and the scope for disputation is vast.*

—B. *Alden Thresher*

In 2001 the Regents of the University of California approved a new policy requiring the "comprehensive review" of student applications to undergraduate programs. UC president Richard C. Atkinson applauded the change, claiming it would enhance the university's ability to select "a class of thoroughly qualified students who demonstrate the promise to make great contributions to the university community and to the larger society beyond."[1] Gone was the requirement that each UC campus admit 50% to 75% of its entering class based solely on academic factors such as grades, test scores, and completion of college preparatory courses. Instead, all student records were to be judged in terms of 14 criteria, which consisted of 10 academic factors and four "supplemental" factors. These supplemental criteria, while not new to the UC admissions process, assumed a much greater role under comprehensive review. Most controversial was the requirement that academic accomplishments be evaluated "in light of an applicant's experiences and circumstances," which included "low family income, first generation to attend college, need to work, disadvantaged social or educational environment, [and] difficult personal and family situations."[2]

In 2003 John Moores, then the chair of the UC Board of Regents, authored a scathing report charging that this admissions process resulted in the selection of significant numbers of poorly qualified students, "perhaps at the expense of extraordinarily well-qualified applicants."[3] In a subsequent opinion piece in *Forbes*, he asserted that 359 students were accepted to UC Berkeley in 2002 with total SAT scores below 1000 (roughly the national average at the time) and that about two-thirds of these low scorers were Black, Hispanic, or Native American.[4] At the same time, "some 1,421 Californians with SAT scores above 1,400 applying to the same departments . . . were not admitted. Of those, 662 were Asian-American." This finding led Moores to ask, rhetorically, "How did the university get away with discriminating so blatantly against Asians?" His answer: the "fuzzy factors" used in comprehensive review.[5]

Moores's report ignited a firestorm. The UC Board of Regents voted to censure its own chair; the chancellor of UC Berkeley, Robert Berdahl, accused Moores of undermining confidence in Berkeley's admissions practices and of subjecting admitted students to "derision";[6] and a group of Berkeley professors joined with civil rights advocates to challenge the report's heavy emphasis on SAT scores.[7] But Moores had his supporters too, ranging in prominence from Ward Connerly, UC Regent and staunch foe of affirmative action, to the unknown head of a test preparation firm, who told the *San Francisco Chronicle*, "John Moores has received a lot of flak . . . for one reason: Berdahl and the UC system are scared to death that he will reveal the sloppiness of the new UC admissions system."[8]

Overlooked in much of the uproar was the fact that the University of California never claimed that comprehensive review would result in the selection of students with the strongest scholastic credentials, as traditionally defined. After all, maximizing the high school grades or test scores of the entering class could be easily achieved using a computer and would hardly require the detailed consideration of applications mandated by comprehensive review. The comprehensive review process was intended to take into account "accomplishments beyond the classroom that illustrate qualities such as leadership, intellectual curiosity, and initiative."[9] And in fact, the admissions process was very much in line with an explicit policy of the University of California Regents: to "seek out and enroll" a student body that is not only talented but "encompasses the broad diversity of backgrounds characteristic of California."[10]

The Moores debacle provides a useful starting point for defining the concepts of fairness and effectiveness of admissions. We need some rough working definitions of these terms, to be explored and refined throughout this book. I use "effectiveness" to refer to the degree to which admissions policies and procedures achieve their intended goals. In the Moores case, for example, one stated goal of UC admissions was to enroll an entering class with a "diversity of backgrounds characteristic of California." At least in principle, the degree to which diversity goals are attained can be addressed through statistical analysis. Did the ethnic and socioeconomic makeup of the entering class mirror that of the population of California? Was the demographic composition different from what it had been in previous years?

Fairness pertains to whether the goal itself and the means through which it is implemented are ethical and just. For example, should admissions procedures incorporate compensation for past or present social injustice? Is achieving diversity a legitimate goal of university admissions policy? Is it fair to consider a candidate's contribution to diversity when evaluating his application? If so, how can a candidate's contribution to diversity be properly evaluated? Is it ever fair to use decision criteria that vary across groups? Obviously, data analyses alone cannot answer these questions. One measure of the depth and complexity of the controversy surrounding fair admissions practices is the fact that, in cases spanning more than 40 years, the Supreme Court has yet to offer a comprehensive, unambiguous ruling on the legitimacy of race-based preferences in admissions.

Collectively, fairness and effectiveness roughly correspond to what is called validity in the educational and psychological testing field. In discussing admissions testing, validity expert Michael Kane recently observed that "the claims made for admissions-testing program[s] go beyond accurate prediction [of success] and involve . . . assumptions about the overall effectiveness of the program in promoting the goals of the institution and broader social goals. In particular, selection programs generally assume that the attributes evaluated by the testing program involve skills / competencies that are needed for effective performance and are not simply correlated with the [success] measure, that the assessment procedures and the [success] measure are free of any identifiable sources of bias, . . . and that they have consequences that are, in general, positive for the institution and society."[11] A tall order! In this book, I consider many of the same issues, but with reference to the entire enterprise of college admissions, not only the admissions testing component.

The effectiveness of the selection criterion is a key factor in evaluating its fairness. It is possible to argue that a particular screening criterion is fair if it serves a legitimate goal of the selection process, even if its impact falls disproportionately on certain demographic groups. However, if a criterion has a disproportionate effect and is also demonstrably invalid for its intended purpose, it must be judged unfair.

Consider an example from outside the world of college admissions: the English literacy tests to which some American voters were subjected until they were curtailed by the Voting Rights Act of 1965 and finally banned permanently in 1975.[12] These tests had the indisputable effect of preventing disproportionate numbers of minority-group members from voting. However, defenders argued that the tests served a legitimate purpose—to ensure that voters had the skills necessary to understand the voting process—and therefore, the disproportionality of their effects did not invalidate them. In *Lassiter v. Northampton Election Board,* a 1959 Supreme Court case addressing this issue, the Court held in favor of a North Carolina literacy test, arguing that "the ability to read and write . . . has some relation to standards designed to promote intelligent use of the ballot. . . . Literacy and intelligence are obviously not synonymous. Illiterate people may be intelligent voters. Yet, in our society, where newspapers, periodicals, books, and other printed matter canvass and debate campaign issues, a State might conclude that only those who are literate should exercise the franchise."[13]

However, the Supreme Court came to an opposite conclusion in *Katzenbach v. Morgan,* a 1966 case that addressed the legality of literacy tests that prevented large numbers of Puerto Ricans living in New York City from voting. These tests had been prohibited by the Voting Rights Act of 1965, but a lawsuit was filed arguing that the Voting Rights Act itself was unconstitutional. In the Court's opinion supporting the prohibition of the tests, Justice William Brennan noted that one of several arguments Congress could have considered was that "as a means of furthering the intelligent exercise of the franchise, an ability to read or understand Spanish is as effective as ability to read English for those to whom Spanish language newspapers and Spanish language radio and televisions programs are available to inform them of election issues and governmental affairs."[14] In other words, not only was the impact of the tests falling disproportionately on certain groups—in this case, native Spanish speakers—but the tests were not functioning effectively as a device for distinguishing poorly informed and well-informed voters. Today it is, of course, widely acknowledged that literacy tests were thinly disguised attempts to prevent Blacks and immigrants, among others, from voting. Both the discriminatory nature of literacy tests and their ineffectiveness for their alleged purpose were succinctly summarized in a 1970 Supreme Court case by Justice William O. Douglas, who noted that Congress had "concluded that such tests have been used to discriminate against the voting rights of minority groups and that the tests are not necessary to ensure that voters be well-informed."[15]

In recent years some of the SAT's most vehement critics have made a strikingly parallel argument about the SAT. "A more reliable way to disguise social selection as academic merit has not been invented," according to sociologist Joseph A. Soares, who goes on to argue that the SAT doesn't predict college grades but does correlate with socioeconomic status.[16] (We will return to the specifics of these controversial claims later on.) And according to journalist Peter Sacks, "the SAT has proven to be a vicious social sorter of young people by class and race, and even gender—and has served to sustain the very upper-middle-class privilege that many of the exam's supporters claim to oppose."[17]

Similar but less strident language appeared in *Facts and Fantasies about UC Berkeley Admissions*, the rejoinder to the Moores report prepared by a group of Berkeley faculty members and an array of other entities, including civil rights groups, the testing watchdog organization FairTest, and the Princeton Review Foundation, which is associated with the test-coaching company of the same name. *Facts and Fantasies* decried Moores's faith in SAT scores as an index of academic talent, describing the SAT as "an effective tool of social stratification at Berkeley" and noting that the "wealth preference" and racial gaps on the SAT are significantly more extreme than on other admissions criteria.[18] Furthermore, according to *Facts and Fantasies*, the SAT is "a weak predictor of grades" and "has virtually no value in predicting graduation rates" at Berkeley.[19] Here again we see the connection between effectiveness and fairness: Heavy reliance on the SAT (the policy attributed to Moores) is claimed to be unfair because of the alleged dual failings of disproportionate impact on certain race and income groups and limited utility for identifying successful students.

This linkage is embedded in the federal legal principles known as disparate impact law. For purposes of evaluating admissions criteria, the particular laws that have historically been invoked are Title VI of the Civil Rights Act of 1964, which prohibits discrimination on the basis of race, ethnicity, and national origin, and Title IX of the Education Amendments of 1972, which prohibits gender discrimination. These statutes apply to programs that receive federal financial assistance.

As described in a briefing report prepared for the Regents of the University of California in 2008, "there is a three-part test for assessing disparate impact complaints. A violation of law may occur if: 1) There is a significant disparity in the provision of a benefit or service that is based on race, national origin or sex; and 2) The practice at issue does not serve a substantial legitimate justification (i.e., is not educationally necessary); or 3) There is an alternative practice that is equally effective in meeting the institution's goals and results in lower disparities."[20]

Although the Civil Rights Act prohibits only intentional discrimination, the federal regulations that have been used to interpret it have, on occasion, allowed selection practices to be challenged in court if they created race-based differences in outcomes, even if no discrimination was intended.[21] According to a 2015 legal analysis of the application of Title VI in educational contexts, "a prohibition on disparate impact presumptively invalidates a policy that has a discriminatory effect on a protected racial group, regardless of the policy's intent."[22] In practice, however, court rulings have been divided as to whether disparate impact without discriminatory intent is sufficient to justify a legal challenge under the Civil Rights Act.[23]

In a 2002 paper, William Kidder, then a researcher with Testing for the Public, a test preparation company, and Jay Rosner, executive director of the Princeton Review Foundation, recommended that lawsuits based on claims of disparate racial impact be filed against colleges to curtail their use of the SAT. They noted that "because ETS and similar test producers are not recipients of federal financial assistance and are not subject to [federal] civil right statutes, suing colleges and universities on a disparate impact theory over their use of SAT in admissions is the only judicial remedy."[24] (Kidder is now associate vice chancellor at UC Riverside.)

Assuming that a racial disparity in admission rates could be demonstrated and could be attributed to the SAT, the challenge for the defendant—the college—would be to demonstrate that the SAT was educationally necessary. Even if a college successfully argued that this was the case, the plaintiffs could still claim that an equally effective alternative was available that would have a lesser racial disparity.

Here again, we return to the issue of effectiveness in the course of evaluating a fairness claim. The effectiveness issue, in turn, is linked to the institution's goals. As Kidder and Rosner acknowledge, "In analyzing whether 'a substantial legitimate justification' exists for over-reliance on the SAT despite its disparate impact, a key consideration is that there must be a fit between a university's mission and its admission practices."[25]

Ideally, we could examine a college's admissions policy and determine whether it flows from the school's stated educational mission. Unfortunately, as previous admissions researchers have noted, "mission statements are not things of beauty or rigor."[26] They can be vague, incomplete, or self-serving. In fact, in attempting to infer an institution's mission, it is often helpful to consult its admissions policy. This intrinsic circularity means that we cannot treat a school's stated mission and its admissions policy as independent pieces of information and then analyze their interrelationship. Indeed, according to education historian Harold Wechsler, "admissions policies and 'institutional goals' have a reciprocal effect on each other. Every college attempts to devise an admissions policy that will attract and select students who will help it fulfill its mission. But at the same time the students who are finally admitted make demands on the college that are not entirely anticipated—demands that force modifications in the institution's goals."[27]

Distinctions are often made between the mission of private universities and that of public universities, especially the land grant universities. But in reality these differences have faded over time. In 1862 the first of two Morrill Acts (named after Vermont congressman Justin Morrill) was signed by President Abraham Lincoln. It provided for federal grants of land to the states for "the endowment, support, and maintenance of at least one college where the leading object shall be, without excluding other scientific and classical studies, and including military tactics, to teach such branches of learning as are related to agriculture and the mechanic arts . . . in order to promote the liberal and practical education of the industrial classes in the several pursuits and professions in life."[28]

But the 69 land grant institutions have, to varying degrees, drifted away from their original mission.[29] The list includes Massachusetts Institute of Technology, Cornell, and the University of California, which hardly fit the image of schools that serve the "industrial class" today. And although public universities are sometimes regarded as havens for talented low-income and working-class students in their states, a 2010 report from the Education Trust, an advocacy group, claims that this is no longer true: "Driven by commercial ranking systems that reward them more for who they exclude than for who they educate, and anxious to attract the out-of-state and other full-pay students who can help make up for declining state investments, public research-extensive universities [a category that includes 102 institutions] have become less and less representative of the high school graduates in their states." Instead, the students attending these schools "have come to resemble the student population their private counterparts serve."[30] The report shows that in 2007 these 102 institutions spent nearly as much in student grant aid on students in the top 40% of the income distribution (family incomes exceeding $80,400) as they did on students in the bottom 40% (incomes of up to $54,000).[31] In short, in terms of their admissions and financial aid policies, funding sources, and goals, public and private universities are more similar than they once were.

We focus here on the stated purposes of colleges' admissions policies. What principles do schools currently use to allocate educational opportunities? We can then attempt to evaluate these principles and the ways in which they are implemented.

## The Goals of College and University Admissions Policies

In this section, I outline five perspectives on the goals of college admissions that have emerged from the public discourse, the admissions research literature,[32] and the mission statements, admissions descriptions, and other publications of the postsecondary institutions themselves. The admissions policies of most colleges and universities incorporate a mix of these goals. We will revisit the legitimacy and fairness of these purposes throughout this book.

What do colleges and universities seek to achieve through their admissions policies? One obvious and frequently invoked purpose of admissions is to *fulfill institutional needs*. A straightforward application of this principle is that if the school needs more players for the lacrosse team or more oboists for the orchestra, it will seek to admit applicants with the required talents. Most institutions, regardless of their educational mission, place at least some weight on needs of this kind.

In a somewhat more controversial application of this principle, some colleges argue that a particular type of student body is needed to facilitate the kind of education they wish to offer. For example, Antioch College, my alma mater, says in its mission statement that "diversity in all its manifestations is a fundamental component of excellence in education." Similarly, the California College for the Arts says, "We believe that a culturally diverse campus is integral to academic excellence."[33] These statements argue for diversity not (only) as a matter of social justice, but as a prerequisite for a high-quality education. In a 2003 survey by the National Association for College Admission Counseling (NACAC), 74% of responding colleges and universities included a commitment to diversity in their mission statements. In addition to racial and ethnic characteristics, the dimensions on which diversity was sought were geographic location (including international status), socioeconomic status, first-generation status, gender, age, religion, special talents, and academic interests.[34]

On the other side of the coin, some institutions seek a student body that is homogeneous—at least on certain dimensions—in order to further their missions. These include colleges that focus on a particular course of study (say, performing arts schools or military academies), single-sex schools, religious institutions, and historically Black colleges and universities. For example, according to Howard University's mission statement, the school "provides an educational experience of exceptional quality . . . to students of high academic standing and potential, with particular emphasis upon educational opportunities for Black students."[35] And the "College Prep Checklist" on Brigham Young University's website includes as its first two bullets "Live the standards of the LDS Church" and "Attend and graduate from LDS seminary." The university, which is supported by the Church of Jesus Christ of Latter-day Saints, requires that "each applicant . . . be endorsed by his or her ecclesiastical leaders as one who is worthy to attend BYU and is living in harmony with the Honor Code and the Dress and Grooming Standards."[36]

Also among the institutional necessities that must be fulfilled is a school's need to stay afloat financially. It is an uncomfortable fact that some schools do take into account students' ability to pay (or to promote parental donations) when deciding who gets in. A 1999 College Board report notes that although many admissions professionals object to the idea of considering students' finances when making admissions decisions, "the realities of the modern world preclude, for some institutions, the luxury of taking the ethical high ground for all of their prospective students."[37] In the NACAC report on college admissions for 2015, about half of the responding schools acknowledged that "ability to pay" was of at least limited importance in making admissions decisions and about half the schools said the same about "alumni relations." Private institutions were more likely than public ones to rate these factors as being important.[38]

Institutional attention to students' financial status can take many forms. To reduce their student support budgets, colleges may deny admission to students because of their financial need or may accept them but offer inadequate aid packages, a course of action called "gapping."[39] And it is no secret that institutions may accept academically unimpressive applicants whose parents are expected to make large donations. These applicants may include legacies—children of alumni—as well as children of wealthy or socially prominent individuals. Mitchell Stevens, the sociologist who studied the admissions process at Hamilton College, recounts how an admissions officer's interest was piqued when she saw the occupation of an applicant's father: prime minister.[40] One of the key chroniclers of the rule-bending that takes place in the quest for funds is journalist Daniel Golden, who has noted that there is even an established term for students who are accepted with an eye toward their parent's future donations: "development admits."[41]

The institutional-needs perspective involves judging properties of the incoming class as a whole. If an oboist with stellar academic credentials can be persuaded to attend, it may not be necessary to accept an oboist with a marginal background. If a sufficient number of admits can pay full tuition, it may be unnecessary to accept a questionable applicant whose family is sure to contribute a hefty sum.

A second perspective on admissions policy holds that selections should be made in order to *reward past performance*. The idea of admission as a reward was articulated in 2003 by Edward M. Kennedy, then the ranking Democrat on the Senate education committee, who stated that "college admission systems should promote diversity, reward achievement, and be fair."[42] Although colleges rarely acknowledge granting admission as a "reward" for "deserving" students, many do use these terms when describing scholarships. For example, Muhlenberg College states that its merit scholarships were established in "an effort to recognize and reward outstanding academic achievement . . . [M]erit awards . . . are offered solely on the basis of academic and extracurricular achievement in high school and promise for excellent scholarship and extra curricular contribution on the college level."[43]

The type of past performance that is to be rewarded need not be narrowly defined in terms of grades and test scores; it can encompass virtues such as dedication to community service or "hard work." In fact, from some perspectives it is the work and not the result that is relevant, leading the authors of a book on admissions to ask rhetorically, "If the important thing is what people can take credit for . . . [s]houldn't we subtract [people's] initial endowments (natural and environmental) from their performance to discover their true merit?"[44] The notion of rewarding struggle—the "A for effort" idea—is particularly appealing, which is why it is not uncommon for colleges to include in their admissions criteria the ability to overcome adversity, such as being in the family's first generation to go to college.

A third possible purpose of admissions is to *identify and nurture the most talented students*. Exemplifying this goal, Yale College states that its mission is

"to seek exceptionally promising students of all backgrounds ... and to educate them, through mental discipline and social experience, to develop their
intellectual, moral, civic, and creative capacities to the fullest."[45] This admissions criterion will not necessarily lead to the same decision as the one designed to reward past performance. A dedicated but unimaginative student
might be admitted as a reward for his diligence and hard work under the
second goal, while a brilliant but capricious applicant might be admitted
under the third goal with an eye to harnessing his talent.

A fourth possible objective of admissions is to *expand college access and promote social mobility*. This goal not only permits but demands the consideration of characteristics like race, financial status, and family educational
background. In their landmark 1998 book, *The Shape of the River*, William G.
Bowen, former president of Princeton, and Derek Bok, former president of
Harvard, referred explicitly to one aspect of this mission, noting that "our
country continues to need the help of its colleges and universities in building
a society in which access to positions of leadership and responsibility is less
limited by an individual's race than it is today."[46] An institution that explicitly mentions access in its mission statement is the State University of New
York, which strives to "provide to the people of New York educational services of the highest quality, with the broadest possible access, fully representative of all segments of the population." The SUNY mission statement also
includes the unusual promise to establish "tuition which most effectively
promotes the university's access goals."[47]

Finally, the most broadly defined admissions purpose is to *maximize the
benefit to society*. This noblest of goals is difficult to translate into practice,
given that people's lifetime accomplishments are not well predicted by their
attainments at age 18. How, then, can schools pick the applicants who will
produce the greatest benefit to humanity? Nevertheless, making the world
of the future a better place is, in fact, a stated goal of some institutions. For
example, MIT states that its mission is "to advance knowledge and educate
students in science, technology, and other areas of scholarship that will best
serve the nation and the world in the 21st century." The statement continues,
"We seek to develop in each member of the MIT community the ability and
passion to work wisely, creatively, and effectively for the betterment of
humankind."[48]

## Philosophical Perspectives on Selection

Can we turn to philosophers, past or present, to resolve the dilemma of how to fairly admit students to college? Harvard economist Robert Klitgaard considered this question in his 1985 book on admissions and concluded (in short) that the answer was no.[49] It is appealing to imagine that our selection decisions could be simplified by invoking a canonical principle or two. Unfortunately, the rules that have been proposed in this context often rely on premises that are not universally agreed upon (thus producing rather than resolving controversy) or are too vague to translate neatly into practice.

In another book, as part of a chapter on philosophical aspects of fairness in assessment, my coauthor Neil Dorans and I considered how three major philosophers—Aristotle, Robert Nozick, and John Rawls—might have approached college admissions.[50] What would their views have been on the consideration of grades, test scores, ethnic and socioeconomic background, and access to educational opportunities in making admissions decisions? According to Aristotle, just distribution depends on the purpose of the good that is being distributed. If flutes are being allocated, said Aristotle, the best flutes should go to the best flute players. Presumably, the men who can best fulfill the purpose of the university should be selected to attend.[51] (Women and slaves would have been excluded from consideration.) If the university's purpose is to nourish scholarly excellence, as Aristotle would likely have argued, then imposing purely academic criteria would be reasonable and fair. According to the libertarian philosophy espoused by Nozick, protection of individual rights is paramount and inequality is not in itself unjust. If an applicant can boost his chances of college admission by buying his way into a first-rate high school, enrolling in the best SAT prep courses, and hiring a high-priced admissions coach, the libertarian sees no objection. Rawls's perspective is harder to characterize. He believed that we don't deserve to be rewarded for our talents because we can't take credit for nature's endowments. More controversially, he also took the position that we don't deserve to be rewarded for hard work because the ability to put forth effort is itself a function of opportunity and luck. From a Rawlsian viewpoint, neither a mathematical prodigy nor an applicant brimming with course credits, extracurricular activities, and volunteer jobs would automatically "merit" admission. Some aspects of today's admissions practices, then, would clash with Rawls's beliefs. Based on his writings on the formulation of social policies, we conjectured that Rawls would favor a flexible admissions policy that allowed candidates multiple ways of demonstrating their eligibility. Ultimately we concluded that the three philosophical perspectives provided useful lenses through which to view college admissions. We found Rawls's views to be the most appealing and the most consistent with the zeitgeist. But they certainly don't lead in any obvious way to simple answers or universal principles for the admissions process.

The challenges of trying to develop overarching principles on which to judge admissions policies are exemplified in the book *Leveling the Playing Field*. In their fascinating analysis of college admissions, philosophers Robert K. Fullinwider and Judith Lichtenberg propose two governing principles for allocating coveted college slots: First, "other things being equal, it is desirable to enhance educational opportunities for those whose opportunities have been significantly limited." Second, "individuals should be neither helped nor hindered in their efforts at educational advancement by factors irrelevant to the legitimate goals of educational institutions."[52]

Although I find these principles to be consistent in spirit with my own views, they nevertheless invite a thousand questions: Starting with the first principle, what "other things" must be equal in order to take into account candidates' disparate educational opportunities? How do we know whose opportunities have been limited—is it sufficient to know a candidate's race and family income? And if we (not unreasonably) believe that remaining financially sound is a legitimate goal for a university, does the second principle allow us to accept an academically deficient applicant whose parents promise a large donation? To address the financial loophole, the authors rule out financial solvency as a legitimate goal because it is not relevant to the core missions of educational institutions. Fair enough. But much remains to be clarified about the second principle: What *are* the legitimate goals of educational institutions? If redressing social wrongs is *not* a legitimate goal, the second principle might be said to contradict the first. In particular, unless fostering diversity or compensating for racial discrimination are considered to be legitimate educational goals, a premise that is by no means universally endorsed, the second principle would seem to rule out affirmative action. But raising doubts about affirmative action is clearly not the authors' intent. Indeed, they stipulate that affirmative action does serve a legitimate goal, contending that it is needed to produce an integrated society.[53] Left unanswered are the specific questions on which reasonable people can disagree: Should an applicant get automatic preferential treatment for being Latino? poor?

male? Or for having struggled with a childhood illness? Is it OK to use bonus points or quotas in implementing preferences?

Developing philosophical principles is one thing; translating them into an admissions policy is another. Still, an effort to articulate the arguments about what constitutes fairness in college admissions is necessary to any serious consideration of admissions systems and may serve to narrow the range of acceptable policies. Hence, we will occasionally return to some philosophical perspectives throughout the book.

## Statistical Perspectives on Selection

How can statistical analysis help in evaluating admissions policies? As I noted earlier, certain questions can be addressed in a straightforward way through data analysis: Given a particular applicant pool, which of several competing policies produces the entering class with the highest average high school grades? Which results in the largest number of Black and Latino students? What is the graduation rate for a particular entering class or for students admitted through a particular program? What kinds of jobs do the students get after graduating?

But the potential contributions of the field of statistics to admissions policy go beyond these sorts of simple analyses. Of particular interest is a collection of statistical methods for determining whether particular groups of applicants are treated fairly in selection processes. Although questions of fairness need not involve comparisons of demographic groups, most public debates about the fairness of admissions policies have, in fact, focused on the question of whether members of one applicant group (say, Black students, White students, women, or students with disabilities) are treated equitably in comparison to their peers. Much of the important statistical thinking about selection fairness appeared under the rubric "culture-fair selection" in the late 1960s to the mid-1970s, following an era of significant civil rights legislation. A dozen or so statistical models for fair selection were proposed, including two that will be described here—the decision theory model and the equal prediction model.[54] But first we consider the most basic conception of fairness—the equal performance model.

## Equal Performance Model

The simplest of the quantitative fairness definitions, which is not usually stated in formal statistical terms, embodies the assumption that in order to be fair, any measure used in the admissions process—indeed, any educational measure or assessment—should yield the same average scores or success rates for all applicant groups. I'll call this the equal performance model.

Given the enormous range in family income and school resources among the communities in our country, along with the strong relationship between race and socioeconomic status (SES) and the effects of racism more generally, any expectations of equivalent academic skills seem either naively optimistic or disingenuous. Research shows that even in early childhood, socioeconomic factors are a strong predictor of cognitive functioning.[55] Furthermore, childhood poverty rates vary dramatically across ethnic groups. U.S. government figures for 2014 reveal dismally high child poverty rates of 30 to 36 percent for Black, Hispanic, and American Indian children, compared to an already troubling 11 to 12 percent for their White and Asian counterparts.[56] It is not surprising, then, that even at the starting gate—in kindergarten—low-SES children perform poorly in school, and Black and Hispanic children perform more poorly in math and reading than White and Asian children.[57] For older children, both family and school-level SES have been found to be related to student-teacher ratios, teacher experience and credential status, access to college preparatory courses, and student achievement.[58] The ELS results I have already presented, for example, show large ethnic and socioeconomic gaps in high school grades and admissions test scores.

In the view of most testing professionals, group differences in test scores warrant examination and could in fact point to biases or other problems in the test, but they are not in themselves evidence of such flaws. However, although the equal performance characterization of fairness is explicitly rejected by the 2014 *Standards for Educational and Psychological Testing*,[59] it has gained a degree of acceptance outside the testing profession.

Endorsement of the equal performance principle often takes the form of automatically interpreting any group differences in test scores as a manifestation of unfairness or bias. For example, under the headline "The ACT: Biased, Inaccurate, and Misused," FairTest claims that "race, class and gender biases give White, affluent, and male test-takers an unfair edge." To support the "class" part of the argument, the 2007 "fact sheet" goes on to note that "ACT scores are directly related to family income: the richer students' parents are, the higher are average scores." (The race argument gets a bit muddled when FairTest tries to explain the high scores of Asians: "If the ACT were not biased, Asian Americans, who take more academic courses than any other group, would likely score even higher.")[60]

The equal performance perspective has been advanced not only in the media but inside academia. For example, Janet Helms, a psychology professor at Boston College, argues in essence that racial differences in test scores are spurious and that this "contamination" should be statistically "removed." After applying her "research strategy for removing racial variance from test scores" to SAT math data, she concluded that "idealizing Blackness [a measure of racial identity] lowered the students' actual mean score by slightly more than 100 points."[61] Helms's statistical strategy was intended to "restore" these points.

The equal performance model has also surfaced in the legislative realm. A bill introduced in the California senate stated that "a test discriminates . . . if there is a statistically significant difference in the outcome on test performance when test subjects are compared on the basis of gender, ethnicity, race, or economic status." Had the bill passed, test sponsors could have been fined $750 per test taker for administering an exam that was discriminatory under this definition.[62]

## Alternatives to the Equal Performance Model

For purposes of discussion, let's consider a simplified version of the admissions situation. We will assume that only two groups of applicants are under consideration—say, Black and White applicants, or men and women—and that we want to derive an admissions policy that treats the two groups in an equitable way. We'll also assume that admissions decisions are made on the basis of a single quantity, called the test. The "test" in this case is not necessarily a standardized test score; it could be a high school grade-point average (GPA), a combination of test scores and GPA, or some type of numerical rating or "index." Indexes of this kind, which can take into account letters of recommendation, extracurricular activities, and awards, are in fact used by many colleges in determining admission. Finally, we'll suppose that first-year college grade-point average (FGPA) is a fair and reasonable numerical measure of college performance.

*Decision theory model.* Nancy Petersen and Melvin Novick, who conducted key research on selection in the 1970s, argued that selection decisions should be made using decision theory, a branch of statistical analysis that emerged in the mid-twentieth century.[63] Decision theory can be used to formalize the decision maker's explicit judgments about the *utility*—the usefulness or value—associated with various courses of action. Then, in theory, these judgments can be used to make decisions that maximize the *expected utility* of the overall selection process.

The decision theory models proposed for application in the admissions context have typically been very simple ones in which it is assumed that college performance can be classified as successful or unsuccessful. In our example, success would be defined as an FGPA that exceeded a criterion value. Admissions officials would need to make a priori judgments about the utility associated with four possible decisions: accepting a successful candidate, accepting an unsuccessful candidate, rejecting a candidate who would have been successful, and rejecting a candidate who would have been unsuccessful. The actual values of the utilities are unimportant; what is significant is their *relative* values. Negative numbers are often used to represent undesirable outcomes—accepting unsuccessful candidates or rejecting successful ones.

Much of the research on the use of decision theory in college admissions is based on the assumption that an institution wishes to compensate for cultural or racial discrimination experienced by some applicants—the disadvantaged group. In a 1976 study, Petersen illustrated the application of a decision theory approach for this compensatory purpose, using actual student data. In one scenario she used data from a college with about 2,500 students, 305 of which were considered disadvantaged. ACT scores and college GPA for "the first academic unit" (which I'll call FGPA) were available for each student. On average, both the scores and FGPA were substantially lower for the disadvantaged group. A successful college outcome was defined as an FGPA of at least 2.00.

The goal of Petersen's analysis was to solve for the minimum ACT score that should be required for future disadvantaged and advantaged applicants, assuming that one-third of the applicant pool could be accepted. The resulting minimum scores in this type of analysis are those that will be optimal under the stated assumptions about the utility, or value, of the various kinds of decisions that are made about the applicants. In this example, it was assumed to be a worse error to reject a potentially successful applicant than to accept a potentially unsuccessful applicant. Also, rejecting a potentially successful applicant was assumed to be worse for disadvantaged applicants (a utility of −5) than for advantaged applicants (−3), while the loss associated with accepting a potentially unsuccessful applicant was assumed to be the same for both applicant groups (−1.5). A correct decision to accept a potentially successful candidate was assumed to be worth 3.5 points for disadvantaged applicants and 1.5 for advantaged applicants, while a correct decision to reject an unsuccessful applicant corresponded to a utility of 1.5 for both groups. These specifications led to a minimum ACT requirement of 15.2 (on a scale of 1 to 36) for the disadvantaged group and an ACT minimum of 21.4 for the advantaged group. These minimums, in turn, produced a selection rate of 36% for the disadvantaged group and 33% for the advantaged group.[64]

When the utilities differ across applicant groups, as they do in this example, different qualifying scores on the test will generally result. The utilities chosen here set a lower bar for the disadvantaged group than for the advantaged group. Of course, imposing cutoffs that vary across student groups flies in the face of a frequently invoked principle of fairness in admissions—that all procedures and policies should be applied uniformly. Yet this aspect of the model is the essence of its appeal: It provides a formal justification for treating groups differently.

The beauty of the decision theory approach to selection is that it requires that institutional values be made explicit. But this feature is also its Achilles' heel. College administrators are likely to be reluctant to assign numerical values to the goals of the admissions process, especially when race is involved. Even if they agree to do so, conflicts about these values are likely to occur. Commenting on just this situation, the eminent psychometrician Lee Cronbach remarked, "Make no mistake. The issues will not be settled by mathematical specialists. Utility theory cannot be expected to crank out a just answer to a question of resource allocation [if utility values cannot be agreed upon]."[65]

Another drawback of the approach (though not an intrinsic one) is that incorporating race in the manner described in this example would almost certainly be prohibited by Supreme Court rulings on affirmative action admissions policies. In the employment context, the use of test-score cutoffs that differ by race, color, sex, or national origin was explicitly banned by the Civil Rights Act of 1991.[66] Given the mathematical complexities of the model, the difficulties in persuading institutions to articulate their utility values, and the controversies associated with the use of race, it is not surprising that the decision theory approach has not gained traction. We now turn to a model that is applied frequently by university institutional research offices and testing companies.

*Equal prediction model.* One widely studied category of admissions procedures is based on the statistics of prediction, discussed in detail in Chapter 3. For now, we need consider only a very basic prediction model. Suppose we apply linear regression, a standard form of statistical analysis, to predict FGPA using our "test." We start with a set of students who already have FGPA values, and we then try to "predict" those values using our test scores. If the prediction works well (the predicted values of FGPA are sufficiently close to the actual values), the prediction equation can then be used to predict performance for new applicants.

According to the fairness definition that I call the equal prediction model, a prediction equation may be used in the admissions process only if it "works the same way" for all student groups. That is, this model requires that a particular test score lead to the same predicted FGPA, regardless of which student group (male, female, Black, White, and so on) the applicant belongs to. This concept of fairness is largely based on the work of psychologist T. Anne Cleary, whose 1968 article "Test Bias: Prediction of Negro and White Students in Integrated Colleges" is considered to be a milestone in the area of selection fairness.[67]

Suppose that in analyzing our data, we found that predicted FGPAs were systematically too high for one group (say, men) and too low for another group (women). This particular pattern does, in fact, occur on the SAT, though the differences are ordinarily quite small.[68] While Cleary might have labeled this finding as test bias, we would call it predictive bias today: According to the 2014 edition of the *Standards for Educational and Psychological Tests*, "the term *predictive bias* may be used when evidence is found that differences exist in the patterns of associations between test scores and other variables for different groups, bringing with it concerns about bias in the inferences drawn from the use of test scores. Differential prediction is examined using regression analysis."[69]

The distinction between test bias (the term used by Cleary) and predictive bias (the term used in the *Standards*) is significant because it highlights the fact that different prediction equations can arise from factors that go beyond the test itself. Differential prediction can occur because the test isn't perfectly precise[70] and excludes important predictors of college performance such as the student's degree of effort or motivation. For example, it has been conjectured that women work harder in college than men, hence performing better than men who share the same test score. Another possibility is that the quantity that is being predicted—FGPA in this case—differs systematically for the groups in question. For example, because women and men tend to differ somewhat in their choice of majors, their FGPAs may not be comparable.

That statistical approaches to selection can lead to very different results was clearly demonstrated in an interesting study that had its roots in a legal case involving university admissions. In 1971, Marco DeFunis, a White student rejected by the University of Washington Law School, filed a lawsuit claiming that he was a victim of racial discrimination because minority candidates with lesser academic qualifications than his own had been admitted. The case has much in common with the landmark *Bakke* case. It is less well known because it was declared moot by the U.S. Supreme Court in 1974. By that time DeFunis had almost completed his degree at the UW Law School, where he had been provisionally admitted.[71]

Researchers Hunter Breland and Gail Ironson sought to determine what the UW Law School admission rates would have been under fair selection rules that had been proposed in the educational and psychological literature. They started by using past research to make some plausible assumptions about the qualifications and expected law school performance of minority and majority applicants. (According to UW criteria, minority students were those who identified themselves as Black American, Chicano American, American Indian, or Philippine American.) Using the actual numbers of majority and minority applicants to the UW Law School in 1971 and the total number of applicants who were admitted, Breland and Ironson applied three of the best-known "culture fairness" rules to the data. In essence their analyses addressed the question, "What would the admission rates have had to be for minority and majority applicants in order to meet this fairness definition?" They considered four cases, each corresponding to a set of assumptions about minority- and majority-group qualifications and performance.

For majority students, the resulting admission rates were similar (ranging from 17% to 18%) for all rules and cases and were only slightly different from the actual admission rate (15.5%). However, for minorities the admission rates decreed by the statistical models ranged from 0% to 16% over the various cases and rules.[72] More significantly, these model-based admission rates were far lower than the actual admission rate for minorities: 52.9%. Thus, three seemingly credible rules for fair selection did not agree with each other, and none of them yielded results that remotely resembled the outcomes evidently regarded as fair by the University of Washington.

## Defining College Success and Candidate Groups

Two major issues that are pertinent, not only to our three statistical selection models but to the development and evaluation of admissions policy in general, involve the measurement of college success and the identification of applicant groups that should be accorded a special status. More specifically:

- How should candidates' college "success" be defined and measured?
- What constitutes a "group" of candidates, and which groups warrant special consideration?

We will consider these questions briefly here and revisit them in later chapters.

### How Should Successful College Performance Be Defined and Measured?

What does it mean for a student to be "successful" in college? Presumably a successful student will gain expertise in her chosen field, earn satisfactory grades, and graduate in a reasonable time period. A variety of other possible criteria come to mind. Did she participate in her college community? Did she find the college experience satisfying? Did she have good job prospects upon graduation? Did she learn to be a better-informed citizen of the world?

In a 2012 review, psychologist Steven E. Stemler listed several outcomes that colleges themselves deemed important, including the development of capabilities in writing and speaking, in quantitative, logical, and ethical reasoning, in citizenship, and in intercultural literacy.[73] (Stemler also offers the startling suggestion that alumni giving might be a useful index of college success, claiming that "if a class that is having their 25th reunion donates a large sum to the university, admissions officers may take this as a sign that their admissions process worked fairly well." To his credit, Stemler does acknowledge that "the relationship between alumni giving and student learning may be tenuous, at best.")[74]

Despite this very wide array of possible definitions, the most common success measure in the admissions testing literature, by far, is first-year college grade-point average (FGPA). More than 25 years ago, SAT critics James Crouse and Dale Trusheim estimated that more than 3,000 studies had already been conducted to evaluate the ability of the SAT and high school grades to predict FGPA.[75] The same success criterion has typically been used for studies of the ACT, for research on innovative admissions measures, such as the assessments of creativity and practical skills developed by psychologist Robert Sternberg, and for investigations of various "noncognitive" factors proposed for use in the admissions process, such as "emotional control" and "social activity."[76]

What accounts for the ubiquity of FGPA in admissions research? First, it is important to keep in mind that in the admissions testing literature, the usual goal is to evaluate particular measures as predictors of success, rather than to evaluate the students themselves. Ideally, this evaluation should be based on as many students as possible, which argues in favor of data that can be collected early in students' college careers, before significant numbers of students drop out or transfer elsewhere. Another advantage of FGPA is that it tends to be more comparable across students than GPA data collected in subsequent years, after students' academic programs have become more differentiated. Some admissions studies, however, have used later grades or grades in particular courses as success measures.[77]

Grades clearly have disadvantages that weigh against their availability and convenience. Because they reflect only a small portion of a student's college activities and accomplishments, grades provide a rather narrow measure of college success. In addition, grades can be inconsistent, inaccurate, and possibly biased. It is well known, for example, that the stringency of grading practices varies across institutions, academic programs, and individual courses (though adjustments to correct this problem are sometimes possible).[78] In addition, grades lack precision—particularly letter grades, which have only a few possible levels—and may reflect factors unrelated to student accomplishment, such as institutional requirements constraining the distribution of grades or departmental traditions of assigning only A's and B's. In addition, grades may reflect biases against particular groups of students or even particular individuals.

A key success criterion used in some studies is whether or not the student graduated.[79] In their acclaimed book on college completion, *Crossing the Finish Line*, William G. Bowen, Matthew M. Chingos, and Michael S. McPherson assert that college graduation rates are "presumptively the single most important indicator of educational attainment."[80] Forty years ago, Warren Willingham, then a research director at ETS, elegantly summarized the pros and cons of graduation as a measure of academic success. Although he was referring to graduate education, his remarks are equally applicable at the undergraduate level: "Regardless of what other judgments a faculty may make about a . . . student, the acid test is whether he or she is granted the degree. Consequently, this is probably the single most defensible criterion of success. On the negative side, one must wait a long time for this criterion. Another difficulty is the fact that whether or not a student graduates may frequently depend upon extraneous influences."[81]

Another frequently mentioned indicator of college success is postcollege accomplishment. Did the student ultimately expand the horizons of knowledge or promote the betterment of humankind? Or, on a smaller scale, did the student experience success in his chosen career? Although this type of criterion is appealing, the practical problems are daunting: How should career accomplishments be defined and measured? Income is one possible criterion, but a mediocre business executive may earn many times more than a brilliant professor. Supervisor ratings are notoriously imprecise and subjective, and customs for awarding prizes and other kinds of recognition differ widely across fields. Also, when should career success be assessed? Too early and the student will not have had the opportunity to realize her goals. Too late and it will be impossible to establish a link between her career and her college experience.[82]

In my analyses of data from the Education Longitudinal Study that appear in later chapters, I will focus on grades, graduation, and the attainment of postbaccalaureate certificates or degrees. Although each of these measures has its flaws, they should, collectively, provide a useful perspective on students' college success. How grades and degree completion reflect on the fairness and effectiveness of admissions procedures is, of course, a much more complex question. This is true not only because of the countless life events that can affect a student's accomplishments, but because of another intervening factor—the student's college education itself. That is, the role of postsecondary institutions is not merely to select the "best" students through a feat of skillful prediction (the scenario cynically described by Alden Thresher), but to actually provide a coveted good called a college education. Presumably this college experience itself will have an impact on the student's achievements.

## What Groups of Candidates Warrant Special Consideration?

Another issue that needs to be addressed in the course of studying admissions policy is which groups of applicants warrant special consideration, possibly including preferential treatment. What, exactly, constitutes a "group"? This question has provoked facetious suggestions that preferential treatment could be demanded by atheists, short people, those with a particular blood type, or even candidates whose defining characteristic is having been rejected by a previous selection procedure.[83]

In reality, the motivation for implementing preferential treatment is typically related to public concern, legal considerations, or both. The categories identified in federal law (race, ethnicity, and national origin in Title VI of the Civil Rights Act of 1964 and gender in Title IX of the Education Amendments of 1972) are important in this context. In addition, there has been increased public concern in recent years about the underrepresentation of low-income students in higher education, particularly at selective colleges. In fact, the types of preferential treatment that are most frequently in the public eye today are those based on socioeconomic disadvantage and on race (more specifically, membership in an underrepresented minority group). Even if we as a society were to agree on the legitimacy of considering these factors in admissions (a big if), we would still have to make some specific decisions: How is socioeconomic disadvantage to be gauged? Is it simply a question of measuring financial resources, or should other factors be considered? Do members of underrepresented ethnic or racial groups automatically merit preferential treatment? This last question was famously answered in the negative by then-senator Barack Obama, who said in 2007 that his daughters "should probably be treated by any admission officer as folks who are pretty advantaged."[84] In most cases, however, these determinations are more difficult to make.

## Transparency

Another key fairness principle to which college admissions systems should adhere is transparency. The goals of the admissions process and the basis on which decisions are to be made should be clear to applicants. Applicants should be made aware of what data are to be considered and how these data are to be weighted and combined to arrive at a decision. They should also know about any special preferences and exceptions that are in effect.[85] This transparency principle can be seen as an extension of standards currently in place for testing. The *Standards for Educational and Psychological Testing* note that to the degree possible, test takers should be informed in advance about "the test, the testing process, the intended test use, test scoring criteria, [and] testing policy" and that "the greater the consequences to the test taker, the greater the importance of ensuring that the test taker is fully informed about the test."[86] In the college admissions context, the entire candidate evaluation procedure is the "test."

The "holistic" or "comprehensive" review systems used by many elite schools can be legitimately challenged on the grounds that they lack this sort of transparency. As Harvard psychology professor Steven Pinker has noted, "anything can be hidden behind the holistic fig leaf."[87] The University of California, for example, lists intellectual curiosity as a desirable candidate characteristic. But how is intellectual curiosity to be evaluated, and how important is it to the admissions decision? Similarly, what is the definition of diversity—a stated goal of the admissions process—and how are applicants' contributions to diversity taken into account? The UC comprehensive review process also includes consideration of disabilities, difficult personal and family situations, and low family income (among many other criteria).[88] But how much do these factors count? How many grade points or SAT points is a parental divorce worth? How about an asthma problem? How low does the family income have to be before it becomes a plus in the admissions process?

In 2013 a Stanford writing and ethics instructor who served as an "external reader" (an initial screener) for Berkeley's admissions office raised some similar questions in an opinion piece in the *New York Times*. In her eyes, the process was "opaque and secretive," "confusingly subjective," and characterized by "fundamental unevenness." Hardships, she said, sometimes counted more than achievements.[89]

Holistic admissions policies have sparked legal actions as well. A complaint filed in 2015 with the U.S. Department of Education and the Justice Department by a coalition of Asian-American groups charges that "Harvard's Holistic Evaluation Approach disproportionately penalizes Asian-American applicants by using stereotypes and racial biases during the admission process. Harvard's admissions officers often unreasonably perceive Asian-Americans' academic strengths as weaknesses. In addition, they unjustifiably give Asian-American students low scores in non-academic criteria." The complaint, citing the work of Daniel Golden, compares the treatment of Asian Americans to the discrimination against Jews by elite universities in the 1920s and 1930s.[90]

Are the Harvard policies discriminatory against Asians? Or are they mistakenly assumed to depend much more on grades and test scores than they actually do? What nonacademic factors are considered in the admissions process, and are they reasonable? The description of Harvard's admissions criteria that appears on its website is quite lengthy, yet remarkably uninformative. Harvard evidently considers questions such as the following: "Where will you [the candidate] be in one, five, or 25 years? Will you contribute something to those around you? What sort of human being are you now? What sort of human being will you be in the future? . . . Are you a late bloomer? How open are you to new ideas and people?"[91] But what evidence is used to gather (or guess at) this information? How important is it to the admissions decision, relative to more traditional criteria, such as grades, test scores, and the rigor of the applicant's high school courses? And where do diversity considerations come in?

The Supreme Court's *Grutter* decision gave the green light to the consideration of race in admissions, provided it was part of "a highly individualized, holistic review of each applicant's file, giving serious consideration to all the ways an applicant might contribute to a diverse educational environment."[92] As a result of this terminology, "holistic review" has become linked in a very real way with the use of race in admissions. A new American Council on Education (ACE) report by Lorelle L. Espinosa, Matthew N. Gaertner, and Gary Orfield, goes so far as to say that "holistic review is now a required practice for institutions that wish to consider race in admissions." And among 338 colleges that responded to an ACE survey, 97% of those that used race in admissions implemented holistic review, compared to 69% of those that did not use race. Those that used holistic review as a strategy for increasing diversity rated it as very effective.[93]

Holistic admissions also played a role in *Fisher v. University of Texas,* which the Supreme Court considered for the second time in 2015. The case concerned the legality of the affirmative action procedure used by UT Austin to supplement the Top Ten Percent Plan in effect in Texas. This supplementary admissions program, is in fact, holistic review, used to admit a quarter of the entering class. In 2012 the president of UT Austin told the *New York Times* that the holistic review was not "designed or motivated by adding to ethnic diversity." He said it was not intended to benefit applicants from private or suburban schools either. Interestingly, though, the Black and Hispanic students interviewed by the *Times* believed that the holistic admissions program helped affluent White candidates, whereas the White and Asian students thought that it helped Black and Hispanic applicants.[94] Similarly, a new plan to solicit letters of recommendation from applicants to UC Berkeley ("adding one more factor to the holistic mix," according to the *Los Angeles Times*) has been criticized both as another opportunity for privileged students to gain an advantage and as a covert affirmative action program, intended to aid students of color.[95] Holistic admissions, it seems, is a sort of Rorschach image on which students and administrators project their anxieties about the admissions process.

In 2005 sociologist Michael Hout published the results of a study of UC Berkeley's comprehensive review process, commissioned by Berkeley officials. Hout used ratings from Berkeley's comprehensive review process to infer, retrospectively, the weights that were, in effect, used by application readers. I say "in effect" because the study does not tell us what mental process the readers went through. What it does show is which student characteristics were most highly related to the scores (ranging from 1 to 5) their applications received. According to Hout's analysis, the largest influence by far was high school grades, including whether candidates had a "perfect 4.0" GPA, whether they were top-ranked in their high schools, and whether their grades trended downward (a negative factor). Other major influences were the applicants' scores on Advanced Placement tests and on the SAT Subject Test in Writing and the difficulty of their senior programs in high school.[96] None of these findings seem problematic in themselves; what is troubling is that an elaborate retrospective analysis was needed to determine which factors were most associated with readers' scores. Ideally the weights assigned to each factor would result from an intentional policy and would be accessible to applicants.

An issue Hout did not address was the extent to which readers agreed when rating an application. Examining the agreement is one way to evaluate the degree to which a rating process is well-defined and replicable. In early 2014, I contacted the Office of Planning and Analysis at UC Berkeley (where I received an MA and a PhD), requesting this information. In one of these messages I said, "As I understand it, each reader assigns a score on a 1-to-5 scale to each application, and all applications are read by two (or more?) readers. So it would be interesting to look at the $5 \times 5$ table and compute various indexes of agreement between the two readers." Although the lead policy analyst at first seemed willing to supply information, no results were ever provided and my fourth email went unanswered.[97] A year later my question was answered, at least in part, by an article in the *Los Angeles Times*, which noted that engineering professor Panos Papadopoulos, outgoing chair of the academic senate at Berkeley, had explored this issue. Papadopoulos had the files of top applicants reread to see if the initial ratings held up. The rescored candidates had initially received the highest possible rating—a 1— and had been automatically admitted as a result. On the rereading, 40% were assigned a rating of 2 or 3 instead.[98]

Berkeley has argued that its admissions process is transparent, and in some respects it is. The list of factors is public, as is the general procedure followed by the readers. But as Hout noted, "guidelines prescribe what the readers consider as they decide on a read score [but] leave it up to the readers to figure out how much weight each factor gets."[99] And if Berkeley collects information on reader agreement, they certainly aren't anxious to make it public.

Summarizing his view of the status quo at selective schools, a former dean of admissions noted, "Elite institutions . . . admit whomever they want for whatever reasons might be important to them at the time. Why? Because they can."[100] But that is not as it should be. Candidates shouldn't be forced to play the game without knowing the rules.

# CHAPTER TWO

# Admissions Tests and High School Grades: What Do They Measure?

The content of higher education has not only advanced; methods of selecting those to benefit from it have improved at least as fast. Each ten-year age-cohort of the élite has . . . had more innate capacity than the previous one. . . . Intelligence tests and aptitude tests [are] objective, and a good deal more reliable than the older forms of examination.

—M. *Young*

If this scenario sounds a bit off kilter, that's because it comes from the satirical essay *The Rise of the Meritocracy,* originally published in 1958. The author was British sociologist Michael Young, who coined the now-ubiquitous word "meritocracy." Young describes a smoothly running but nightmarish world in which every aspect of life—schooling, work, compensation, marriage—is controlled by test scores under a system headquartered in Eugenics House. Eventually the tests themselves become unnecessary when a Nobel prize-winner demonstrates that the intelligence of children can be accurately predicted from the intelligence of their ancestors. As a result, "intelligence trends and distributions have actually been calculated for the next 1,000 years."[1]

Although Young seemed to view a preoccupation with cognitive assessment as a British phenomenon, interest in testing was growing rapidly across the Atlantic. In 1947, about a decade before Young's essay was published, Educational Testing Service (ETS) was founded in Princeton, New Jersey. Its first annual report, submitted by its president, Henry Chauncey, included the following ode to testing: "With respect to knowledge of individuals, the possibilities of constructive use [of tests] are far greater than those of misuse. Educational and vocational guidance, personal and social adjustment most

49

certainly should be greatly benefited. Life may have less mystery, but it will also have less disillusionment and disappointment."[2] "The field of testing is exceedingly broad and the opportunities for ETS almost limitless."[3] (Interestingly, according to Nicholas Lemann, author of *The Big Test: The Secret History of the American Meritocracy,* Young contacted Chauncey in 1959, requesting an interview, but the two never actually met.)[4] Although Chauncey's claims about the benefits of tests sound naive and outmoded today, some would say that the "all tests all the time" scenario is not that far removed from present-day America. Journalist Peter Sacks sees it this way: "Like a drug addict who knows he should quit, America is hooked. We are a nation of standardized testing junkies."[5]

In reality, though, America is ambivalent about tests. This is reflected in two simultaneous trends in admissions testing: On one hand, both the SAT and the ACT programs recently reported record numbers of test takers,[6] and in recent years states have begun to use college admissions tests as part of their state assessment programs. As of early 2016, 21 states required students to take the SAT or ACT, and three more gave students a choice of four tests, including the SAT and ACT. Twelve states were using the SAT or ACT in their federally mandated accountability reports on high school students.[7] On the other hand, more and more colleges have gone "test-optional" during the last decade. The National Center for Fair and Open Testing, a watchdog organization better known as FairTest, puts the total number of test-optional schools at nearly 850, while acknowledging that its list includes institutions that merely "deemphasize" tests.[8]

The legitimacy of using admissions tests as a selection tool rests primarily on claims that test scores can contribute to the prediction of students' college grades. In the remaining chapters of this book, I will consider in detail the use of test scores, grades, and other factors to predict college success. For now I'll examine some broader questions: How did the SAT and ACT come to be used in college admissions? What are the pros and cons of admissions tests? Are high school grades a better and more equitable measure of students' academic skills? How do grades and test scores shape the characteristics of the entering class?

## The SAT

The first SAT, administered by the College Board in 1926 to about 8,000 students, was a wholesale departure from the exams that had been developed by the Board at the beginning of the century. Instead of a weeklong battery of essay tests, the first SAT takers were faced with 315 questions to complete in 97 minutes.[9] A major factor in this change of direction was the expansion in attempts to scientifically measure intelligence that occurred during World War I. "With millions of young draftees as their victims, the psychologists had a field day," according to a history of the College Board, a membership organization that was founded in 1900 and now includes over 6,000 educational institutions.[10] The postwar period brought with it a surge of enthusiasm about the possible uses of this "scientific" testing in civilian life. One possible application was in college admissions. As the College Board secretary put it in 1924, "The Board wishes to ascertain in regard to the boys and girls entering college not merely whether they have stored in their memories the contents of the textbooks in general use but primarily whether they have made a start . . . on the road from childhood to intellectual maturity."[11]

The 1926 SAT consisted mostly of multiple-choice questions similar in form to those included in the Army Alpha tests, which had been developed for selecting and assigning military recruits during the war. (In fact, I found one question from the Army Alpha that appeared intact in the 1926 SAT: "A certain division contains 3000 artillery, 15,000 infantry, and 1000 cavalry. If each branch is expanded proportionately until there are in all 20,900 men, how many will be added to the artillery?")[12] The Army Alpha tests, in turn, were directly descended from IQ tests, which had made their American debut in the early 1900s.

In the 1920s one of the staunchest advocates of IQ tests was Princeton psychology professor Carl Brigham, who had been involved in testing military recruits during World War I. Brigham's most prominent writings reflected the belief that racial and ethnic groups could (and should) be scientifically ordered from most to least intelligent using average test scores. Based on his analysis of data from World War I army recruits, Brigham concluded that immigrants were less intelligent than native-born Americans and that each succeeding wave of immigrants was less intelligent than the last. He rejected the idea that unfamiliarity with English could have affected the test results. Also, said Brigham, Americans of Alpine or Mediterranean heritage were inferior in intelligence to those of Nordic heritage. "The Jew" and "the negro" deserved special mention because of their woefully deficient intelligence.[13]

Brigham later renounced his key findings, acknowledging that further research had led him to recognize that test scores are influenced by "schooling, family background, familiarity with English, and everything else, relevant and irrelevant."[14] He also realized that information is obscured by adding up the scores on disparate tests, as he had previously done. Although he denounced his earlier work as "pretentious" and "without foundation,"[15] it is the work he is best known for, particularly his 1923 book, *A Study of American Intelligence*. Brigham's work fit smoothly into the racial theories promoted by the thriving eugenics movement. According to a 1961 biography, he "was greatly influenced by the writings of Madison Grant and by Charles W. Gould, prominent racists of the 1920's, and [his] broader conclusions generally conformed to their theories."[16] In his 1923 book (in which he formally acknowledged the contributions of both Grant and Gould),[17] Brigham argued that "legal steps" should be taken to prevent the deterioration of the nation's intellectual capacity. He advised that "immigration should not only be restrictive but highly selective." But the "really important steps," according to Brigham, required "prevention of the continued propagation of defective strains in the present population. This is the problem which must be met, and our manner of meeting it will determine the future course of our national life."[18]

Brigham was not merely one of many early promoters of cognitive tests; he was the man behind the SAT. As a College Board advisor, he chaired the commission appointed to prepare and score what the Board regarded as its first "psychological test." (The commission decided it was wise to avoid the term "psychological" in the test's title and decided on "scholastic aptitude" instead.) Brigham ultimately became a paid member of the College Board staff, while retaining his academic appointment at Princeton.[19] To this day, the library at ETS headquarters bears his name.

This ancestral linkage to intelligence tests and, indirectly, to eugenics, may be one reason the SAT attracts more controversy than its competitor, the ACT, despite the fact that scores on the two tests have typically had a correlation exceeding .9. (The correlation measures the strength of association between two quantities on a scale that ranges from −1 to 1.)[20] In his 1999 book *The Big Test*, Nicholas Lemann sometimes seemed to suggest that the SAT was a cleverly disguised IQ test. Henry Chauncey, the first president of ETS, remarked that Lemann "doesn't say precisely that it is an IQ test. . . . But he always goes back to talking about IQ tests, so readers get the impression that the SAT measures native ability, which of course, it doesn't."[21] The objectionable lineage of the SAT was explicitly mentioned as a detriment by Richard Atkinson, then president of the University of California, in his consideration of the role of the SAT in UC admissions. In a 2001 speech in which he called for replacing the test with exams linked to the high school curriculum, he mentioned the perception that "the SAT was akin to an IQ test—a measure of innate intelligence."[22] In a subsequent article he noted that the SAT and similar tests "have a historical tie to the concept of innate mental abilities and the belief that such abilities can be defined and meaningfully measured." According to Atkinson, a cognitive psychologist by training, "neither notion has been supported by modern research."[23]

While some critics see the SAT as irredeemably tainted by its past association with Brigham and his ilk,[24] a 1992 congressional report on educational testing noted that "it was not just the hereditarians and eugenicists who were attracted to such concepts as 'intelligence' and the 'measurement' of mental ability; many of the early believers in the measurement of mental . . . processes were progressives, egalitarians, and communitarians committed to the betterment of all mankind."[25] A prime example is Alfred Binet, the French psychologist who created the Stanford-Binet intelligence test. Rejecting the prevailing belief in the immutability of intelligence, he ultimately devoted himself to using his tests to improve children's education. Several decades later, Harvard president and educational reformer James Bryant Conant saw admissions tests as a counterweight to admissions policies based on wealth and ancestry. Conant played a key role in the founding of ETS and became its first chairman of the board.[26]

A major revision of the SAT occurred in 2005, following a nationwide controversy about the test's utility and fairness in which Richard Atkinson's 2001 speech featured prominently.[27] The version of the SAT that was introduced in 2005 consisted of three sections: critical reading, math, and writing. The critical reading section substituted short reading questions for the analogies that had formerly been part of the verbal section. The math section incorporated more advanced mathematical material than its predecessor and eliminated certain question types. The new writing section included both multiple-choice questions and an essay.

Another overhaul has just taken place: a newly redesigned SAT had its debut in 2016. The president of the College Board, David Coleman, promised "an assessment that mirrors the work that students will do in college so that they will practice the work they need to do to complete college." Coleman previously led the development of the Common Core State Standards for K–12 education, which have been adopted by 42 states and the District of Columbia[28] but remain highly controversial. Although he formerly pledged that the redesigned SAT would be closely aligned with the Common Core,[29] those claims no longer appear on the College Board website.

The 2016 SAT has a more complex structure than its precursor and yields a plethora of scores and subscores. ("More scores equals more you," says the SAT Web page.) The mandatory portion includes reading, writing and language, and math components. The main scores are two "section scores" that range from 200 to 800—one in "evidence-based reading and writing" and one in math—and a total score that is the sum of the section scores. Scoring on the mandatory components is based on the number of correct answers; there is no penalty for wrong answers as in the past. Among the new scores now being offered are two "cross-test" scores—"analysis in history/social studies" and "analysis in science." These scores are based on selected questions in the mandatory portions of the test. An optional essay component yields scores in reading, analysis, and writing.[30]

In mid-2016, concordance tables and an online "score converter" were made available that were intended to allow score users to compare scores on the 2016 SAT to scores on the previous version.[31] Scores on the new test tend to be higher than on the old. For example, using the online tool and plugging in "old SAT" scores of 500 on each of the three sections yields a total score on the new SAT of 1090 (560 on evidence-based reading and writing and 530 on math). The College Board also offered a translation to ACT scores, which was immediately disputed by the chief executive of ACT Inc., who also criticized the linkage between the two versions of the SAT. In an unusual public exchange, ACT asserted that further research was needed in order to establish trustworthy concordances; the College Board claimed otherwise.[32] Interpretation of the new SAT scores is likely to remain the subject of intense scrutiny as colleges ramp up for the next application season.

In addition to the SAT itself, the SAT program also includes 20 SAT Subject Tests (formerly called the College Board Achievement Tests, and later, the SAT II Subject Tests), which assess the candidate's knowledge in such areas as U.S. history, math, biology, chemistry, physics, French, Spanish, Chinese, and Hebrew. The SAT and SAT Subject Tests are owned by the College Board and are administered by ETS under a contract with the Board.

The content of the SAT and the claims about what it is intended to measure have evolved during the test's nine decades of existence.[33] ("SAT" originally stood for "Scholastic Aptitude Test," and later, "Scholastic Assessment Test." "SAT" is no longer considered to be an acronym, but the full name of the test.) Although the original developers of the SAT spoke unabashedly of aptitude and intellectual capacity, the current version of the SAT is described as measuring students' "readiness" for college work, "focusing on the core knowledge and skills that evidence has shown to be critical in preparation for college and career."[34]

Some observers have speculated that one possible motivation for the College Board's most recent changes to the SAT was the ACT's gain in market share. And indeed, the SAT seems to be growing more similar to the ACT.

## The ACT

It was in 1959 that the SAT acquired a competitor—the American College Testing Program, which was established in Iowa City by representatives of 16 states. About 75,000 students took the test that year. (Today the test is simply "the ACT," and the company is also known as "ACT." Like "SAT," "ACT" is no longer considered an acronym.) ACT was founded by E. F. Lindquist, a University of Iowa statistician and the director of the Iowa Testing Programs, and Ted McCarrel, the University of Iowa admissions director and registrar.

Why develop a new college admissions test? In Iowa testing circles, the SAT was considered to be geared toward privileged students applying to elite Eastern institutions; the ACT, by contrast, "would be designed for anyone who wanted to go to college." In its early years the ACT was administered primarily in Midwestern states, but it is now accepted by all U.S. four-year colleges and universities.[35]

From the beginning the ACT differed from the SAT in terms of both content and underlying philosophy: Whereas the SAT included only verbal and mathematical sections, the ACT was more closely tied to instructional objectives. The content of the ACT is informed by regular surveys of high school and college instructors and curriculum experts. Today, the test consists of four multiple-choice sections: English, mathematics, reading, and science. Students receive a score in each subject area, as well as a composite score. The ACT program also includes an optional 30-minute essay test, first administered in 2005. Students who elect to take it receive a writing test score and an English language arts score, based on the English, reading, and writing results. The ACT recently began providing a "STEM score" as well. Although the acronym ordinarily refers to science, technology, engineering, and mathematics, the ACT STEM score refers to the student's performance on the math and science sections of the test. In 2016, ACT also began to offer new reporting categories that "are aligned with ACT College and Career Readiness Standards."[36] The ACT remains a paper-and-pencil test, except in some states and districts that offer the ACT to all students. A computerized version has been offered as an option in some schools participating in these programs.

Taking a not-so-subtle dig at the College Board, the ACT website says, "We know The ACT has significant impact on people's lives. Because of this, we work hard to avoid unnecessary risks that might come with large-scale changes or total product reinvention."[37]

## High School Grades

Undergraduate institutions typically regard grades in college preparatory courses as the most important factor in admissions decisions. The precise manner in which grades should be incorporated, however, is the subject of ongoing debate. One area of contention is how to take into account the well-established fact that grading standards vary substantially across high schools.[38] Is this a flaw, to be "adjusted away," or a property to be exploited? Another defining characteristic of grades is the fact that they reflect more than mere academic performance. Does this limit their utility or is it actually an advantage? What do we know about the pros and cons of grades? What is their ideal role in the college admissions process?

One common use of high school grades in admissions is as a predictor of college grades. Many institutions statistically combine high school GPA, test scores, and other factors to predict students' first-year college grade point averages (FGPAs). Brigham's "Princeton bogie grade," which used scores on the College Board essay tests, SAT scores, and high school grades to predict FGPA at Princeton, was probably the first effort of this kind.[39] How do high school grades stack up against admissions test scores as a predictor? One way to measure the utility of a predictor is to examine the correlation between the predictor and the quantity that is to be predicted—in this case, college grades. Although a 2008 College Board study showed the SAT and high school GPA to be about equally strong as predictors,[40] high school grades have typically been found to be a somewhat better predictor than test scores when evaluated from this perspective. Even Brigham, father of the SAT, "had concluded by 1928 that the correlation between freshman [college] grades and the Scholastic Aptitude Test was slightly lower than that . . . between college grades and previous school grades."[41] In recent years the signaling function of grades has also been promoted. Using high school grades as an admissions criterion conveys the message to students, parents, and teachers that academic performance in high school is important.

High school grades, however, have two distinct disadvantages as predictors of college grades. First, they are not very useful for making distinctions at the high end of the scale. For example, consider the fact that in 2015 an astonishing 37,200 applicants to UC Berkeley had high school GPAs of at least 4.0.[42] (Extra points are given for honors and Advanced Placement classes.) Second, high school grades can lead to systematic prediction errors because of the differences in grading standards across schools. A student with a high school GPA of 3.0 (on a 0–4 scale) from a top-notch high school may be well prepared for college, whereas a student with the same GPA from an inferior school may not be. Ignoring these high school effects can lead to overly optimistic predictions of college performance for students from low-quality schools and pessimistic predictions for students from superior schools. These kinds of distortions can occur even in the presence of a substantial correlation between high school and college grades.[43] From the prediction perspective, the nonequivalence of grades across high schools is a problem to be corrected. Attempts to adjust for these between-school differences date back to Brigham's attempt to create a universal high school grade scale called the Converted School Grade.[44] In recent years much more sophisticated methods have been developed, but there is no general agreement as to whether or how grades should be adjusted.[45]

In any case, the role of high school grades in college admissions is not limited to its contribution to the prediction of college grades. If an undergraduate institution does not seek to predict college achievement, the variation in grading standards across high schools need not be an obstacle. In fact, certain admissions policies exploit the fact that some schools grade more stringently than others. In particular, "percent plans" stipulate that students with the highest grades in their schools receive certain advantages in college admission. For example, the Top Ten Percent Plan enacted in Texas in 1997 ensures that high school graduates whose grades put them in the top 10% of their class will be automatically admitted to any public university in the state.[46] The percent plans are intended to increase racial and socioeconomic diversity on campus. Some critics have taken a cynical view of these plans because they succeed only to the degree that low-income students and ethnic minorities are concentrated in lower-quality schools. In an impoverished and ineffective high school, a student who otherwise would have no chance of attending his preferred college might be near the top of his high school class and hence eligible for automatic admission. Percent plan advocates would point to this situation as evidence of a successful policy. Testing proponents might argue that this situation exemplifies the need for considering standardized test scores along with high school grades in admissions.

What exactly do grades—in particular, high school GPAs—measure, and why do they sometimes tell a different story from scores on standardized tests? Warren Willingham, then a senior researcher at ETS, and his colleagues studied these very issues. According to Willingham, grades have much in common with test scores, but have three distinguishing characteristics. First, as mentioned above, grades are affected by the contexts in which they are assigned. Not only do grades vary across schools and teachers, they also inflate and deflate over time. A second difference is that grades reflect "scholastic engagement," which includes characteristics we might call industriousness, conscientiousness, and perseverance. Willingham refers to the third distinguishing factor as teacher judgment. By this he means that grades are influenced by the particular aspects of the student's performance that the teacher chooses to evaluate: "Individual assessment by the teacher can be based more closely on the specific material that each student has studied and what each has learned than is possible with a standards-based test."[47]

It may seem benign or even advantageous for grades to measure studiousness, motivation, or other factors related to schoolwork. However, grades can reflect unwanted influences as well. Some nonacademic factors may be intentionally incorporated by instructors; other influences may not be conscious. As a college lecturer recently observed, an instructor "might assign higher grades because a student (1) is very nice; (2) has done well in other work for the class or prior classes; (3) seems hardworking and conscientious; (4) seems very interested in the class; (5) seems eager (or desperate) for a high grade; (6) needs a high grade for some important purpose; (7) has a certain gender or ethnic status; (8) is attractive; (9) looks, speaks, or acts like a very intelligent person; or (10) is connected to the instructor in some way (e.g., the child of a friend or colleague)."[48]

Research on grading practices has shown that, in addition to academic performance, teachers take into account such factors as attendance, effort, completion of assignments, and classroom behavior.[49] Studies and informal observations involving college students have suggested that grades can also be influenced by the student's physical attractiveness and charm. (One article declares "Beauty is talent." Another asks, "Are we grading on the curves?")[50] Some research on younger students has found that boys receive lower grades than girls because of classroom misbehavior.[51] A 2014 study of high school students found that young women and students with limited English proficiency tended to earn higher grades than other students, after taking test scores and school characteristics into consideration, while low-income students earned lower grades.[52]

Alleged bias in grading became an issue when New York State began to give equal weight to high school GPA and SAT scores in awarding college scholarships in the late 1980s. An outcry ensued, with school districts accusing each other of padding their own students' GPAs. Ironically, the use of grades in the scholarship decisions had been intended to satisfy critics who objected that using SAT scores alone to pick the winners led to bias against girls. But one superintendent said of the new system, "I'm not supporting S.A.T.'s as a way to award scholarships because they are discriminatory against girls, but grades are discriminatory against boys."[53]

## Grades, Tests, and Group Differences

Some researchers have explicitly addressed the question of whether grades are more fair than standardized test scores and have concluded that the answer is yes. For example, Robert T. Brennan and his colleagues sought to investigate "the *relative* equitability of high-stakes tests to the prevailing gold-standard measure of school achievement—teacher-assigned grades. According to [this] definition, if a high-stakes test creates a greater gap between groups as defined by their race/ethnicity or gender, then we would consider the high-stakes test to be less equitable. . . ."[54]

Based on elaborate statistical analyses, the authors, who acknowledged that the students' "true abilities" were unknown, found that grades were generally more equitable than test scores—in this case, scores on the tests that make up the Massachusetts Comprehensive Assessment System. Surprisingly, though, they noted that despite this conclusion, they "explicitly do not assert that this demonstrates that high-stakes tests are more biased than grades or even biased at all."[55] This statement reinforces their evident belief that "equitability"—a synonym for fairness—can be defined simply in terms of score differences. Not only does Brennan's conclusion seemingly endorse the equal performance model described earlier, it also requires us to accept grades as the ideal measure (the "gold standard") of students' academic skills, despite what is known about their susceptibility to distortion.

Arguing from the opposite perspective—using test scores as the standard—a 1994 U.S. government report based on the National Education Longitudinal Study showed that eighth graders with similar scores on math and reading tests received grades that varied widely with the poverty level of the school. In reading, "students in high poverty schools . . . who received mostly A's in English got about the same reading score as did the 'C' and 'D' students in the most affluent schools." In math, "the 'A' students in the high poverty schools most closely resembled the 'D' students in the most affluent schools." The report contends that this apparent leniency in grading in high-poverty schools is unfair to students because it fails to give them an accurate picture of their own achievement and thus deprives them of the opportunity to improve their skills.[56]

Along with potential upward or downward biases, there is another factor that needs to be taken into account when comparing group differences in grades and test scores—their relative precision. One way to think about this is in terms of signal-to-noise ratio. In engineering, this ratio compares the strength of a "signal" (often an electrical signal) to the level of background "noise." In the case of grades and test scores, we can think of the signal as "academic skills." The noise is anything that interferes with our assessment of the signal (*measurement error*, in psychometric terms). Because they are affected by many nonacademic factors, including the teacher's stringency and the student's attitudes and classroom behavior, grades are relatively noisy measures. SAT and ACT scores are less noisy (more *reliable*, psychometrically speaking) in that they are less susceptible to these sorts of extraneous influences. This in itself does not mean tests measure "the right thing" or that they are more appropriate for use in admissions. What it does mean is that they are more consistent and precise. All other things being equal, a less precise measure will yield smaller group differences. In other words, because grades are noisier than test scores, they will tend to blur any distinctions among groups in academic performance.

## Admissions Test Scores and SES

As the Brennan study demonstrates, one argument for the fairness of grades relative to test scores in college admissions is that differences among ethnic groups tend to be smaller. A second argument hinges on the relationship between these measures and socioeconomic status (SES). Some test critics argue that ideally, predictors of college performance should be unrelated to SES, and grades are viewed as coming closer to this standard. For example, two University of California researchers asserted in a 2007 paper that "compared to high-school grade-point average . . . , scores on standardized admissions tests such as the SAT I [an earlier name for the SAT] are much more closely correlated with students' socioeconomic background characteristics" and used this claim to support their conclusion that "high-school grades provide a fairer, more equitable and ultimately more meaningful basis for admissions decision-making. . . ."[57]

What do the data tell us about these pronouncements? Every year, the College Board publishes SAT results categorized by the test takers' family income. Let's consider the SAT math results for 2015. For the highest income category—more than \$200,000 per year—the average score is 587, well above the national average of 511. For the lowest income category—less than \$20,000—the average score is 455—a difference of 132 points. The corresponding gaps between the highest and lowest income levels are 137 for critical reading and 137 for writing. One way to evaluate the magnitude of these disparities and to compare them to income gaps on tests with different score scales is to translate them into standard deviation units. The standard deviation is a measure of how spread out the scores are. Roughly speaking, the standard deviation of a collection of values—say, test scores—is the average distance of a value from its mean. Dividing the income gaps by their respective standard deviations, we find that the math, critical reading, and writing gaps are all slightly more than one standard deviation unit. Results from 2015 show a gap of 1.3 standard deviations between the highest and lowest income groups on the ACT composite,[58] and the results I presented earlier show a similar admissions test score gap for the ELS senior cohort of 2004. As I have noted, gaps of 0.8 standard deviations or more are considered large in behavioral science research.

These results clearly illustrate that SAT and ACT scores are associated with socioeconomic status. But why is this the case? Two hypotheses often advanced by testing commentators are what I call the content and coaching hypotheses.[59] The content hypothesis is that the test questions are not well tied to the high school curriculum and focus on material that is more familiar to students from wealthier families. (The fact that the SAT long ago contained an analogy question using the word "regatta" is sometimes cited in this connection. The infamous regatta item is even featured in the Wikipedia entry for the SAT.) The coaching hypothesis says that because coaching, or test preparation, is more easily available to affluent test takers (indisputably a fairness issue), the scores of these students become inflated, creating an association between test scores and socioeconomic status.

So do we still see an association with SES on tests that are based on skills acquired at school or tests for which no coaching is available? The ELS survey itself provides an ideal example of such an assessment. One component of the survey is a math achievement test, which was developed to measure the acquisition of mathematics skills and concepts. ELS results are never reported for individual students, classrooms, or schools and thus create no incentive for coaching. The ELS math assessment, then, allows for a test of both the content and coaching hypotheses.

A government report shows that, despite the absence of esoteric content and the unavailability of test coaching, performance on the ELS math assessment is strongly related to socioeconomic status. Consider the 2004 results for the ELS high school seniors. Results are provided in terms of five achievement levels. Level 4 requires "understanding of intermediate-level mathematical concepts and / or multistep solutions to word problems such as drawing an inference based on an algebraic expression or inequality." Level 5, which very few students attained, involves more advanced material. Seventy percent of students in the highest SES category scored at the intermediate level or above (Levels 4 or 5), compared to only 43% of those in the second-highest SES category, 29% of those in the third category, and 19% of those in the bottom category.[60]

Why do these vast differences occur on a school-based achievement test for which there is no coaching? One clue lies in patterns of course-taking. Students who took precalculus in the last two years of high school scored better than their peers, and this was especially true of those who also took calculus. But while 30% of those in the highest SES category took precalculus, only 11% of those in the lowest SES category did so. The report notes that "students with more socioeconomic and educational resources" are likely to have had "experiences and instruction at earlier stages in school [that] gives them the foundational skills to move through the hierarchy at a pace that ensures their enrollment in courses like precalculus and calculus."[61] The home lives of these students also offer educational experiences not available to children from low-SES families. Every step of the way, wealthier students have learning opportunities that facilitate their educational progress.

In terms of content fairness, admissions tests—and standardized tests in general—have improved over the last 25 years because of rigorous monitoring. All reputable testing companies use expert reviews to eliminate potentially offensive or unfair items and also conduct statistical analyses to determine whether test questions give some groups an unfair edge by including material that is unrelated to the skills being tested. The legendary "regatta" item (which required test takers to know that the relationship between "oarsman" and "regatta" was analogous to the relationship between "runner" and "marathon") was objectionable because, in addition to testing verbal skills, it also assessed familiarity with an elite sport. This question would not appear on the SAT today. For one thing, analogy items were eliminated from the SAT in 2005 following criticism that they were too far removed from classroom learning. But more importantly, ETS test developers (who create SAT questions under a contract with the College Board) must follow the ETS Guidelines for Fairness Review of Assessments, which state that "if specialized knowledge of a sport is needed to answer an item, the item should not appear in a general skills test."[62] The document also warns against including questions involving military topics, regionalisms, religion, specialized tools, or U.S. culture except when necessary for the assessment of a particular skill. (For example, a history test could include questions about war.) If a regatta-type question were created and somehow survived the initial screening, it would then be subjected to statistical analyses that compared the performance of various pairs of groups, such as men and women, Black and White test takers, and Hispanic and White test takers. Evaluations of this kind, called differential item functioning analyses, seek to determine whether, for example, men and women who have similar overall scores on the relevant section of the test nevertheless tend to perform differently on certain test questions. This can be an indication that the question is assessing a skill that is not relevant to the intended purpose of the test. Questions judged to be problematic after a subsequent committee review are modified or eliminated.[63]

## Grades and SES

Over the last century, hundreds of studies have examined the association between socioeconomic status and academic achievement. All types of academic measures are found to be correlated with SES, including number of course credits completed, teacher ratings of students, participation in extracurricular academic activities, persistence in school, and also grades.[64] For example, the ELS results presented earlier show a marked socioeconomic gap in high school GPA for the 2004 senior class. These relationships are unsurprising in light of the overwhelming evidence that educational quality varies with SES. So why is high school GPA ordinarily found to have *smaller* associations with SES than SAT or ACT scores do? Certain technical factors help explain this disparity. First, all other things being equal, we would expect high school GPA to have a smaller correlation with SES than admissions test scores do if only because they are less precise (or more "noisy").[65]

But the correlations between academic measures and SES that are typically reported are potentially misleading for another reason: They confound the answers to two different questions. The first question is, "To what degree do individual students with high academic performance tend to come from families with high income?" The second question is, "To what degree do high schools with high *average* performance also tend to have high *average* family income levels?" It is nearly always the first question—about the student-level relationship—that is of primary interest.

To understand this distinction, it may help to consider an example from outside education. Suppose we are interested in the relationship between home value and temperature. We collect data from three cities: San Diego, Denver, and Minneapolis. San Diego, with an average annual temperature of 64, has a Zillow home value index of about $500,000, while Minneapolis, with an average temperature of 46, has a home price index of about $200,000. Denver is in between, with an average temperature of 50 and a home price index of about $300,000.[66] If we compute a correlation between the three average temperatures and the three home price indexes, we find that it exceeds .99—an almost perfect correlation. The higher the temperature, the greater the home value. So would we be correct in assuming that within these cities, the houses in the sunnier locales sold for higher prices? If we did make that conclusion, we would be falling prey to a well-known statistical fallacy—believing that relationships observed for groups (here, cities) must also hold for individuals (in this case, houses).[67] In fact, there might be no relationship at all between home values and temperature within cities, or there might even be a negative relationship. Knowing the between-city relationship (the near-perfect correlation) doesn't tell us anything about the within-city relationship.

Now let's make the highly implausible assumption that we could obtain data from 1,000 home sales in each city, as well as the outdoor temperatures at each house at the time of sale. We could then recompute the correlation based on these 3,000 pairs of temperature / home-value data instead of just the three pairs we had before. However, we still would not know what the relationship was between temperature and price *within* the cities. Instead, we would now have a mixture of between-city and within-city information that would be hard to interpret. If we wanted to know what the within-city relationship was, our best approach would be to compute the correlation within San Diego, the correlation within Denver, and the correlation within Minneapolis and then take the average.

In the educational situation, the high schools correspond to the cities. We can think of family income as corresponding to home values, and academic measures (grades or test scores) as corresponding to temperature. The within- and between-high-school components of the correlations can be statistically disentangled if it is possible to determine which high school each student attended.[68] If so, we can get at the student-level relationships between income and academic performance by calculating the correlations of interest within each high school and averaging the results across schools (taking school size into consideration).

In a study I conducted with my colleague Jennifer Green, we used these ideas to explore the relationships between socioeconomic factors (family income and parent education) and academic factors (high school GPA, high school class rank, and SAT math and verbal scores). We had College Board data on nearly 100,000 students—a random sample of SAT takers from 2004. These students came from more than 7,000 high schools, and we knew which school each student attended.

Ordinarily, analyses of the correlations among these factors are computed after combining the data from all students, without taking account of which high school each student attended. When we followed these procedures, we found the typical pattern: SAT scores appeared to have substantially higher correlations with SES (.31 to .38) than did high school GPA (.17 to .21) or class rank (.14 to .20). Further analyses were needed to tell us how much of these relationships was at the student level. When we calculated the student-level correlations within high schools and then took the average, we found that the association with SES ranged from .20 to .25 for SAT scores, from .12 to .18 for high school GPA, and from .15 to .21 for class rank. The SAT correlations still tended to be larger than the others, but not dramatically so. College Board researchers obtained comparable results using SAT data from 2007.[69]

It seems reasonable to conclude that high school grades are somewhat less correlated with SES than are SAT scores. But this is a matter of degree rather than a qualitative difference, and is not, in itself, sufficient to support the belief that that high school GPA is a more authentic indicator of academic skills. A measure of academic performance that is unrelated to socioeconomic factors has yet to be discovered.

## The Role of Coaching in College Admissions

Test coaching has always been an incendiary topic, and the flames have been fanned both by test preparation firms, which promised huge score gains, and by testing companies, which for many years took pains to claim that coaching was ineffective. Even the Federal Trade Commission weighed in during the 1970s, taking aim both at coaching companies, which were said to "have a universal propensity for . . . making unsubstantiated advertising claims," and at standardized tests, in part because of their alleged coachability.[70]

Just how effective is coaching in improving admissions test performance? In order to be credible, test-coaching research must compare the gains of coached groups to the gains of uncoached groups who simply take the test a second time, and must incorporate information about the characteristics of coached and uncoached students. (Randomly assigning students to coached and uncoached conditions, which would allow the assumption that the groups were equivalent, is not ordinarily feasible.) The most trustworthy studies of SAT coaching are remarkably consistent in their conclusions, finding average gains (on a 200-to-800 scale) of 6 to 9 points on the verbal section and 14 to 18 points on the math section.[71] (These studies are based on the pre-2005 SAT. No later coaching studies are available.) Published studies on ACT coaching are rare, but indicate average coaching gains of no more than 1.5 points on the composite scale, which ranges from 1 to 36.[72]

Despite the fact that average gains are modest, coaching has implications for fairness for the obvious reason that test takers don't have equal access to test preparation services, particularly the more expensive versions. As of 2016, The Princeton Review offers individual tutoring packages that cost up to $7,800. Also available is an "SAT honors" prep course that costs $1,999 and requires a previous score on the new SAT of 1250, combined across the two main sections. (Yes, a test preparation course with its own admissions criteria!) For those whose scores or wallets don't make the grade, there are other options, including a self-paced online course "starting at $299."[73]

Although the public conversation on coaching for college admission typically focuses on test preparation, the coaching phenomenon is actually much larger. Thanks to the rapidly growing independent admissions counseling industry, paid help is available not only on admissions tests, but on the entire admissions process. These admissions consultants don't work for high schools; they are hired by parents. According to the New York Times, the "going national rate" in 2009 was $185 per hour, but some consultants were found to charge more than $40,000 per student,[74] and much higher rates have been reported recently. In addition to providing advice on how and where to apply, private admissions counselors typically edit (cynics would say "compose") students' college applications. One owner of a high-end admissions consulting business, who collects hundreds of thousands of dollars from some clients, told Businessweek that his employees find internships and volunteer opportunities for college candidates, edit their essays and résumés, and proofread their applications. He described his role as that of a good sculptor, bringing out "the natural beauty of the stone."[75] Countering this poetic description, Bob Laird, former director of undergraduate admissions at UC Berkeley, told the Chronicle of Higher Education that "private admissions consultants have ... powerfully increased the advantages that wealthy students and families already have in the college-admissions process."[76]

In a 2010 article, sociologist Claudia Buchmann and her colleagues suggested that test coaching can be seen as part of "shadow education," defined as "educational activities outside of formal schooling."[77] This is even more true of private admissions counseling. Indeed, shadow education can affect every piece of the admissions process. For example, grade coaches have been around for centuries and are often very expensive. We don't call them that of course; we call them private tutors. Arguably, tutoring is usually intended to produce actual learning, not merely boost grades, but the distinction can be a bit fuzzy. For example, consider this online ad for a national chain of tutoring programs: "Grade CHANGER—Ace the Next Report Card with Sylvan."[78]

The only antidote to the inequities of shadow education is greater access to free or low-cost test preparation and college counseling services. An example is a five-year program created by the California legislature in 1998. Funds were allocated to high schools to offer ACT and SAT prep courses aimed at students from low-income households. Students could be charged no more than $5 for at least 20 hours of instruction.[79] In an encouraging development, the College Board has entered into a partnership with the Khan Academy, a nonprofit provider of instructional videos, to offer free online tutoring for the redesigned SAT that debuted in 2016. The Board's president said he sought to dismantle the culture of costly test preparation that "drives the perception of inequality and injustice in this country." If the tutoring lives up to the promise that it will give students "deep practice and [help] them diagnose their gaps at absolutely no cost," it could be a useful learning tool.[80] Following suit, ACT announced in late 2015 that it would offer low-income students free access to its newly redesigned online test preparation program, as "part of ACT's commitment to helping increase college access, opportunity and success for low-income students." Students who don't qualify as low-income will have to pay for the program, which is a collaboration between ACT, Inc. and coaching giant Kaplan Test Prep. It will include video tutorials as well as live instructional sessions to which students can tune in.[81] While these efforts by testing companies are unlikely to cause the demise of commercial coaching programs, they may serve to undercut their value.

On a larger scale, some noncommercial college access programs have been successful in preparing low-income and minority students to apply for and attend four-year colleges by providing counseling, supplementary instruction, test preparation, assistance with applications, campus visits, and scholarships.[82] Increasing support for services of this kind—ideally integrated into high school and even middle school programs—is the only way to reduce the "shadow education" advantages enjoyed by students from affluent families.

## Using the ELS Data to Study Admissions Using Test Scores and High School Grades

To examine the effects of using test scores and high school grades as admissions criteria, we can compare the composition and accomplishments of entering classes selected using high school GPA only, admissions test scores only, and an equally weighted composite of GPA and test scores.[83] For each of the admissions criteria, we will consider two rules—a broad selection rule that involves choosing the top 41% of applicants using the criterion in question and a narrow rule that involves selecting the top 10%. To apply the broad rule using the test-score model, for example, we rank-order the applicants in terms of their test scores and then admit the top 41%. The admission rate for the broad rules matches the enrollment rate for the actual ELS applicants: Forty-one percent of the ELS senior cohort members who applied to the competitive colleges actually enrolled in one. The selection rate for the narrow rules is similar to the admission rates at Brown, Caltech, and Dartmouth. Tables 2-1 through 2-5 contain the results of applying the various models. The hypothetical entering classes can be compared to the actual enrollees.

Tables 2-1 through 2-3 show the characteristics of the entering classes in terms of gender, ethnicity, and socioeconomic status. One of the most dramatic differences among the admissions models involves the percentage of women. Table 2-1 shows that about 53% of the enrollees were women (mirroring the percentage of women among applicants). The smallest percentage of women—about 45%—occurred for the narrow version of the test-score rule. The percentage of women was much higher when high school GPA only was used for selection than when test scores or a combination of the two was used. Under the broad version of the high school GPA rule, 62% of those selected were women; under the narrow rule, nearly 65% were women. Further analysis showed that, among the applicant group, women were more likely to be from the lowest socioeconomic quartile than were their male counterparts. Therefore, it's possible that women were also more likely to have attended high schools with lenient grading practices, contributing to their disproportionate representation in this entering class.

Table 2-2 shows that the three broad selection rules produced fairly similar ethnic characteristics. In all cases, the percentage of underrepresented minorities (URMs) was smaller than the 12% observed for the enrollees. This finding suggests that the actual admissions and enrollment processes for the applicants to the competitive colleges were, not surprisingly, based on more than simply test scores and grades and may have had an affirmative action component. The three narrow rules differed considerably from the broad rules and from each other. The percentages of URMs were lower for the narrow rules than for the corresponding broad rules. In particular, the narrow test score and composite rules yielded fewer than 3% URMs. The narrow high school GPA rule yielded more URMs—about 9%—but the representation of Asians was only about 7%, compared to about 17% for the narrow test-score rule. Under narrow selection, then, the ethnic composition of the entering classes depended heavily on which admissions criterion was used.

The results for socioeconomic status in Table 2-3 show that the broad rules based on test scores and on the composite yielded results that were similar to each other and quite similar to the results for the enrollees: Almost two-thirds of the entering classes were from the highest SES level. The broad rule based on GPA produced a class with about 59% at the top SES level; the corresponding percentage for the narrow GPA rule was 61%. By contrast, the narrow test-score rule yielded a class with 77% from the top level, and the narrow composite rule yielded 70%.

All these patterns are consistent with the initial findings I presented from the ELS survey, which showed substantial socioeconomic and ethnic gaps in high school GPA among the applicants to the competitive colleges, and even larger gaps for test scores. Also, women were seen to have better high school grades and slightly lower test scores than men.

What about the academic accomplishments of the various entering classes? Table 2-4 gives the averages and standard deviations of test scores and high school grades for each entering class. The scores and grades for the six models tended to be higher than those of the actual enrollees, particularly for the narrow rules. Within each admission rate (broad or narrow), the test-score rule produced the highest average test score, the GPA rule produced the highest average high school GPA, and the composite rule produced results in between.

Table 2-5 shows that average first-year college GPA (FGPA) was higher for all the admissions rules than for the enrollees. Average grades were higher for the narrow rules than for the broad rules and higher for the GPA and composite rules than for the test-score rules. Four-year college graduation rates ranged from 61% to 70% and six-year rates ranged from 82% to 88%. For the most part, the graduation rates under the six admissions scenarios tended to be better than the rates observed for the enrollees. Graduation rates for the narrow admissions models were better than those for the broad rules, and the rates for the GPA and composite models were better than those for the test-score models. The narrow composite-based rule produced the highest four-year and six-year graduation rates—70% and 88%. Although these completion rates may not seem particularly high, they far exceed the national graduation rate for students who entered four-year institutions in 2004. According to the National Center of Education Statistics, the overall four-year graduation rate was a mere 38%. The six-year rate was 58.4%. Detailed NCES results for students who began college in 2007 showed that graduation rates rose steadily as the selectivity of the college increased. Research has shown that more selective schools have higher graduation rates than less selective ones even when differences in students' entering credentials are taken into account. These superior completion rates may occur because favorable peer influences, high faculty expectations, and high-quality educational and financial resources are more characteristic of selective schools.[84]

Perhaps the most interesting finding concerns the percentages of students who completed a postbaccalaureate credential by 2013, nine years after high school graduation. The vast majority of the credentials received were either master's degrees or "professional doctorates," which included degrees in law, medicine, and dentistry. Among the enrollees, the completion rate for a postbaccalaureate credential was 28%, and for five of the six entering classes in Table 2-5, the percentages ranged from about 30% to 35%. But for the class selected using the narrow GPA rule, the completion rate was much higher—about 42%. Most of these credentials were master of science degrees or law degrees.

## Conclusions

As the ELS analyses show, selection methods based on high school GPA, test scores, and a combination of the two can produce very different entering classes. Strict selection yielded better academic credentials and college outcomes than broad selection, but produced classes that were less diverse. Rules based only on test scores produced classes that were less diverse and had slightly lower graduation rates, first-year college grades, and graduate degree completion rates than methods based on high school GPA or on a combination of GPA and test scores. One possible reason for the differences in outcomes is that high school grades summarize four years of academic accomplishments and may reflect students' motivation and perseverance as well as their cognitive skills. In their book on college graduation, William G. Bowen, Matthew M. Chingos, and Michael S. McPherson conjecture that grades also reflect coping skills, time management skills, and "the ability to accept criticism and benefit from it."[85] This viewpoint is consistent with past research that has found high school grades to be related to "personality factors," including conscientiousness and grit. In one study in the Netherlands, grades were found to be more highly correlated with these properties than with IQ test scores.[86] Whereas test scores provide a snapshot of students' academic skills, high school grades represent students' performance over the long haul.

One factor to keep in mind when considering the results in Tables 2-1 to 2-5 and throughout this book is that the students selected by the various admissions models differ from each other and from the enrollees in terms of the schools they attended and the fields they studied. For the six rules I studied in this chapter, I examined these issues in some detail. In terms of college competitiveness, all the enrollees by definition attended schools in the "most competitive" (39% of enrollees) or "highly competitive" (61%) Barron's categories. But those selected using the various admissions models included students who attended schools at all six Barron's levels of competitiveness. For all admissions rules in this chapter, 63% to 78% of students attended schools in the top two categories, and fewer than 4% attended schools below the "competitive" category. Students selected using the narrow rules were more likely to attend the "most competitive" schools than those selected using the broad rules, and among the narrow rules, those selected using test scores or the composite were more likely to attend these schools than were the students selected using GPA. The impact of these differences on college outcomes is not obvious. On the one hand, it may be easier to earn high grades at less competitive colleges. On the other hand, as I mentioned earlier, research indicates that attending selective colleges actually facilitates graduation, even after taking students' initial qualifications into account. Among the highly qualified students included in my research, nearly all of whom attended selective schools, field of study is likely to have had more impact on college outcomes than the school's competitiveness rating. Therefore, it was reassuring to find that, for all six rules and for the enrollees, there was little variation in students' first college majors. For all these groups, the most popular initial fields of study were engineering, biological sciences, social sciences, and business. For all three broad rules and for the enrollees, each of these fields drew 9% to 14% of students, with only minor variations across the rules. The classes selected by the narrow rules were slightly more likely to be in engineering and social sciences and less likely to be in business than those selected by the broad rules. Differences among the narrow rules, although slightly more substantial than the differences among the broad rules, were still remarkably small.[87] It seems fair to conclude that the academic disparities among the "entering classes" are largely due to the selection criteria themselves.

Beyond the differences in the characteristics of the admitted students, what are the pros and cons of using GPAs and test scores in college admissions? As critics point out, admissions tests assess only a narrow range of skills and do so mostly through the use of a single question type—multiple-choice. These aspects of admissions tests can and should change. Already, both the ACT and the SAT have begun to offer writing tests, addressing one deficiency noted in a review of admissions testing conducted by the National Research Council in 1999.[88] Within a few years, both tests will likely be given primarily via computer, which will expand the types of test questions that can be included. Computerized test questions today can involve multistep math problems, interactive graphs, and even tasks in which test takers communicate with automated mentors and peers to arrive at a solution. In 2009 the government-sponsored National Assessment of Educational Progress administered a science test to students in grades 4, 8, and 12 that included interactive computer tasks requiring students to "solve scientific problems in a computer-based environment, often by simulating a natural or laboratory setting."[89] Some of these novel question types are likely to make their way into admissions tests in the future. Because of technological advances, it is also possible to use computers to score student responses consisting of several paragraphs of text, or even a graph or diagram. This means that even for tests administered on a large scale, like admissions tests, questions need not be restricted to a multiple-choice or short-answer format. Of course, it is important that admissions policy makers and test makers not be seduced by the dazzle of new assessment technology in making the transition to computerized testing. Valid and fair measurement must remain the primary goal.

Another concern often raised about admissions tests is that test scores are sometimes used in inappropriate ways, despite the cautions routinely issued by testing agencies. Some misuses may result from the fact that test scores can give the impression of being much more precise than they are. In fact, because of factors collectively referred to as measurement error, individuals would not be expected to get exactly the same test score on repeated test administrations even if the previous testing experience could be purged from their memory. Scores can be affected by test takers' moods, testing conditions, and lucky guesses. These factors, among others, reduce the precision (or *reliability*) of the test score. Grades are generally even less precise, but tests are more likely to give an illusion of exactitude, if only because there are many possible scores.

A College Board publication advises that institutions that use tests in admissions should "ensure that small differences in test scores are not the basis for rejecting an otherwise qualified applicant" and should "guard against using minimum test scores unless used in conjunction with other information such as secondary school performance and unless properly validated."[90] But this advice lacks specificity. How large does a score difference need to be to allow the conclusion that two applicants' skills are different? How would the use of a minimum test score be properly validated? Research has shown that these principles are sometimes violated, either because the institutions are not aware of them or because they regard them as unimportant. In a recent NACAC survey, admissions directors at 1,075 four-year schools were asked to describe their uses of admissions tests. There were 246 respondents, 89% of whom stated they used admissions tests. Twenty-four percent of ACT users and 21% of SAT users reported using scores "to define a cut-off threshold for admission." A substantial proportion of admissions directors also reported that for applicants with above-average SAT scores, a small score increase (say, from 600 to 610 in critical reading) would "significantly improve" the likelihood that the applicant would be admitted.[91] These misuses can lead to statistically unjustifiable decisions. Testing companies may need to be much more specific and proactive in publicizing guidelines for test use. In its critical review of admissions testing in 2008, NACAC went one step further, recommending that the College Board and ACT conduct periodic audits to ensure that institutions are using test scores properly.[92]

An advantage of admissions tests is their ability to provide efficient comparisons of students whose high school grades are influenced by the schools they attended, the classes they chose, their rapport with their teachers, and many other extraneous factors. Test scores can also provide a means of evaluating home-schooled and international candidates and can help to distinguish among the many applicants to elite colleges who share a GPA of 4.0 or above. As test proponents like to point out, admissions tests can sometimes serve to identify talented students with weak academic backgrounds—those who used to be called "diamonds in the rough" before that label came to be seen as disparaging.

In contemplating the advantages and disadvantages of GPAs and SATs, it is useful to note that high school grades actually "contain" test scores. Sociologist Christopher Jencks once remarked that using grades rather than SAT scores in admissions amounted to nothing more than "substituting tests designed by high school teachers for tests designed by the Educational Testing Service."[93] It's also important to keep in mind that neither test scores nor grades need be part of the admissions process. Author Alfie Kohn, a fierce SAT opponent, has expressed an almost equally strong antipathy toward grades. In a 2001 opinion piece in which he mused hopefully about an end to the SAT, he pointed to the "ominous threat" that a fading SAT would lead to a greater emphasis on high school grades. "There is a widespread assumption that less emphasis on scores as an admissions criterion has to mean more emphasis on grades, as though nature has decreed an inverse relationship between the two," he said. "But for grades to be given more emphasis would be terribly unfortunate." Kohn pointed to the unreliability and subjectivity of grades, as well as the possibility that, if grades were emphasized in admissions, students would focus on "grooming their transcripts" rather than on learning. He particularly decried the use of class rank (central to the percent plans), arguing that a focus on relative academic standing causes students to view their peers as obstacles to their own success.[94] And SAT critic Lani Guinier, who has been railing against the "testocracy" for many years, also condemns grades in her latest book, noting that it is "important to remember that the current prevailing notion of merit in college admissions—as a function of standardized-test scores and secondary school grades—is neither objectively true nor natural."[95]

*Table 2-1.* Percentages of Women and Men for Enrollees and Six Admissions Models

| Gender | Enrollees | Broad Selection Rules | | | Narrow Selection Rules | | |
|---|---|---|---|---|---|---|---|
| | | Test Score | High School GPA | GPA-Test Score Composite | Test Score | High School GPA | GPA–Test Score Composite |
| Women (%) | 53.4 | 50.0 | 62.0 | 57.2 | 44.7 | 64.8 | 53.5 |
| Men (%) | 46.6 | 50.0 | 38.0 | 42.8 | 55.3 | 35.2 | 46.5 |

*Note:* Some column totals are not exactly 100% because of rounding.

*Table 2-2.* Percentages of Students in Each Ethnic Group for Enrollees and Six Admissions Models

| Ethnic Group | Enrollees | Broad Selection Rules | | | Narrow Selection Rules | | |
|---|---|---|---|---|---|---|---|
| | | Test Score | High School GPA | GPA–Test-Score Composite | Test Score | High School GPA | GPA–Test Score Composite |
| Asian (%) | 12.1 | 12.7 | 10.4 | 12.3 | 16.5 | 6.8 | 15.6 |
| Underrepresented minority (%) | 12.4 | 7.3 | 10.1 | 7.9 | 2.5 | 8.8 | 2.5 |
| More than one race (%) | 3.8 | 2.6 | 2.4 | 2.0 | 1.6 | 3.9 | 1.5 |
| White (%) | 71.7 | 77.5 | 77.1 | 77.8 | 79.4 | 80.6 | 80.4 |

*Note:* Some column totals are not exactly 100% because of rounding. Results for Black, Hispanic, and American Indian students were combined to conform with Institute of Education Sciences data security requirements.

*Table 2-3.* Percentages of Students in Each of Four Socioeconomic Categories for Enrollees and Six Admissions Models

| Socioeconomic Status (SES) | Enrollees | Broad Selection Rules | | | Narrow Selection Rules | | |
|---|---|---|---|---|---|---|---|
| | | Test Score | High School GPA | GPA–Test-Score Composite | Test Score | High School GPA | GPA–Test Score Composite |
| Highest (%) | 63.6 | 64.9 | 58.7 | 64.0 | 77.0 | 61.0 | 70.4 |
| Second highest (%) | 20.8 | 22.8 | 22.5 | 22.4 | 16.5 | 22.3 | 21.8 |
| Second lowest (%) | 11.4 | 8.9 | 12.9 | 9.5 | 3.9 | 13.9 | 4.7 |
| Lowest (%) | 4.2 | 3.4 | 5.9 | 4.1 | 2.7 | 2.8 | 3.0 |

*Note:* Some column totals are not exactly 100% because of rounding.

*Table 2-4.* High School GPA and Test-Score Data for Enrollees and Six Admissions Models

|  | Enrollees | Broad Selection Rules | | | Narrow Selection Rules | | |
|  |  | Test Score | High School GPA | GPA–Test-Score Composite | Test Score | High School GPA | GPA–Test-Score Composite |
|---|---|---|---|---|---|---|---|
| High school GPA |  |  |  |  |  |  |  |
| Average | 3.5 | 3.5 | 3.8 | 3.7 | 3.7 | 4.0 | 3.9 |
| Standard deviation | 0.4 | 0.4 | 0.2 | 0.2 | 0.3 | 0.0 | 0.1 |
| Test score |  |  |  |  |  |  |  |
| Average | 1245 | 1325 | 1249 | 1303 | 1452 | 1297 | 1431 |
| Standard deviation | 150 | 89 | 144 | 111 | 54 | 133 | 68 |

*Table 2-5.* College First-Year Grade-Point Average (FGPA), Graduation Rates, and Postbaccalaureate Attainment Rate for Enrollees and Six Admissions Models

|  | Enrollees | Broad Selection Rules | | | Narrow Selection Rules | | |
|  |  | Test Score | High School GPA | GPA–Test-Score Composite | Test Score | High School GPA | GPA–Test-Score Composite |
|---|---|---|---|---|---|---|---|
| College FGPA |  |  |  |  |  |  |  |
| Average | 3.2 | 3.3 | 3.4 | 3.4 | 3.5 | 3.6 | 3.6 |
| Standard deviation | 0.6 | 0.6 | 0.5 | 0.5 | 0.5 | 0.4 | 0.4 |
| College Graduation |  |  |  |  |  |  |  |
| 4-year graduation rate | 64.3 % | 60.8 % | 65.2 % | 64.7 % | 61.6 % | 64.0 % | 69.6 % |
| 6-year graduation rate | 83.7 % | 81.8 % | 86.6 % | 85.4 % | 85.5 % | 86.6 % | 88.2 % |
| Postbaccalaureate attainment rate | 28.0 % | 30.2 % | 35.2 % | 33.2 % | 30.0 % | 41.8 % | 33.8 % |

# Performance Predictions and Academic Indexes

> To predict a certain behavioral outcome, for example, "How well will this student do in college?" would it be better to ask for a forecast from the admissions officer who has studied the student's record, interviewed him about his goals and aspirations, and then thought about the problem in a judicious, rational, and informed way? Or would a more accurate prognostication be made if we turned the test and file data over to the statistician who would put them through his prediction equations and formulas in order to give an answer to our question?
>
> —*Harrison Gough*

Seventy-five years of research says that we should bet on the statistician. Studies have repeatedly found statistical methods to be more accurate than "human" approaches in predicting academic success.[1] But statistical prediction is often viewed with great skepticism, particularly when human behavior, such as college performance, is the target. In this chapter I address several questions: How are statistical prediction equations derived for admissions purposes, and how well do they work? What are the pros and cons of this kind of formulaic prediction, and how does it compare with predictions of college performance made by experts? And if it's legitimate to engage in forecasting college success, how should the predictors themselves be selected?

Carl Brigham was probably the first to statistically forecast college performance. As described in his biography, Brigham "experimented with various combinations of examination marks, test scores, and school grades to find the best predictor. . . . The result was the so-called Princeton bogie grade. The bogie grade was the predicted freshman average grade of an applicant for admission to Princeton. It was originally based on the weighted average of the College Board examinations marks, the Scholastic Aptitude Test score, and school grades, these three factors being combined by a multiple regression equation. Brigham reported that it produced a correlation of about .75 with the student's actual grade average for his freshman year."[2]

Since the development of the bogie grade, thousands of statistical studies have been conducted with the goal of predicting college grade-point average. Some of these studies are conducted by testing companies for purposes of investigating the validity of admissions tests as predictors of college achievement;[3] others are carried out by faculty researchers studying the admissions process. But the majority of these analyses are performed by the admissions offices or institutional research departments of colleges and universities.[4]

Some institutions use the analysis results to develop academic indexes for use in admissions, very much analogous to the Princeton bogie grade. For example, in order to qualify for automatic admission to Iowa State University, the University of Northern Iowa, or the College of Liberal Arts and Sciences at the University of Iowa, students from Iowa high schools must have a score of at least 245 on a measure called the Regent Admission Index, or RAI. The RAI, described as "a score derived from a mathematical equation that includes four factors which have been shown to be predictors of academic success," is defined as follows: RAI = 2 × ACT composite score (or SAT equivalent) + 20 × high school GPA + 5 × number of core courses completed + high school percentile rank. (High school percentile rank is the percentage of students whose GPA is below the student's GPA.)[5] Other institutions use similar indexes as part of the admissions process, although the formulas themselves are not usually provided. In her 1997 book, former Dartmouth admissions officer Michele Hernández professed to "reveal one of the central mysteries of the Ivy League admissions process"—the use of an index based on test scores and high school class rank. Nearly 15 years later, the New York Times likened the index to "the most furtive of secret fraternity handshakes," although by then, unofficial online calculators had sprung up that allow prospective applicants to estimate their index values.[6] The University of California, too, uses an admissions index based on test scores and high school grades in evaluating in-state applicants. A prospective applicant can obtain her index value using a calculator on the admissions website.[7]

As we will see, the academic indexes are, in essence, a type of performance prediction. These indexes, which are used primarily by large institutions, can serve several functions in the admissions process. In rare cases they may serve as the sole basis for a university's admissions decisions. In other institutions, they may be part of a triage process in which some applicants are automatically admitted, some are denied, and the remainder are referred to application readers. Like the bogie grade, most academic indexes have their roots in regression analysis, a standard statistical procedure used in a variety of applications, such as forecasting a company's financial performance using the firm's characteristics or predicting a nation's average life expectancy based on its resources.[8]

## How Are Regression Equations for Predicting College Performance Derived?

In most efforts to predict college performance, the outcome to be predicted is first-year college GPA (FGPA) and the predictors are admissions test scores and high school GPA. For now, we'll assume this is the case. The regression model is estimated using data from students who have already completed one year of college and have FGPA values. In the resulting equation, each predictor—let's say score on the evidence-based reading and writing section in the new SAT, SAT math score, and high school GPA—is multiplied by a weighting factor and then summed up (along with an additive term) to obtain the predicted FGPA. Regression analysis is guaranteed to produce the best weighting of the predictors in the sense that the predicted FGPAs will correspond as closely as possible to the actual FGPAs for the students in question.[9] The obtained equation might look like this one, which I constructed as an example:

$$\text{Predicted FGPA} = 0.82 + 0.39 \times (\text{High school GPA}) + 0.000975$$
$$\times (\text{SAT evidence-based reading and writing score}) + 0.00078$$
$$\times (\text{SAT math score})$$

How might a university use these results? The equation could be applied in future years to predict the FGPA for each college applicant. For example, a candidate with a high school GPA of 3.5, an SAT evidence-based reading and writing score of 650, and an SAT math score of 600 would have a predicted FGPA of about 3.29, obtained by plugging the GPA and test scores into the equation. The candidate's predicted FGPA, along with other information in her application packet, could then be used in deciding whether to admit her. Alternatively, the equation could serve as the basis for developing an academic index in which the predictors are assigned the same relative weights as in the regression results. For example, multiplying each of the regression weights by roughly 5,128 produces the following index, which seems a little less daunting than the original equation:

$$\text{Index} = 2000 \times (\text{High school GPA}) + 5 \times (\text{SAT evidence-based reading}$$
$$\text{and writing score}) + 4 \times (\text{SAT math score})$$

The index is not interpretable as a predicted FGPA, but it still represents predicted performance (on a new scale) and allows candidates to be compared. The university can also use the results to assess the usefulness of SAT scores and high school grades as admissions criteria.

## How Accurate Is the Statistical Prediction of College Grades?

The effectiveness of a particular regression equation is ordinarily evaluated on the basis of the correlation coefficient, which measures the degree to which the predicted FGPAs correspond to the actual FGPAs.[10] Correlation coefficients lie between 0 and 1 when two factors are positively correlated (one factor tends to be high when the other is high). When there is more than one predictor, the statistic is technically called the *multiple* correlation, but it is often referred to simply as "the correlation." In research involving the prediction of human behavior, correlations greater than .5 are typically considered large; values of .3 to .5 are considered moderate, and values less than .3 are considered small.[11]

What does current research say about the value of college admissions tests and high school grades in predicting FGPA? An examination of large-scale studies published in 2000 or later reveals some consistent patterns. The multiple correlation of (pre-2016) SAT score (critical reading and math scores considered together) or ACT score (all four main section scores considered together) with FGPA is typically about .3 to .4.[12] For both the SAT and the ACT, including the writing component as a predictor tends to boost the correlation by about .02.[13] The correlation between high school GPA and FGPA is usually slightly higher. Considering ACT or SAT scores as predictors along with high school grades yields correlations with FGPA that average about .5. (A study of a pilot version of the redesigned SAT that was unveiled in 2016 produced results quite consistent with these.)[14]

A 2008 College Board study of the utility of the SAT as a predictor of college grades can serve as an illustration of the kind of information that can be gleaned from research of this kind.[15] The study involved the version of the SAT that debuted in 2005, which included three sections: critical reading, math, and writing. The research was based on data from about 150,000 students from 110 institutions. All analyses were performed separately within each school and then averaged, taking the size of the institution into account. Results showed that using only high school GPA as a predictor yielded a correlation of .36; using only the SAT produced a correlation of .35. When high school GPA and SAT scores were used in combination, the correlation rose to .46.

Is the increase from .36 to .46, attained by including the SAT, an important gain? Test critics have argued that it is not. But in a setting where highly accurate prediction is not possible, admissions officers may perceive even a modest increment as worthwhile. The higher the correlation, the greater the precision of FGPA predictions and the smaller the risk of mistaken admissions decisions (assuming the candidate's likely FGPA is considered to be an important factor). From an institutional perspective, in fact, admissions tests may be seen as a bargain, given that the applicants themselves pay to take the tests.

Occasionally test scores are found to do a better job than high school grades in predicting students' grades in the first year of college. For example, the 2008 College Board study found the SAT to be slightly more predictive than high school GPA in certain kinds of institutions, including those with admission rates under 50% and those with fewer than 2,000 undergraduates. In two large University of California studies, SAT scores were found to outdo high school grades as predictors of FGPA for certain entering classes.[16]

The predictive value of high school grades and test scores tends to vary to some degree over student groups. In the College Board research, SAT scores and high school GPA were more highly correlated with FGPA for women than for men. In general, correlations were also higher for White students than for other ethnic groups and for those who gave their best language as "English only." These results are consistent with patterns found in previous studies.[17] These correlations may vary from one student group to another for several reasons.[18] The most frequently advanced explanation is that in some groups, SAT scores and high school grades may not correspond as closely to students' academic skills as in other groups. The same could certainly be true for college grades. Even if test scores and grades are equally accurate for all groups, it is possible that for some groups the relationship between test scores and FGPA is more likely to be diminished because competing responsibilities or interests interfere with college performance.

Finally, the disparate correlations could result from differences in the first-year classes chosen by various groups, since students' FGPAs are based on the grades they earn in these classes.

## Statistical Versus Human Prediction of Human Behavior

Although the statistical prediction of human behavior has a long history and is regarded as routine in some settings, it has also generated a fair amount of controversy and an extensive literature, including the classic 1954 volume *Clinical versus Statistical Prediction*, by the psychologist Paul Meehl. Disputes have arisen about the validity of statistical judgment in fields as diverse as psychiatric diagnosis, criminology, and—as recently noted by political wunderkind Nate Silver—baseball performance. Statistical prediction is often regarded as distasteful on principle, and possibly even threatening. As psychologist Harrison Gough put it in 1962, opponents of statistical prediction consider it to be "atomistic, pedantic, artificial, static, and pseudo-scientific" compared to prediction procedures based on human judgment, which are viewed as "dynamic, meaningful, deep, genuine, and sophisticated."[19] And in a 1979 article in the *Yale Law Journal*, Barbara Underwood offered another reason for the distrust of statistical prediction as a means of distributing societal benefits, including admission to college: In the eyes of the public, any "attempt to predict an individual's behavior seems to reduce him to a predictable object rather than treating him as an autonomous person." The very same issue arose in a discussion of baseball performance documented by Silver 33 years later: Statistically predicting performance was seen as impinging on free will.[20]

But the dichotomy between "human" or "clinical" approaches and statistical techniques is a false one—human judgment may be aided by statistics, and statistical prediction models are developed by humans. A better way to pose the question is to ask whether human judgment is enhanced by statistical methods in the prediction of academic performance. According to more than seven decades of research, the answer is yes. In perhaps the earliest of such studies, conducted in 1939, psychologist Theodore Sarbin compared two methods of predicting college grade-point average. One method used a statistical prediction equation, derived using regression analysis. The only predictors were the students' high school ranks and college aptitude test scores. The other method used the judgments of counselors, who based their predictions on their own interviews of the students, along with the students' high school records, admissions test scores, and scores on achievement, personality, and vocational interest tests. Sarbin found that the regression equation had a slight edge in terms of accuracy—the counselors tended to overestimate the students' future grades.[21] This study and others like it led Sarbin to a conclusion sure to enrage those with an aversion to statistical approaches: In his judgment, statistical prediction was the scientific gold standard. "Human" prediction, such as that performed by a clinical psychologist, was merely a crude approximation to that ideal.

Several decades later, the authors of a 2013 meta-analysis of studies predicting academic or work performance (including six analyses predicting GPA) noted that excessive attention to prominent cues and "inconsistency in use of weights without a compensating gain in insights will cause experts to form judgments with less predictive power than mechanical combination of the same set of cues." Why would human judgment be less effective than a mechanical combination of data? Let's first consider how excessive attention to certain cues could be a problem. Suppose an admissions officer champions Ed, a quiet and studious applicant, who is admitted and indeed proves to be a stellar student. A new applicant, Jed, has a similarly serious manner and in fact looks a bit like Ed. The admissions officer might, consciously or not, support Jed because of these superficial characteristics. Inconsistent weighting of cues could occur if, say, the admissions official generally regards high school performance as extremely important, but tends to be more lenient for applicants who are particularly charming or attractive. Beyond these quirks of reasoning, human judges' decision-making capabilities can be impaired by other factors that don't affect computer algorithms, like headaches and bad moods.

The pervasive finding that statistical methods are more effective than human judgment for combining multiple data features has been characterized as demonstrating that the "model of man" is superior to the man himself. In other words, a statistical model derived from human judgments actually outperforms human judgments.[22] The meta-analysis, conducted by Nathan Kuncel of the University of Minnesota and his colleagues, revealed a "sizable" advantage in favor of the statistical approach in admissions decision-making situations where the human and statistical prediction methods were based on the same information.[23] Sarbin's research showed that even when counselors had access to much more information, they did not predict college grades as accurately as statistical equations.

## Why Isn't Statistical Prediction of College Performance Better Than It Is?

Even though research shows that statistical prediction of behavior is generally more accurate than unaided human prediction, it is still less precise than we would wish. Psychologist Robyn Dawes, who wrote extensively on this topic, described a dean's opinion of the use of statistical prediction in admissions decisions: In reflecting on the fact that the statistical approach led to a correlation of .4 with a measure of student performance, whereas the admissions committee's judgments yielded a correlation of .2, the dean commented, "Twice nothing is nothing."[24]

In regression analysis, the square of the multiple correlation can be interpreted as the proportion of variation in the predicted quantity (say, college grades) that is "explained by" or associated with the predictors (say, test scores and high school grades). So if these predictors, used together, produce a multiple correlation of only .4, as in the Dawes quote and in typical prediction studies, they "explain" only 16% of the variation in college grades. Why aren't the predictions more accurate? One reason is that high school GPA and test scores do not constitute perfectly precise measures of students' preparation, nor is FGPA a perfect measure of their accomplishments. Grades, in particular, tend to have relatively low signal-to-noise ratios.[25] But the modest correlations also result in part from the intrinsic unpredictability of human behavior. Students with identical high school grades and SAT scores will still differ in their choice of classes, their motivation to succeed, and the amount of effort they devote to their academic work, and these factors are among those that contribute to the "unexplained" 84% of the variation in FGPAs.

Social scientists' efforts to predict other forms of human behavior are plagued by similar problems. Why are we not better able to predict who will succeed on the job, who will avoid committing a parole violation, or who will benefit from psychotherapy? The reason is that, in all these cases, an infinite number of factors can intervene—factors that could not be evaluated in advance. The promising job applicant is laid off during a financial downturn. The high-risk parolee receives unexpected family support. The deeply depressed psychotherapy client is able to benefit from a new drug. Dawes noted that many of his psychologist colleagues found this unpredictability hard to accept and rejected statistical prediction because it made the reality of poor prediction explicit. Clinical prediction, by contrast "allows us the comforting illusion that life is in fact predictable and that we can predict it."[26]

But there's more to this story of inaccurate prediction. The models typically used to predict college performance do not represent social scientists' best attempts at prediction. If all available predictors were included, the multiple correlation would be larger. Instead, the models used in the admissions context are intentionally incomplete, or *sparse*—they include only those factors the institution considers to be equitable, legal, and publically acceptable in terms of their impact. In general, the included predictors will involve skills or talents that are likely to facilitate college success. The models are intended to maximize prediction, given that all included factors are considered legitimate from these perspectives.[27]

Suppose a college simply admitted the applicants with the highest predicted first-year grades. What factors might be regarded as unacceptable for use in these performance predictions? Consider what would happen if an applicant's race and family income, along with high school grades and test scores, were used in formulating these predictions.[28] Research consistently shows that race and income are related to college grades and graduation rates, with White, Asian, and high-income students performing better than their counterparts from other groups.[29] The most obvious explanation for these differences is the effects of poverty and racism on earlier educational experiences and opportunities. Researchers, social theorists, and politicians have, of course, offered an array of possible reasons for group differences in academic achievement, including cultural, attitudinal, linguistic, environmental, and biological factors. Whatever the reasons, selecting students using performance predictions based in part on race and SES would mean that a Black student who grew up in poverty would have lower predicted college grades than a wealthy White student with identical high school grades and test scores. The expected impact would be precisely contrary to the goals of both socioeconomic and race-based affirmative action: In general, members of ethnic and socioeconomic groups that are already underrepresented would be less likely to gain admission. This selection process would be widely rejected because it inhibits diversity by perpetuating past disadvantage.

But using race or SES in this way is unfair on a more fundamental level. Factors used to predict college performance for purposes of making admissions decisions should measure college-relevant skills. It is not sufficient for these characteristics to merely be *predictive* of college success. It is particularly unfair to predict performance using characteristics that are not under applicants' control, thus depriving them of the opportunity to improve their chances of selection. Of course, a similar argument is made in opposition to affirmative action: Those who don't receive preferences are disadvantaged by characteristics not under their control. Isn't this the same issue dressed up in different political clothes? No, it's not. Using race or SES to calculate predicted performance amounts to saying to a Black student or an applicant from an impoverished family, "We're predicting a lower performance for you because of the past performance of others like you"—a kind of racial profiling. In contrast, justifying affirmative action does not require that any conjectures be made about the relative college performance of various student groups and does not involve the disparagement of groups that are ineligible for admissions preferences. The most compelling rationale for affirmative action stems from a social justice goal: A candidate's race or socioeconomic status is considered in pursuit of the ideal of a fully integrated society. I discuss alternative justifications for affirmative action policies, including the diversity rationale favored by the Supreme Court, in more detail in Chapter 4.

## SAT Scores and Performance Predictions

Taking the idea of unacceptable predictors one step further, test critics have asserted that admissions test scores—particularly SAT scores—are themselves illegitimate predictors of college performance because in essence they are proxies for wealth or income, rather than measures of relevant applicant skills. In reporting on the SAT changes planned for 2016, MSNBC's Chris Hayes opened the segment by declaring that the SAT "tests for a really weird thing . . . it tests for how much money your parents make." Similarly, in her 2015 book *The Tyranny of the Meritocracy*, Harvard law professor Lani Guinier argues that "SAT scores are accurate reflections of wealth and little else"; and testing opponent Peter Sacks claims that "one can make a good guess about a child's test scores by looking at how many degrees her parents have and what kind of car they drive." (Both Guinier and Sacks seem to take credit for coining the term "the Volvo effect" to describe this phenomenon.) In his blast at elite schools, *Excellent Sheep*, former Yale professor William Deresiewicz jumps on the bandwagon, declaring that "the SAT is supposed to measure aptitude; what it actually measures is parental income . . . and even more, parental wealth." Even the *Wall Street Journal,* hardly a bastion of liberal thought, published a piece in 2014 calling the exam the Student Affluence Test.[30]

During the last 15 years, a flurry of claims and counterclaims has emerged about the role of socioeconomic status and SAT scores in the prediction of college grades. The authors of a 2001 University of California report claimed their analyses of UC data showed that the predictive value of SAT scores declined when the education and income level of students' parents were included as predictors in the regression equation. The researchers interpreted this to mean that "much of the apparent relationship between the SAT I and UC freshman grades is conditioned by socioeconomic factors."[31] In other words, they maintained that, to a large degree, the SAT is predictive of FGPA, not because it measures skills that are needed in college, but because it measures SES, which in turn is related to college grades. The authors compared the SAT I (which we now simply call the SAT) unfavorably with the SAT II (the subject-matter exams now called the SAT Subject Tests), asserting that the Subject Tests were "less sensitive" to SES. These findings were invoked to support UC president Richard Atkinson's 2001 proposal that the SAT should be eliminated from the UC admissions process in favor of tests focusing on students' classroom achievement. In a similar vein, economist Jesse Rothstein made waves in 2004 with his claim that SAT scores provided a surreptitious way for schools to use family background in admissions decisions. According to Rothstein, considering SAT scores amounted to "laundering family background, which turns a disallowable characteristic into a characteristic with another name."[32]

It's a well-established fact that SAT scores are related to family background. But is the SAT predictive of college grades largely *because* of this link? If so, that would imply that the skills assessed by the test were mostly unrelated to college performance. Subsequent analyses have not supported that idea, however, showing instead that even when the effects of SES are statistically controlled, SAT scores—and high school grades—largely retain their value as predictors of FGPA. In fact, the conclusions of the 2001 UC report did not follow from the analyses. The UC researchers added both SAT Subject Tests and socioeconomic factors to their prediction equations and seemingly confused the effects of these two modifications. As one highly respected commentator noted, "the reduction in the size of the regression weight for the SAT I was due more to the inclusion of the SAT Subject Tests in the prediction equation than it was to the inclusion of the SES measures."[33]

Most of the UC analyses from 2001 were fairly coarse in that they combined data for seven UC campuses and four entry years (1996–1999). When my colleagues at UC Santa Barbara and I conducted a finer-grained analysis of the data, we found that incorporating SES in our prediction equations did not, in fact, produce a consistent decline in the predictive value of SAT scores, nor were SAT scores "more sensitive" to socioeconomic factors than SAT Subject Test scores.[34] An elaborate reanalysis subsequently conducted by Paul Sackett of the University of Minnesota and supported by the College Board arrived at the same conclusion. Based on analyses of the UC data, as well as other large multi-institution datasets, Sackett and his colleagues concluded that "SAT score retained the vast majority of its predictive power above and beyond high school GPA even after SES was added to the model." That is, adding SES to the equation did not substantially reduce the regression weight for SAT scores. To cement their point, they added that "it is not the case that the SAT is nothing more than a proxy for SES."[35] A meta-analysis of data from 50 institutions led ACT researchers to a parallel conclusion. They found that ACT scores and high school GPA "had much stronger relationships with 1st-year [college] GPA than SES . . . had. This finding . . . provides additional evidence against the testing critics' assertions that test scores are mere measures of SES."[36]

## Beyond the Correlation Coefficient

Although they're usually the coin of the realm when it comes to evaluating predictive effectiveness, correlations have some technical pitfalls and limitations. One complicating factor is the impact of *restriction of range*. A basic drawback of typical studies of admissions criteria is that only a portion of the applicants is available for analysis. Suppose we want to examine the usefulness of high school GPA as a predictor of FGPA at a particular college. Students who were rejected by the college because of low high school grades will not, of course, have FGPA values at that school. This restriction of the range of the high school grades (and, as a result, of the college grades as well) curtails the size of the correlations. As a result, the apparent association between high school GPA and FGPA is smaller than it would be if all applicants could be included in the analysis.

To understand the impact of range restriction, consider the case of men's basketball performance. It's sensible for a team coach to prefer tall players, everything else being equal, because they have an obvious advantage in the game. However, once a team is selected, a player's height is not generally a good predictor of his performance. Why? Because the range of height is severely restricted among the team members. Among these extremely tall players who don't vary much in height, other factors, like speed, power, and agility, are likely to be much more predictive than height. An analysis of the relation between basketball performance and height that appears on the Web sums it up nicely: "We expected taller players to be better at basketball. . . . However, our assumption was wrong, and in the end all of the basketball players were tall." Psychologist David R. Caruso and his colleagues used a detailed analysis of 2012 statistics from the New York Knicks and the Boston Celtics specifically for the purpose of illustrating restriction of range. They found that, far from being positively correlated with game performance, height actually had a negative correlation with points earned (whether the focus was on points per game or points per minute of playing time). That is, there was a tendency for taller players to earn fewer points. If a researcher wanted to study the relationship between height and basketball performance among adult males in general, then using data from professional basketball teams would yield a distorted picture.[37]

Similarly, correlations computed in admissions research will produce a more pessimistic picture of predictive effectiveness than is warranted, assuming that the goal is to estimate the usefulness of predictors in selecting students *from the overall applicant pool*. To compensate, statistical adjustments are sometimes applied in an attempt to estimate how big the correlation would have been if the range had not been restricted. Adjusted values can be considerably higher than unadjusted ones. For example, when the correlations obtained in the 2008 College Board study are adjusted, the predictive value of high school GPA rises from .36 to .54, the correlation for SAT scores rises from .35 to .53, and the correlation for high school grades and SAT scores combined increases from .46 to .62.[38] These statistical "corrections" are only approximate because they depend on unrealistically simple assumptions about the selection process.

## Practical Effectiveness

For nearly a century it has been understood that the usefulness of a predictor depends not only on its correlation with the target of prediction but also on the selection ratio—the proportion of individuals to be chosen. In a classic

1939 article, H. C. Taylor and J. T. Russell demonstrated that "under the conditions found when tests are used for selection of employees or students, correlation coefficients within the range of .20 to .50 [are more effective than generally recognized] ."[39] Their criterion for *practical effectiveness* was the proportion of those selected who are satisfactory. For example, suppose that 50% of the applicants to an elite college are satisfactory in terms of their expected college grades, but the school can accept only the top 10% due to space limitations. Let's suppose that an admissions test score is our only selection criterion, so we will simply choose those applicants whose test scores are in the top 10%. If we foolishly use a test that has no relationship to college grades—a correlation of zero—only 50% of our selected students are expected to be satisfactory, because that is the overall percentage of satisfactory applicants. But if our test has a correlation of .35 with college grades—certainly a realistic level—74% of the selected applicants are expected to be satisfactory.[40] If the correlation is .50, the percentage rises to 84. And the smaller the selection ratio, the greater the payoff a particular correlation will yield. In concluding, Taylor and Russell stated, "We believe that it may be of value to point out the very considerable improvement in selection efficiency which may be obtained with small correlation coefficients."[41] More than 75 years later, the phenomenon they described is still not widely recognized.

## Systematic Errors in Predicting FGPA

We can get yet another perspective on the relative utility of potential predictors by investigating the pattern of prediction errors for major student groups. Suppose a college uses data from all of its freshmen to obtain a single regression equation for use in predicting FGPA for admissions purposes. Will this equation work equally well for all students, or might it lead to predicted college grades that are too high for some groups and too low for others? As it turns out, prediction patterns of this kind do often occur, whether test scores or high school grades are used as predictors.

Regression analysis produces a predicted FGPA for each student, along with the difference between this predicted value and the FGPA actually earned by the student, called the prediction error. If a student was predicted to have an FGPA of 3.0, but earned an FGPA of only 2.5, we say that his prediction error was 0.5 or, more specifically, that his FGPA was *overpredicted* by 0.5. Regression analysis has the property that the average prediction error for the entire group on which the analysis is based will be zero. But a prediction model—even one with a high multiple correlation—can still produce predicted FGPAs that are systematically "off target" for certain student groups.

Research conducted during the last 50 years has shown that when a single regression model is estimated for all students combined, with GPA and test score as predictors, FGPA tends to be *overpredicted* for African American and Hispanic students: The predicted FGPAs from the regression analyses tend to be higher than the grades these students actually earn.[42] As former college presidents William G. Bowen and Derek Bok put it in their landmark book *The Shape of the River,* "far from being biased *against* minority students, standardized admissions tests consistently predict higher levels of academic performance than most blacks actually achieve."[43]

Various theories have been offered about the reasons for this counterintuitive phenomenon, including hypotheses involving unwelcoming or racist campus environments and unfavorable student attitudes, as well as more narrowly technical explanations: These kinds of prediction errors can occur simply because predictors are measured imprecisely.[44]

My own research suggests that these ethnic-group prediction errors can be attributed at least in part to high school quality. One clue about the source of these distortions is that ethnic-group overprediction is typically more severe when high school GPA alone is used as a predictor than when high school grades and SAT scores are used in conjunction. Could this be because African-American and Latino students are more likely to attend lower-quality high schools with less stringent grading? If high school grades are inflated for students in inferior schools, this distortion could lead to misleadingly high predicted FGPAs.

Along with my collaborator Igor Himelfarb, I sought to investigate the role of high school quality and determine whether it explained the patterns of prediction errors. We studied more than 70,000 students who enrolled in 34 undergraduate institutions in 2006. These students had attended a total of about 5,800 high schools. Because direct information about instructional quality was not available, we used the socioeconomic status (SES) of the school—the average parental education and the poverty level in the district—as a rough index of a high school's merit.[45] Previous studies have shown that school-level SES is related to instructional quality and student achievement.[46] We found that students in lower-SES schools tended not to do as well as predicted in college (overprediction), whereas students in higher-SES schools performed better than predicted (underprediction). As we hypothesized, African-American and Latino students were much more likely to have attended low-SES high schools than other students. Roughly 70% of African Americans and Latinos had attended low-SES schools, whereas fewer than half of White and Asian American students had done so. We conjectured that including the SES index in our prediction equations would reduce the size of the ethnic-group prediction errors. To explore this idea, we applied three alternative models for predicting FGPA and then evaluated the accuracy of prediction for various groups.

When only high school GPA was used to predict FGPA, the predicted FGPA values for African-American students were higher than actual FGPAs by a quarter of a grade point on average, a large discrepancy, given that FGPA is reported on a 0–4 scale. For Latino students, the distortion was almost as large. When SAT scores were included along with high school grades, prediction errors were substantially reduced, a reflection of the fact that SAT scores, unlike grades, have essentially the same meaning across schools. Finally, when the high school SES index was added to the prediction model, average prediction errors decreased further, falling below a tenth of a grade point for all ethnic groups.[47]

The results supported our hypothesis that one reason African Americans and Latinos tend to have predicted college grades that are higher than their actual grades is that they are disproportionately represented in suboptimal high schools, where a high GPA does not ensure a high level of achievement. The overprediction of FGPAs was particularly large when high school GPA was the only predictor. Prediction models that included SAT scores and the high school SES index essentially "adjusted for" the disparity in grading standards across high schools.

Systematic prediction errors also occur for men and women, although they have tended to be smaller than those for Black and Latino students. When prediction equations include both SAT scores and high school grades, women's FGPAs are typically underpredicted by about 0.06, on average, whereas men's grades are overpredicted by the same amount. Unlike the ethnic-group errors, prediction errors tend to be slightly larger when the SAT is included than when high school grades alone are used as a predictor. Some evidence suggest that this pattern of errors occurs because women tend to select college majors that are more leniently graded than those chosen by men, making it easier for them to earn high FGPAs. Some research has found that prediction errors are smaller in more selective colleges, where there may be fewer differences between men and women in terms of the courses they take. Other research points to the idea that women are more diligent and studious in college than their male counterparts.[48]

These patterns of overprediction and underprediction show that the effectiveness of a predictor cannot be fully characterized by a correlation coefficient, or even a correlation coefficient accompanied by a selection ratio.

## Using the ELS Data to Examine FGPA Prediction

To illustrate the phenomena of over- and underprediction, I performed some regression analyses using my sample of applicants to selective schools from the Education Longitudinal Study. The goal was to derive the best equation for predicting first-year college grade-point average (FGPA) using the equally weighted composite of high school GPA and admissions test score described in Chapter 2. I also wanted to determine whether a single prediction equation could provide a good fit to the data for different groups of applicants.[49] In the first set of analyses, I considered applicants who were underrepresented minorities (URMs) or White. In the second set, I examined the regressions for men and women. The correlation between the composite and FGPA was about .55, a value slightly larger than the typical multiple correlation obtained when high school GPA and admissions test scores are used to predict FGPA. In addition, the strength of the relationship was about the same for all four applicant groups, a desirable finding. However, both sets of analyses resulted in systematic prediction errors: Even though the *strength* of the relationship was the same, the predicted FGPA value corresponding to a particular composite score varied with group membership.

Let's first consider the URM–White comparison. Applicants who were in neither group were excluded from the analysis, resulting in a sample of 870 applicants that was 24% URM. Using data from both groups combined resulted in the following equation:

$$\text{Predicted FGPA} = 2.99 + 0.25 \times \text{Composite score}$$

How would this equation be applied? Let's consider an applicant with an admissions test score of about 1150 on the 400-to-1600 SAT scale and a high school GPA of 3.25. Because these values are the averages for the ELS applicant group, this candidate would also receive an average score on the composite, which is scaled so that its average value is zero. If we plug a composite score of zero into the regression equation, we can see that this applicant has a predicted FGPA of 2.99, a B. However, my analysis results showed that using a single equation for both URMs and Whites did not yield an ideal fit to the data.

More specifically, the analyses showed that although the strength of the relationship between the composite and FGPA (represented by the factor of 0.25 in the equation) was about the same for the two groups, the additive value of 2.99 was too high for URMs and slightly too low for White students. As a result, the equation led to predicted FGPAs that were, on average, too high by 0.09 FGPA points for URMs (overprediction) and too low by 0.03 points for Whites (underprediction).[50] As I mentioned earlier, this pattern is consistent with previous findings on the prediction of college grades, and a plausible (though perhaps incomplete) explanation is that applicants who are Black, Hispanic, or American Indian are likely to have attended lower-quality schools, on average, than White applicants. This disadvantage is unlikely to be fully captured by high school grades and test scores. Therefore, URMs might not perform as well in college as White students with the same composite scores.

The regressions for men and women were based on all 2,190 applicants to selective colleges. About 52% were women. The best-fitting equation was found to be identical to the one obtained in the URM–White analysis. But again, this combined-group equation did not provide an optimal fit to the data. On average, women's FGPAs were underpredicted by 0.11 grade-points, while men's FGPA were overpredicted by 0.12 points.[51] Like the results of the URM–White analysis, the underprediction of women's college grades, along with the corresponding overprediction for men, is consistent with previous research. As I noted earlier, some possible explanations are that women are more conscientious about their studies or are more likely to major in areas with relatively lenient grading policies (hence affecting their FGPAs). One feature of the ELS findings that departs from typical research results is that the prediction errors for men and women were larger than the prediction errors for URMs.

The disparities between groups in these prediction equations violate the equal prediction model of fairness: For these college applicants, basing an admissions decision on the academic composite alone would be unfair because the predicted college performance for individuals with the same composite score varies with ethnicity and sex. This conclusion does not imply that either the high school grades or the test scores are biased (although bias is not ruled out). Instead, the results suggest that the prediction equation may be incomplete. If we included such factors as quality of high school, rigor of high school curriculum, hours per week spent studying during college, major field of study, and perhaps family resources, we would probably find that a single equation would fit the data better. In other words, if we could match the applicants on all these factors, in addition to composite score, the prediction errors found in these analyses would likely be substantially diminished. This is the pattern we observed in the Zwick and Himelfarb study when we added a rough measure of high school quality to the equation we used to predict FGPA. But again, it's important to keep in mind that factors that improve prediction accuracy may be highly inappropriate as admissions criteria. Acknowledging that financial resources can help to predict college performance is one thing; systematically denying access to low-income applicants is another.

## Prediction of College Performance Beyond the FGPA

Although the majority of studies of the validity of admissions tests focus on the degree to which they can predict FGPA, research has shown that these tests are useful in predicting grades beyond the first year of college.[52] And according to a number of large studies, admissions test scores are also useful in predicting who will graduate. Recently, both ACT and the College Board have examined graduation rates for test takers who do and don't meet certain college readiness benchmark scores. In the case of the ACT, there are separate benchmark scores for each section: English (18), math (22), reading (21), and science (24). A 2012 study from ACT that included about 19,000 students from more than 1,000 four-year institutions showed that the four-year graduation rate for those who met all four benchmarks was 52%, compared to 18% for those who did not meet any.[53] Similarly, a 2013 College Board study based on more than a million students from two large national datasets showed that students who had attained the college readiness benchmark on the previous version of the SAT (a combined score of 1550 out of a possible 2400 on the critical reading, math, and writing assessments) had a four-year graduation rate of 58%, compared to 31% for those who did not.[54] This finding is consistent with earlier studies showing a relationship between SAT score and graduation, including a 1996 study of more than 75,000 freshmen at 365 institutions that found the SAT to be a valuable predictor even for the 9,000 students with high school GPAs of A or A+.[55]

The relative utility of admissions test scores and high school GPA as predictors of college graduation has been the topic of three substantial data analyses during the last decade. First, in a 2007 report based on roughly 75,000 students who entered the University of California between 1996 and 1999, Saul Geiser and Maria Veronica Santelices found that high school grades were a better predictor of four-year graduation than were SAT scores. Adding admissions test scores to the prediction model yielded only a modest improvement in prediction accuracy.[56] And in their landmark 2009 publication, *Crossing the Finish Line*, William Bowen, Matthew Chingos, and Michael McPherson were even more emphatic in their conclusion that "high school grades are a far better predictor of both four-year and six-year graduation rates than are SAT/ACT scores."[57] Based on their analysis of nearly 150,000 students who entered 68 public universities in 1999, they found that admissions test scores added little to the prediction of graduation, once high school grades were considered. When information about which high school each student attended was included in the analysis, the predictive value of high school grades was even stronger.[58] These supplementary data served to correct for disparities in grading stringency.

As we saw in Chapter 2, my ELS analyses, too, showed that selecting students using only high school grades produced entering classes with higher graduation rates than choosing students solely on the basis of test scores, suggesting that grades are more useful in predicting graduation. However, a 2013 study came to a far more favorable conclusion about the value of SAT scores in predicting graduation. College Board researchers Krista D. Mattern, Brian F. Patterson, and Jeffrey N. Wyatt considered four-year graduation rates among 79,000 students who entered 54 undergraduate institutions in 2006. They concluded that both SAT scores and high school GPA were strong predictors of graduation and that SAT scores contributed meaningfully to the prediction of graduation even after high school grades were taken into account. For example, they found that students with an A average in high school who had total SAT scores of 600 to 890 (on a 600-to-2400 scale) had a college graduation rate of 24%; A students with a score of 2100 to 2400 had a rate of 76%.[59] A similar trend held for those with a B average, though not for those with a C average. The researchers' finding, based on further analyses, that "students with higher SAT scores are more likely to graduate [in four years], even after controlling for HSGPA, institutional control, and institutional selectivity," differs sharply from the results of the Geiser and Bowen studies.[60]

Why did these studies arrive at such divergent conclusions? The analyses differed in a number of ways. In particular, both the Geiser and Bowen studies were based entirely on public universities, whereas only 41% of the institutions in the College Board study were public. Also, the College Board study was based on students' self-reported high school GPA, while Geiser and Santelices used GPA values drawn from a UC database and Bowen's research used a combination of GPAs from institutional records (available for 51% of students) and GPA values that were imputed using various sources of data (available for 41%). In addition, the College Board study used scores on the revised SAT that was introduced in 2005 and included writing scores, whereas the UC study and the Bowen research were based on an earlier version of the test. The Bowen research also included some ACT scores that had been converted to the SAT scale, as in my ELS analyses.[61] And of course, the student cohorts investigated in the three studies entered college in different years, ranging from 1996 to 2006.

Nevertheless, there is some common ground. The College Board study, like the Bowen research, found that high school grades contributed to the prediction of college graduation even after SAT scores were considered.[62] Bowen and his colleagues believe that high school grades are strong predictors of graduation, not only because they measure mastery of course content, but because "high school grades measure a student's ability to 'get it done' in a more powerful way than do SAT scores."[63]

## Conclusions

Why should a university be concerned about applicants' predicted performance? Some schools may wish to consider these predictions to identify academic superstars, but most are likely to be concerned mainly about the optimal use of scarce resources: How can they select students that will make the best use of the limited number of available seats? From this perspective, academic index values and other performance predictions can be a helpful application-sorting tool, particularly at large institutions.

But there are several reasons to be wary of them as well. Correlations and regression coefficients have quirks and flaws that make their interpretation less than straightforward. Range restriction, selection ratios, and systematic prediction errors can have an impact on predictive effectiveness. Although statistical prediction of academic performance has been found to be more accurate than "human" prediction, it is still not very precise and the accuracy of prediction varies somewhat across student groups. Also, the appropriateness of a prediction equation or index can change over time if the characteristics of the applicant pool change. Bob Laird, former admissions director at Berkeley, warns against "the trap of being seduced by a really elaborate formula that employs a lot of variables and gives the illusion of great precision," adding that the temptation to use an approach of this kind "often arises when the faculty chair of an admissions committee is a mathematician or statistician."[64]

In addition, it is not clear that first-year college grades are the ideal target of prediction. In fact, from the point of view of resource allocation, it might make more sense to formulate an academic index based instead on the prediction of graduation. In any case, predictive value alone should not determine whether a particular factor is incorporated in an academic index. The impact of the resulting policy on applicants and on the student body as a whole must be considered. Who will gain and who will lose through the inclusion of a particular predictor? Finally, the role of performance predictions in the admissions decision and the way these predictions are derived should be transparent to the applicant. No secret handshakes!

# CHAPTER FOUR

# Admissions Preferences: Who Deserves a Boost?

To ask whether a society is just is to ask how it distributes the things we prize—income and wealth, duties and rights, powers and opportunities, offices and honors. A just society distributes these goods in the right way; it gives each person his or her due. The hard questions begin when we ask what people are due, and why.

—*Michael J. Sandel*

At the University of California, Berkeley, a few years ago, the campus Republican club sponsored an "Increase Diversity Bake Sale." Pastry prices depended on the buyer's race and gender, with White men paying the most ($2), followed in order by Asian, Latino, African-American, and Native American men (25 cents). Women got a flat discount of 25 cents. The Berkeley College Republicans said their sale was meant to show that "treating people differently based on the color of their skin is wrong." Their clumsy satire spawned a competing piece of political theater involving free cupcakes for all—a nice metaphor—but it also provoked outrage, demonstrations, and threats against the organizers.[1] Affirmative action policies in college admissions are no less controversial now than when they were initiated a half century ago.

Here, we begin by examining the most important legal cases involving race-based affirmative action in admissions. What justifications are offered for affirmative action policies and what are the counterarguments? How effective is "socioeconomic affirmative action"—the granting of admissions preferences to applicants from lower socioeconomic brackets? Is this a legitimate way to improve racial diversity without explicitly using race in admissions decisions? What about the many other preferences that are woven into the fabric of college admissions decisions? In particular, how significant are the "boosts" given to legacies, development admits, and athletes relative to the preferences that stem from presumed disadvantages?

According to one point of view, everyone—regardless of background— deserves a chance to attend the nation's top schools. But from another perspective, no one "deserves" this opportunity: There is no universally accepted definition of merit—no set of qualifications—that automatically entitles the bearer to an education at the school of his choice. I use the word "merit" in its original sense, as a synonym for worthiness or "deservingness," but its meaning is often distorted in the admissions context. The term "meritocracy," repeated endlessly in the public conversation on college admissions, has drifted away from the ironic meaning intended by its originator, Michael Young, and is now used to describe a system in which traditional academic criteria are the sole basis of admissions decisions. Correspondingly, "merit" has come to refer to academic excellence, narrowly defined. The testing watchdog organization FairTest called one of its landmark publications "Test Scores Do Not Equal Merit," a title that is remarkable because it suggests that the opposite point of view might be plausible.[2] The fact is that top grades, volunteer work in a soup kitchen, and superior grit don't automatically equal merit either. There is, in fact, no absolute definition of merit—or, as Berkeley sociologist Jerome Karabel puts it, no neutral definition: "However it is defined, it will benefit some groups while disadvantaging others."[3]

Suppose a college wants to pick the lowest-achieving applicants, on the grounds that they need help—or *merit* instruction—the most. This seems to be a completely justifiable selection principle, both ethically and in terms of maximizing the value added through the provision of a college education. Under this policy, candidates with perfect SAT scores and high school GPAs of 4.0 would, of course, be legitimately rejected. This is what I mean when I say that no one automatically "deserves" admission to a particular school. But at the root of the typical anti-affirmative-action argument is a contrary view—that college applicants who satisfy a particular definition of merit, based primarily on GPA and test scores, are entitled to be admitted in preference to those who do not.

The first official use of the term "affirmative action" came in 1961, when President John F. Kennedy issued Executive Order 10925 calling for "affirmative action to ensure that applicants [for positions with the federal government or its contractors] are employed, and that employees are treated . . . without regard to their race, creed, color, or national origin." The order laid out a clear-cut rationale: Discrimination is contrary to Constitutional principles, and it is the "plain and positive obligation" of the U.S. government to promote and ensure equal opportunity. In addition, it is in the interest of the United States to "promote its economy, security, and national defense" through effective use of its human resources.[4]

The document, which neatly combines egalitarian arguments (the obligation of the government to ensure equal opportunity) with utilitarian ones (the importance of making effective use of human resources), described a relatively uncontroversial form of "affirmative action": People were to be treated without regard to race or color. Today's affirmative action, which is intentionally race-conscious, is far more contentious, as evidenced by the proliferation of legislation, ballot measures, and lawsuits seeking to promote or prohibit it. In the realm of college admissions, affirmative action programs have included the assignment of bonus points in evaluating applications from members of historically excluded groups, the designation of a certain number of spaces in the entering class to members of these groups, and the consideration of race in a less formal way, along with other characteristics. Policies that make use of race in admissions decisions are typically developed by the institutions themselves. However, many such programs have been modified or eliminated as the result of actions by state legislatures or by the courts.

Not surprisingly, California has been a hotbed of affirmative action debate. In 1996 it became the first state to pass an amendment to the state constitution prohibiting public institutions from enacting preferences based on race, gender, or ethnicity. Various bids to overturn the education-related portions of the amendment have been unsuccessful, including a 2011 bill that was vetoed by Governor Jerry Brown (the very bill that provoked the "diversity bake sale") and a bill that was withdrawn from consideration in 2014 after some Asian-American groups protested that it would lead to reductions in Asian enrollment.[5] During the last 20 years, Washington State, Michigan, Nebraska, New Hampshire, Arizona, and Oklahoma have all followed California in enacting legislation banning racial preferences in public education. In Florida, racial preferences are prohibited by an executive order enacted by former governor and 2016 presidential candidate Jeb Bush.[6]

## Affirmative Action Admissions and the Courts

In their rulings on affirmative action in higher education, the courts have created a maze of murky and sometimes conflicting decisions. Not long after affirmative action admissions programs had begun to take root in the late

1960s, a lawsuit was filed against the University of California, Davis Medical School. Allan Bakke, a White man, filed a suit in state court, claiming to be the victim of discrimination because minority candidates with lesser academic qualifications were admitted but he was not. (A similar suit filed in 1971 against the University of Washington Law School, *DeFunis v. Odegaard,* was subsequently declared moot, as I mentioned in Chapter 1.) After the California Supreme Court ordered that Bakke be admitted, the University petitioned the U.S. Supreme Court to review the case. Although *Bakke,* decided by the U.S. Supreme Court in 1978, is by far the best-known court case on affirmative action admissions, the Court's ruling was less than straightforward. Bakke won—his admission to UC Davis was ordered by the Court and Davis's admissions program, which included a separate track for disadvantaged minorities, was declared invalid. Ironically, though, the Bakke decision continues to be cited as a key legal foundation on which affirmative action rests. The reason is that Justice Lewis Powell's opinion (one of six separate opinions that emerged from the case) stated that "the State has a substantial interest that legitimately may be served by a properly devised admissions program involving the competitive consideration of race and ethnic origin."[7] Although UC Davis's application of a mechanical rule for giving racial preferences was declared impermissible, *Bakke* established the principle that the promotion of diversity is nevertheless a legitimate government interest.

Because of its mixed opinions and its lack of specificity about the appropriate means of considering race in admissions, *Bakke* did not provide a strong foundation for subsequent cases. This became abundantly clear in another milestone in the legal history of affirmative action: the case of *Hopwood v. Texas.* In 1992 Cheryl Hopwood, a White applicant rejected by the University of Texas School of Law, filed a suit challenging the admissions process, which involved lower admissions thresholds for minority applicants. (She was later joined by three codefendants.) In its 1996 decision, the U.S. Fifth Circuit Court ruled in favor of Hopwood, saying that diversity was not a compelling state interest, and that race could not be used in admissions, even as one of many factors. The decision verified that a "university may properly favor one applicant over another because of his ability to play the cello, make a downfield tackle or understand chaos theory." Even an applicant's "relationship to school alumni" was stated to be fair game.[8] The use of race, though, was proscribed. The circuit court emphatically rejected *Bakke* as a binding precedent, citing post-*Bakke* Court rulings on race-conscious policies in employment and contracting. Although the *Hopwood* decision had the effect of establishing a new precedent only for the states in the Fifth Circuit—Texas, Louisiana, and Mississippi—it had a chilling effect on affirmative action admissions programs across the country.

The Supreme Court declined (twice) to hear an appeal of the *Hopwood* decision and did not take up affirmative action admissions again until 2003, when it considered two cases from the University of Michigan. Here again, results were complex: In *Gratz v. Bollinger,* a suit filed by Jennifer Gratz and another White applicant, the Court struck down the university's undergraduate admissions policy because it involved the automatic assignment of extra points for minority-group membership. This mechanical procedure was deemed impermissible because it undermined the assessment of applicants as individuals. The second Michigan suit was filed by Barbara Grutter, a White applicant to the University of Michigan Law School. The opinion rendered by Justice Sandra Day O'Connor in *Grutter v. Bollinger* endorsed Justice Powell's opinion in *Bakke,* holding that that the Law School process furthered "a compelling interest in obtaining the educational benefits that flow from a diverse student body." Race could be considered, the Court said, as part of the Law School's "highly individualized, holistic" review of applications. However, any race-conscious policy had to be "limited in time," rather than permanent.[9] The *Grutter* decision had the effect of invalidating the 1996 *Hopwood* ruling.

When the Supreme Court agreed in 2012 to hear *Fisher v. University of Texas at Austin,* many Court watchers hoped that this byzantine complex of decisions might be replaced by a clear-cut, easily interpretable policy. Abigail Fisher, a White applicant, sued UT Austin in 2008, arguing that its admissions policy was discriminatory because it applied less stringent standards to minority applicants in some circumstances. But instead of issuing the hoped-for sweeping decision, the Supreme Court in 2013 vacated an earlier Fifth Circuit Court decision in favor of the university. The Supreme Court, affirming that policies that promote diversity are permissible if they are "narrowly tailored" and if racially neutral alternatives don't exist, sent the case back to the Fifth Circuit so that the admissions policy could be further scrutinized. In mid-2014 the Fifth Circuit Court upheld UT Austin's use of race as one of many factors in admissions decisions. In a surprisingly straightforward ruling, the court said that to forbid the university's use of race "would hobble the richness of the educational experience in contradiction of the plain teachings of Bakke and Grutter."[10]

But the case wasn't over yet. Responding to an appeal from Fisher's attorneys, the Supreme Court agreed in 2015 to rehear the case. In mid-2016 it issued its decision, supporting the university's use of race as part of its holistic review process. Although the outcome was a welcome surprise to proponents of affirmative action, the decision was fairly narrow. Justice Anthony Kennedy, who authored the opinion, pointed out that the UT program was sui generis—one of a kind—because the holistic review process that was under challenge was merely a supplement to the Texas Top Ten Percent Plan, which guarantees admission to top students from every high school in the state. Despite the fact that the ten percent plan was used to admit three-quarters of the incoming class, it was not challenged by Fisher. In his opinion, Kennedy noted that the unusual circumstances of the case "may limit its value for prospective guidance." One legal analyst, noting Kennedy's efforts to confine Court approval to "one case and one plan" for a limited time period, contended that the decision "barely salvaged" the university's use of race as a factor in admissions.[11]

Still, the Fisher outcome was certainly more favorable to affirmative action than the result in *Schuette v. Coalition to Defend Affirmative Action*, decided in early 2014. In that case the Supreme Court upheld an amendment to Michigan's constitution that banned race-based affirmative action in public education, government contracting, and public employment. Groups supporting affirmative action had sued to block the portion of the law concerning education. The justices were sharply divided. In a vigorous dissent, in which she was joined by Justice Ruth Bader Ginsburg, Justice Sonia Sotomayor deplored her colleagues' "refusal to accept the stark reality that race matters." "The way to stop discrimination on the basis of race," she continued, "is to . . . apply the Constitution with eyes open to the unfortunate effects of centuries of racial discrimination. As members of the judiciary tasked with intervening to carry out the guarantee of equal protection, we ought not sit back and wish away, rather than confront, the racial inequality that exists in our society."[12]

## Rationales for Affirmative Action

In the United States, universities have used both informal and explicit policies to limit the admission of people of color, women, Catholics, Jews, and other groups from higher education. In the first half of the twentieth century, excluding African-American students from a university was perfectly legal. Under the Supreme Court's 1896 ruling in *Plessy v. Ferguson*, states were allowed to require people of different races to use separate facilities, as long as these facilities were "equal." According to *Plessy*, segregation was not, in itself, discriminatory. It was not until the 1954 decision in *Brown v. Board of Education* that *Plessy* was overturned. And six years after *Brown*, it took a Supreme Court decision, intervention by U.S. Attorney General Robert F. Kennedy, and 30,000 troops, including U.S. marshals and members of the Army and National Guard, to enforce the admission of a Black man, James Meredith, to the University of Mississippi. Two people were killed and 300 injured in the riot sparked by Meredith's admission.

It was in this climate that President Lyndon Johnson made his remarkable speech about civil rights at Howard University in 1965:

> In far too many ways American Negroes have been another nation: deprived of freedom, crippled by hatred, the doors of opportunity closed to hope. . . . In our time change has come to this Nation. . . . We have seen the high court of the country declare that discrimination based on race was repugnant to the Constitution, and therefore void. . . . [But] you do not take a person who, for years, has been hobbled by chains and liberate him, bring him up to the starting line of a race and then say, "you are free to compete with all the others," and still justly believe that you have been completely fair. Thus it is not enough just to open the gates of opportunity. All our citizens must have the ability to walk through those gates.[13]

During the civil rights era, the rationale for race-based preferences in hiring and admissions was clear. These affirmative action programs were to serve as a means of reparation for slavery and its long and ugly aftermath, and the intended beneficiaries were Black Americans.

In the decades since, arguments in favor of affirmative action have expanded and changed. If the disadvantages suffered by candidates were to be considered in the selection process for schools and jobs, then many groups could claim a piece of what conservative commentator Charles Krauthammer called the "grievance pie,"[14] including Latinos, Native Americans, and Asians. And why should the groups be limited to those based on race or ethnicity? Women, people living in poverty, people with disabilities, and those who face other significant challenges should perhaps be granted preferences as well. This was an expansion—some would say a dilution—of the civil-rights-era concept of affirmative action, but the rationale was essentially the same: The goal of the preferences was to compensate for past or current disadvantages.

But the arguments made by Justice Powell in *Bakke* and by Justice Sandra Day O'Connor in *Grutter* did not rest on principles of reparation or remediation. In fact, as O'Connor noted in her *Grutter* ruling, Powell explicitly rejected UC Davis's argument that it had an "interest" in remediating societal discrimination and in reducing "the historic deficit of traditionally disfavored minorities" in the field of medicine. Instead, Powell stated that race and ethnicity could be considered as part of a university's attempt to select a student body that varied on many dimensions, thus contributing to a "robust exchange of ideas." It is this argument—a university's compelling interest in attaining a diverse student body—that was specifically endorsed in *Grutter*. The *Grutter* Court deferred to the claims made by the University of Michigan and its supporters that diversity yields educational benefits, such as furthering cross-racial understanding, breaking down stereotypes, improving the quality of classroom discussions, and preparing students for a diverse society.[15] Nor did the *Fisher* Court consider social justice rationales for racial preferences in college admissions. In fact, except as an honorific, the word "justice" never appears in either the transcripts of the two Supreme Court hearings of *Fisher* or in the opinions themselves. Instead, as in *Bakke* and *Grutter*, the Court pondered the educational benefits of campus diversity and the role of admissions policy in promoting these benefits.[16] The diversity rationale is sometimes expanded to encompass society in general. Admitting more candidates of color can ultimately lead to a greater diversity of individuals in professional, political, and business roles.

The diversity rationale is quite different from the original justification for affirmative action, but it is perhaps more palatable to those who are not potential beneficiaries. If we assume that the most virulent forms of discrimination and racial hatred have decreased in the last half century, then the reparations rationale becomes weaker over time. Those who receive racial preferences are less likely to have been victims of the most extreme and pervasive forms of racism, and those who pay the price for these preferences are less likely to have been the perpetrators.[17] It may be for this reason that the diversity argument—a justification that invokes the common good—has come to the fore.

But perhaps the strongest argument against DeFunis, Bakke, Hopwood, Gratz, Grutter, and Fisher is that they had no "automatic" right to be admitted in the first place, and therefore no right was being abrogated by university affirmative action programs. This perspective is consistent with John Rawls's philosophical treatise *A Theory of Justice*. According to Rawls's principle of "justice as fairness," our talents do not entitle us to the good things in life, such as admission to the college of our choice. To claim any "moral deservingness" for the good fortune of being endowed with certain talents is not justifiable. In fact, it is no better than claiming a right to societal goods based on "historical and social fortune."[18] Rawls argues that neither can we claim credit for the efforts we make, because effort is itself "influenced by [our] natural abilities and skills and the alternatives open to [us]."[19] Having worked hard for our grades or tests scores, according to Rawls, does not entitle us to a moral gold star.

In a 1977 article titled "Why Bakke Has No Case," the legal scholar Ronald Dworkin views Bakke's lawsuit through what seems to be a Rawlsian lens. Dworkin notes that "there is no combination of abilities and skills and traits that constitutes 'merit' in the abstract."[20] Applicants have no automatic right to be considered on the basis of academic factors alone. What counts in admissions can be determined only after the mission of the institution is defined. This perspective appears to align with Rawls's idea of entitlement, which is different from moral deservingness. Possessing particular characteristics or skills does not allow applicants to claim that they deserve admission in any moral sense. However, once the rules of the game are established—in this case, once the university lays out its mission and its admissions requirements—applicants can legitimately expect that these rules will be followed.[21]

Ideally, then, the university would have a transparent admissions policy. Candidates would know before applying what factors were valued by the university and how these factors were to be weighted and combined in the admissions decision. Assuming that the university had a socially responsible policy and followed its own rules in selecting students, applicants would have no legitimate basis for complaint. Of course, affirmative action opponents would argue that race-conscious policies are not socially responsible and that any preferences should be race-neutral. We now consider one possible race-neutral approach—socioeconomic or "class-based" affirmative action.

## Socioeconomic Affirmative Action

The U.S. Supreme Court's acceptance of certain affirmative action admissions programs has hinged on the presumed unavailability of "race-neutral alternatives" for increasing the enrollment of underrepresented minorities.

(I use the term "race-neutral" as it has typically been used by the courts—to designate a program that does not explicitly consider applicants' race or ethnicity.) Because the status of race-based affirmative action is generally regarded as precarious, interest in (nominally) race-neutral approaches has been growing. In Chapter 5 we will discuss one such alternative, percent plan admissions. Here we address the use of explicit socioeconomic preferences: Can admissions preferences based on socioeconomic background pave the way to racial diversity? Nearly 20 years ago Harvard economist Thomas J. Kane answered with an unequivocal "no." Kane pointed out, using national data from 1992, that Whites and other non-Hispanics vastly outnumbered Blacks and Hispanics among low-income high school graduates (even though Black and Hispanic graduates were much more likely to be poor than were White graduates). This imbalance was even more pronounced for low-income students who were in the top tenth of their high school classes in terms of test scores. Among these students, the "White and other non-Hispanics" group outnumbered the "Black and Hispanic" group by almost five to one. Kane concluded that "there is an inescapable trade-off between race blindness and racial diversity. Class-based preferences do not offer a way out of the quandary."[22]

William Bowen and Derek Bok reaffirmed this position in *The Shape of the River*,[23] and Bowen and coauthors Martin Kurzweil and Eugene Tobin came to a similar conclusion in their 2005 book, *Equity and Excellence in American Higher Education*. Using 1995 data from the applicants to 18 highly selective institutions, they conducted simulation studies in which candidates from low-income families received an admissions preference equivalent to the boost that was at that time being given to legacies in these institutions—a "legacy thumb" on the scale, as the researchers described it. The authors concluded that if this policy were to replace the existing racial preferences, minority admission rates would be expected to fall by roughly half—from 15.5% to 8%.[24] More recently, sociologists Thomas J. Espenshade and Alexandra Walton Radford also concluded that substituting class-based preferences for racial preferences would result in a decrease in minority admissions—from 16% to 10%—based on an analysis of applicant data for 1983, 1993, and 1997 from highly selective institutions.[25]

Now flash forward to a widely publicized 2013 study showing that class-based admissions preferences at the University of Colorado at Boulder (CU) produced a more racially diverse entering class than did race-based preferences. Anticipating a ban on affirmative action in Colorado (ultimately rejected by voters), the admissions office at CU sought to develop a system of admissions preferences based on socioeconomic status (SES). Drawing on the theoretical foundation laid out by Richard Kahlenberg, a key proponent of SES-based preferences, CU researcher Matthew Gaertner developed two types of indexes for use in admissions decisions. The disadvantage index was an estimate of the degree to which an applicant's chances of admission were reduced by socioeconomic circumstances. "Overachievement" indexes measured the degree to which a candidate's admissions test scores and high school GPA exceeded the values that would be expected, given the candidate's socioeconomic background.[26]

Two studies were then conducted at CU to evaluate the new approach. In the first, a system of class-based admissions was applied, for research purposes only, to a set of nearly 500 applications for which actual decisions had already been made under CU's ordinary process, which included racial preferences. Admissions personnel taking part in the study used the index values, under preestablished rules, to give admissions preferences to disadvantaged and "overachieving" applicants. All information about race, as well as candidate names, had been stripped from the applications.

Overall, the admission rate rose slightly under the new approach, from 73% to 77%.[27] As expected, the class-based process resulted in a higher acceptance rate for "low SES" candidates (81%) than did the standard race-based admissions process (72%). For "severely low SES" candidates, the difference was even larger—83% under the new approach, compared to 63% under race-based admissions. More surprisingly, the class-based process also resulted in a higher acceptance rate (65% versus 56%) for underrepresented minorities (URMs), defined as Black, Latino, and Native American students. This is a small difference, resulting from the admission of four more URMs under class-based admissions than under the race-based system.[28] Nevertheless, the fact that the class-based system *increased* the admission rate for URMs is noteworthy because it differs from previous findings. In a second CU study, a system giving preferences based on both class and race was compared to a race-based system, using 1,800 applications. Although the two systems led to identical overall admission rates of 62%, the combined system led to an admission rate of 62% for URMs, compared to 45% for the race-based system.[29]

Why did the CU study lead to such different conclusions from the previous work in this area? First, there may be demographic differences between Gaertner's applicant population and those considered by Kane; Bowen, Kurzweil, and Tobin; and Espenshade and Radford. In addition, these studies used varying definitions of SES. Kane and Bowen used income to determine who received a preference, Espenshade used students' own reports of their social class,[30] and Gaertner used an SES measure that incorporated eight factors, including parental income and education, native language, and the student-to-teacher ratio in students' high schools. Native language may be particularly relevant, given that students whose native language is Spanish are likely to be Hispanic, strengthening the association between the SES measure and ethnicity.[31] Finally, the studies differ in terms of the thresholds used to determine who is eligible for preferential treatment and the size of the boost these applicants receive. As Gaertner notes, the class-based advantages at CU were particularly large: They had the effect of multiplying students' chances of admission by a factor ranging between roughly two and six (relative to applicants with similar grades and test scores who did not receive a class-based adjustment). By contrast, the boosting factor for underrepresented minorities under CU's race-based policy was 1.4.[32]

In any case, admitting a more diverse student body is only part of the battle. How do the students who receive the socioeconomic preferences fare once in college? Gaertner and his collaborator, Melissa Hart, conducted two kinds of follow-up studies to examine the academic progress of the class-based admits. Their earlier work had shown that students admitted by the class-based system but rejected by the race-based system tended to have "substantially lower" high school GPAs and test scores than students who were admitted under both the race-based and class-based systems.[33] In one follow-up study, Gaertner and Hart assessed the two-year progress of about 1,400 students who had been admitted in 2011 using class-based criteria. These students were found to have lower college GPAs, on average (2.5 versus 2.9), than their "baseline" counterparts who had not been admitted using class-based criteria. They also had lower first-year retention rates (76% versus 83%). Among these 1,400 students, those identified solely by the overachievement index performed better than those identified only by the disadvantage index, but still not as well as the baseline students.[34]

Because these 1,400 students had been admitted in 2011, it was not possible to examine their graduation rates in the 2013 follow-up study. To get an idea of what to expect in the long term, the researchers made predictions based on the academic progress of 2,700 similar students who had been admitted in earlier years (2000–2003). These "surrogates" were matched to the actual class-based admits in terms of socioeconomic and academic factors. The surrogates were found to have lower college GPAs and graduation rates than the baseline students. Their six-year graduation rate was 53%, compared to 66% for baseline students. Those identified solely by the overachievement index performed slightly better than the baseline students, while those identified only by the disadvantage index performed quite poorly, with a cumulative GPA of 2.25, a four-year graduation rate of 18%, and a six-year rate of 43%.[35] Invoking class-based preferences, then, is not without its costs. But the researchers argue that with appropriate support services, these lower-performing students can ultimately succeed at CU.

Whether class-based admissions policies will result in an increase in the number of underrepresented minorities will depend on the specifics of the policy and the applicant population. There is, of course, a certain irony in using so-called race-neutral programs for the purpose of increasing racial diversity. As Justice Ginsburg noted in her dissent in *Fisher*, "Only an ostrich could regard the supposedly neutral alternatives as race-unconscious."[36] The fairness of using race-neutral alternatives to achieve racial goals is at issue as well because these strategies violate the principle of transparency. From this perspective, processes that seek to boost the enrollment of underrepresented minorities by "nonracial" means could be viewed as something of a charade. However, the legal constraints on the use of explicit racial preferences, now strengthened by the *Schuette* decision, make it impossible for institutions to seek racial diversity in a transparent way. What is clear is that socioeconomic affirmative action policies will increase the representation of low-income students, an important goal in itself.

## Using the ELS Data to Study Racial and Socioeconomic Affirmative Action

To examine the effects of providing a "thumb on the scale" for certain racial and socioeconomic groups, I used the equally weighted composite of high school GPA and test scores as a starting point. For race-based affirmative action, I added the equivalent of 200 SAT points to the composite values for applicants who are URMs (Black, Hispanic, or American Indian). The size of the boost is consistent with the findings of previous research on the magnitude of preferences that are used in practice.[37] For socioeconomic affirmative action, members of the bottom half of the SES distribution got the 200-point boost. (Recall that in ELS, the SES measure is a composite of mother's and father's education, mother's and father's occupation, and family income.) For both the racial and SES-based affirmative action policies, I again considered two rules—a broad selection rule that involved choosing the top 41% of applicants using the criterion in question and a narrow rule that involved selecting the top 10%. (Of course, the racial affirmative action procedure used here would not actually be permissible today—it is essentially the same approach that was rejected by the Supreme Court in *Gratz*.)

The outcomes of applying the four rules appear in Tables 4-1 through 4-5.[38] Results for the enrollees and for the rules based on the original GPA–test-score composite are included for comparison. As shown in Table 4-1, the race-based affirmative action models yielded classes with a 15% to 16% representation of URMs, exceeding the 12% rate for the enrollees and producing far greater ethnic diversity than the original GPA–test-score composite. However, the results of the race-based models were in some ways disappointing. The percentages of Black and American Indian applicants admitted were small; Hispanics were the primary beneficiaries. Also, Table 4-2 shows that the class selected using the broad race-based affirmative action rule had a socioeconomic profile much like that of the enrollees, whereas the narrow race-based affirmative action rule yielded a class with a large portion of students—about 69%—from the top SES tier. Table 4-3 shows that the race-based rules, as well as the SES-based rules, admitted a somewhat larger percentage of women than actually enrolled in the competitive colleges.

Based on Table 4.2, it is clear that the SES-based affirmative action rules were effective in doing what they were supposed to do, which was to boost the enrollment of those in the bottom two SES levels. The representation of students in those levels was 24% for the broad rule and about 28% for the narrow rule, far exceeding the percentages for the enrollees and the GPA–test-score composite rules. However, although the SES-based rules resulted in somewhat greater percentages of URMs than the GPA–test-score composite, they produced classes with fewer URMs than the enrollees (Table 4-1). In fact, under the narrow SES-based rule, fewer than 6% of the selected students were URMs. I will discuss the reasons for this finding after describing the remaining outcomes.

Table 4-4 shows the academic credentials of the entering classes selected using the affirmative action rules. These students had the same average high school grades as students selected under the corresponding GPA–test-score composite rules: All three broad rules in Table 4.4 had average GPAs of 3.7; the narrow rules had average GPAs of 3.9. Average test scores for the affirmative action classes were slightly lower than those obtained with the corresponding composite rule (broad or narrow). Average test scores and high school grades for all the affirmative action classes exceeded those of the enrollees.

Table 4-5 shows that college grades followed the same pattern as high school grades: All three broad rules led to an average FGPA of 3.4; all narrow rules produced an average FGPA of 3.6. These values exceeded the 3.2 average for the enrollees. For the broad rules, graduation rates for the affirmative action rules were similar to those of the enrollees, but the rate of postbaccalaureate accomplishments was higher. As expected, the classes selected using the narrow rules had higher attainment rates. In particular, the narrow race-based affirmative action rule produced a four-year graduation rate of about 75%, a six-year rate of 90%, and a postbaccalaureate attainment rate of nearly 35%, exceeding the rates obtained with the GPA–test-score composite.

The academic performance results for the affirmative action classes are certainly encouraging and belie the idea that performance must be sacrificed in order to increase diversity. But what of the finding that socioeconomic affirmative action led to a *decrease* in underrepresented minorities relative to the enrollees?[39] This result is consistent with those of Bowen, Kurzweil, and Tobin; Espenshade and Radford; and Kane. We can take a closer look at the ELS data and see why this is the case. To quote Kane himself, "the problem is simply one of demographics." As described earlier, Kane found that among low-income high school graduates with strong academic qualifications, Whites and other non-Hispanics outnumbered underrepresented minorities nearly five to one. Similar patterns hold in the ELS data. Among the ELS senior cohort and among the applicants to competitive schools, there is a clear association between SES and race. But if we look only at those who are most likely to be eligible for admission to a selective college, the association decreases. More specifically, among the applicants the correlation between URM status and SES (top half versus bottom half) is .32, a moderate correlation. But if we focus on those applicants with admissions test scores of at least 1200 (42% of applicants), the correlation is small—only .18. And among those with test scores of at least 1400 (8% of applicants), the correlation shrinks to .07.[40] Another way to quantify the situation is to consider the percentage of low-SES students who are URMs. Among applicants, it's 45%. Among those with test scores of at least 1400, it's only 7%.

It is undeniably true that applicants who are underrepresented minorities are more likely to be poor than White students are. In the senior cohort, nearly 63% of URMs are in the bottom two SES quartiles, compared to 33% of Whites. But this is not the relevant statistic. Even among the senior cohort, low-SES students are more likely to be White than Black, Hispanic, or American Indian. And this disparity becomes greater as the academic requirements are increased. Those who argue that simply giving preferences to low-income students will substantially increase racial diversity may be looking at the wrong statistics.

## Affirmative Action for the Privileged Classes: Legacies, Development Cases, and Recruited Athletes

So far our discussion of admissions preferences has involved special treatment for those who are considered to have a disadvantage because of racial discrimination, poverty, or lack of educational opportunity. Preferences for these applicants are typically justified either as a means of increasing diversity or as a way to compensate for disadvantage. But there are other kinds of "affirmative action" that do just the opposite: They give an edge to those who are already privileged in some respect. Trampling on almost everyone's idea of fair play are the preferences many institutions give to legacies and "development admits." This phenomenon has been extensively documented by journalist Daniel Golden, who notes that at selective schools that "are the gateway to power and influence in our society, affluent but second-rate students regularly get in ahead of candidates with greater intellectual ability or artistic aptitude. These colleges . . . seek donations by reserving slots for children of privilege while turning away outstanding middle-class and working-class applicants." According to Golden, most top U.S. colleges admit legacies at two to four times the rate of nonlegacies. Typically these students come from families that are White and wealthy.[41] Development cases are applicants whose family members, although not alumni, are expected to be a soft touch for fund-raisers. These relatives could be industrial tycoons, Hollywood moguls, or politicians in a position to allocate funding to the institution. The advantages gained by development admits can be worth 300 to 400 SAT points.[42]

Recruited athletes constitute a third privileged class. Contrary to stereotype, recruited athletes are less likely than their fellow students to be from underrepresented minorities or from low-income families, because participants in "rich-person" sports, such as crew, sailing, lacrosse, and fencing, get an edge along with basketball and football players.[43] Just how big is the boost received by recruited athletes? Espenshade and his colleagues, using data from the 1980s and 1990s from three top-tier private institutions, examined various admissions preferences in terms of the SAT bonus they represented. African Americans received a preference equivalent to an extra 230 SAT points (on a 400-to-1600 scale), relative to Whites. Hispanics got the equivalent of an extra 185 points. (An "Asian disadvantage" of 50 SAT points, relative to Whites, was also noted. Although Espenshade attached several cautions to this result, the 50-point figure has featured in recent college counseling sessions for California high schoolers.)[44] Against this backdrop, the bonuses accorded to legacies and especially to athletes were eye-opening. Legacies were given a 160-point advantage over nonlegacies and athletes received a 200-point boost relative to nonathletes.[45]

Bowen and his colleagues used a different approach to illustrate the size of admissions preferences at 19 elite colleges in 1995. They provide a fascinating graphic that shows the admission rates for various kinds of applicants by SAT score. For a given SAT score, those most likely to be admitted were recruited athletes, followed by underrepresented minorities, legacies, and, in last place, applicants who were not members of these special categories. For those with SAT scores (math plus verbal) between 1300 and 1349, for example, roughly 80% of recruited athletes, 75% of underrepresented minorities, and 60% of legacies were admitted, compared to 40% of other applicants.[46] Overall, Bowen estimated that being a recruited athlete boosted a candidate's chances of admission by an average of 30 percentage points, net of other factors. Perhaps the most striking finding was that, at SAT scores below 900, recruited athletes had an admit rate of about 55%, whereas the rates for other applicants were well below 20%. It's no wonder that a former admissions dean called athletic recruiting "the biggest form of affirmative action in American higher education."[47]

Is it fair to give preferences to athletes and children of prospective donors? First let's consider legacies and development cases. Although paving the way for their admission may contribute to a college's financial well-being, no credible argument can be made that this kind of special preference is consistent with the school's educational mission. Legacies and development cases are rewarded for family wealth and social standing and not for any potential contribution to the educational environment of the institution. Nor does this type of preferential admission serve any social justice function— in fact, it's a clear example of privileging the privileged.

And although many institutions regard legacy and development admissions as financial necessities, this need not be the case. After all, many large donations and bequests are made to universities and other organizations without the expectation that a family member of the donor will reap a personal benefit. But because the practice of granting admissions preferences in return for donations is both deeply entrenched and self-perpetuating, it will take a concerted effort to change the culture.

In his 2006 book, *The Price of Admission*, Golden profiled three elite institutions that were flourishing despite giving no legacy or "development" preferences—California Institute of Technology (Caltech), Berea College in Kentucky, and Cooper Union in New York City. "Nobody gets into Caltech because their families are rich, famous, or well connected," according to Golden.[48] At the time of his writing, Berea and Cooper Union not only steered clear of legacy preferences; they offered a full scholarship to all. Cooper Union, however, has fallen upon hard times in recent years. Its financial situation took a severe downturn due to "decades of bad decisions and recent treacherous markets," according to the *New York Times*. The school cut its tuition scholarships in half in 2014, leading to widespread campus upheaval. In 2015, after the president and five trustees quit, New York State's attorney general announced that an independent monitor would be established to oversee the financial management of the college. Unfortunately, Cooper Union's story is now a cautionary tale about the financial challenges facing colleges today. Berea, however, continues to offer all students its Tuition Promise Scholarship, covering 100% of tuition costs. According to the school's website, this support is available because of "the generous support of alumni, friends, organizations and others who believe, as we do, that a student's income should not dictate their outcome."[49] And according to a 2016 report by the Jack Kent Cooke Foundation, "public flagship universities in Texas, California, and Georgia" have also bucked the trend, completely eliminating legacy preferences.[50] Intriguingly, Golden suggests that the British are less fond of legacy preferences than Americans, noting that Euan Blair, son of Oxford alumnus and then-prime-minister Tony Blair, was turned down by Oxford in 2002.[51]

Athletic preferences are less objectionable than legacy and development admits because the athletes are at least being rewarded for their own talents and accomplishments. At some institutions, athletes are considered for admission through the same processes that are used to evaluate other potential exceptions to standard academic requirements. For example, the

Georgia State University website indicates that "students with special talents who do not meet the university admission standards are considered through a special admissions review process." It is also noted that "decisions to deny admission to special talent applicants . . . may be appealed by the chair of an academic department or the Athletic Director," a clear indication that "special talents" include athletic ability.[52]

Except in the case of athletes, there is very little research on the admission of candidates with special talents. In the annual surveys conducted by the National Association for College Admission Counseling, institutions are not explicitly asked about the importance of extraordinary talents in admissions decisions.[53] In a rare consideration of the role of special talents (as distinct from athletic skills), a 1995 report sponsored by several admissions organizations listed the percentage of four-year institutions that reported granting "exceptions to formal academic requirements" for "students with special talents" in 1979, 1985, and 1992. Roughly 300 to 400 public institutions and 600 to 800 private institutions per year responded to the survey. For public institutions, the percentages ranged from 38% to 39%; for private institutions, the percentage was 29% in 1979, dropping to 16% in 1985 and 1992. These percentages were slightly higher than the corresponding ones for athletes.[54]

So if admissions standards can be stretched for other talented individuals, why not for athletes? In fact, the role of an accomplished painter, a gifted poet, or a brilliant Science Olympiad winner within a postsecondary institution is quite different from that of a recruited athlete. Whereas the talents of the painter, the poet, and the scientist help these students to contribute to and benefit from the academic offerings of the college, a significant purpose of athletic recruitment is to encourage donations from alumni and other sports fans. This is particularly true of the "country club sports," which tend to draw wealthy donors.[55] At the same time, many recruited athletes have substantially weaker academic skills than other candidates, and Bowen and his colleagues found that the academic performance of recruited athletes in college tends to be even worse than their weaker credentials would predict, whether or not they are currently playing. One possible reason, they suggested, is that characteristics like "intellectual curiosity or wide-ranging interests, which are normally highly prized by admissions officers, may be sacrificed or at least given less weight" in the interest of maximizing athletic performance.[56]

An extreme case came to light recently at the University of North Carolina at Chapel Hill, where some basketball and football stars were found to read at a grade-school level, requiring help to sound out multisyllable words. Many recruited athletes were able to stay in school by getting credit for bogus independent studies or nonexistent classes "offered" by UNC's Department of African, African American, and Diaspora Studies. The whistle-blowing tutor who brought this to light was accused of defaming the university and was demoted from her administrative position to a low-level paper-pushing job. She eventually resigned because of the difficult atmosphere.[57] But the most serious losses were incurred by the athletes themselves, who were deprived of a legitimate college education.

Similarly, the *New York Times* recently profiled a star athlete with an abysmal high school academic record who was admitted to Southern Methodist University to play basketball. The faculty committee tasked with reviewing "athletic applications" had rejected him but was overruled by the provost. (In explaining the admissions decision to the *Times*, an SMU representative waved the "holistic" banner.) Investigations by the National Collegiate Athletic Association and the Dallas schools revealed that the student's high school had altered his grades with the encouragement of SMU athletic recruiters, leading the NCAA to sanction the university. Again, though, the big loser was the student, who dropped out, evidently blaming himself for the scandal.[58] The UNC and SMU sagas show how university values—and admissions policies—become distorted when victory on the court is allowed to take on outsize importance.

Ironically, Harvard's policy of favoring legacies and athletes served as a successful defense for its unexpectedly low admission rate for Asian Americans, which was investigated by the U.S. Department of Education in the 1980s. The Department concluded that no discrimination had taken place, accepting Harvard's explanation that Asian Americans had a lower admission rate than Whites, despite similar qualifications, because Asians were less likely to be legacies or recruited athletes.[59] Furthermore, Harvard claimed that granting legacy preferences encouraged alumni to make donations and to participate in fund-raising, thus allowing the college to maintain a need-blind admissions policy.[60] More than 20 years later, little has changed. In 2014 an advocacy group filed a lawsuit charging Harvard (along with the University of North Carolina) with "rampant discrimination against Asian Americans" in its admissions process. These cases are now approaching trials in federal district courts.[61] In 2015 a coalition of more than 60 Asian-American groups lodged a complaint with the Office for Civil Rights of the U.S. Department of Education, claiming that Asian-American applicants to Harvard are more likely to be rejected than are similarly qualified applicants from other ethnic groups.[62] Meanwhile, according to the *Harvard Crimson*, "Harvard's acceptance rate for legacies has hovered around 30 percent—more than four times the regular admission rate—in recent admissions cycles."[63]

To sum up, we know that most colleges give an extra boost to legacies and other development admits, claiming that this policy is financially necessary. The *Hopwood* court even gave the seal of approval to preferences for relatives of alumni. Then there are the huge boosts given to recruited athletes—a policy that recently allowed students lacking basic literacy skills to be admitted to a prestigious university. In addition to donation potential and athletic talent, schools routinely give an edge to candidates because of factors unrelated to academic performance. Suppose the candidate is a veteran, for example. Or maybe the applicant is the only one from Alaska or Switzerland. Perhaps his mother is a highly esteemed faculty member the university is trying to retain. Maybe the applicant or a member of her family is a well-known actress or entertainer. (Children from famous families can lend cachet if not cash.) These types of preferences are well known and rarely raise an eyebrow. We might ask, then, why racial preferences provoke so much outrage.

Table 4-1. Percentages of Students in Each Ethnic Group for Enrollees and Six Admissions Models

| Ethnic Group | Enrollees | Broad Selection Rules | | | Narrow Selection Rules | | |
|---|---|---|---|---|---|---|---|
| | | GPA–Test-Score Composite | Composite with Race-Based Affirmative Action | Composite with SES-Based Affirmative Action | GPA–Test-Score Composite | Composite with Race-Based Affirmative Action | Composite with SES-Based Affirmative Action |
| Asian (%) | 12.1 | 12.3 | 11.4 | 13.6 | 15.6 | 12.5 | 14.9 |
| Underrepresented minorities (%) | 12.4 | 7.9 | 15.3 | 9.5 | 2.5 | 15.6 | 5.6 |
| More than one race (%) | 3.8 | 2.0 | 1.8 | 1.9 | 1.5 | 1.4 | 2.3 |
| White (%) | 71.7 | 77.8 | 71.6 | 75.0 | 80.4 | 70.5 | 77.2 |

Note: Some column totals are not exactly 100% because of rounding. Results for Black, Hispanic, and American Indian students were combined to conform with Institute of Education Sciences data security requirements.

Table 4-2. Percentages of Students in Each of Four Socioeconomic Categories for Enrollees and Six Admissions Models

| Socioeconomic Status (SES) | Enrollees | Broad Selection Rules | | | Narrow Selection Rules | | |
|---|---|---|---|---|---|---|---|
| | | GPA–Test-Score Composite | Composite with Race-Based Affirmative Action | Composite with SES-Based Affirmative Action | GPA–Test-Score Composite | Composite with Race-Based Affirmative Action | Composite with SES-Based Affirmative Action |
| Highest (%) | 63.6 | 64.0 | 62.6 | 56.6 | 70.4 | 68.8 | 57.8 |
| Second highest (%) | 20.8 | 22.4 | 22.2 | 19.3 | 21.8 | 19.8 | 14.1 |
| Second lowest (%) | 11.4 | 9.5 | 9.9 | 16.1 | 4.7 | 6.7 | 20.6 |
| Lowest (%) | 4.2 | 4.1 | 5.4 | 7.9 | 3.0 | 4.6 | 7.5 |

*Note:* Some column totals are not exactly 100% because of rounding.

Table 4-3. Percentages of Women and Men for Enrollees and Six Admissions Models

| Gender | Enrollees | Broad Selection Rules | | | Narrow Selection Rules | | |
|---|---|---|---|---|---|---|---|
| | | GPA–Test-Score Composite | Composite with Race-Based Affirmative Action | Composite with SES-Based Affirmative Action | GPA–Test-Score Composite | Composite with Race-Based Affirmative Action | Composite with SES-Based Affirmative Action |
| Women (%) | 53.4 | 57.2 | 57.8 | 57.3 | 53.5 | 55.9 | 56.2 |
| Men (%) | 46.6 | 42.8 | 42.2 | 42.7 | 46.5 | 44.1 | 43.8 |

Note: Some column totals are not exactly 100% because of rounding.

Table 4-4. High School GPA and Test-Score Data for Enrollees and Six Admissions Models

| | Enrollees | Broad Selection Rules | | | Narrow Selection Rules | | |
|---|---|---|---|---|---|---|---|
| | | GPA–Test-Score Composite | Composite with Race-Based Affirmative Action | Composite with SES-Based Affirmative Action | GPA–Test-Score Composite | Composite with Race-Based Affirmative Action | Composite with SES-Based Affirmative Action |
| **High school GPA** | | | | | | | |
| Average | 3.5 | 3.7 | 3.7 | 3.7 | 3.9 | 3.9 | 3.9 |
| Standard deviation | 0.4 | 0.2 | 0.3 | 0.3 | 0.1 | 0.1 | 0.1 |
| **Test Score** | | | | | | | |
| Average | 1245 | 1303 | 1299 | 1295 | 1431 | 1418 | 1411 |
| Standard deviation | 150 | 111 | 117 | 121 | 68 | 85 | 91 |

Table 4-5. College First-Year Grade-Point Average (FGPA), Graduation Rates, and Postbaccalaureate Attainment Rate for Enrollees and Six Admissions Models

| | Enrollees | Broad Selection Rules | | | Narrow Selection Rules | | |
|---|---|---|---|---|---|---|---|
| | | GPA–Test-Score Composite | Composite with Race-Based Affirmative Action | Composite with SES-Based Affirmative Action | GPA–Test-Score Composite | Composite with Race-Based Affirmative Action | Composite with SES-Based Affirmative Action |
| College FGPA | | | | | | | |
| Average | 3.2 | 3.4 | 3.4 | 3.4 | 3.6 | 3.6 | 3.6 |
| Standard deviation | 0.6 | 0.5 | 0.5 | 0.5 | 0.4 | 0.4 | 0.4 |
| College Graduation | | | | | | | |
| 4-year graduation rate | 64.3% | 64.7% | 64.1% | 63.5% | 69.6% | 75.4% | 70.4% |
| 6-year graduation rate | 83.7% | 85.4% | 85.1% | 84.1% | 88.2% | 90.3% | 86.5% |
| Postbaccalaureate attainment rate | 28.0% | 33.2% | 32.9% | 32.8% | 33.8% | 34.9% | 32.9% |

# Percent Plans and Other Test-Optional Admissions Programs

> It is as if people tiptoe around the 800-pound gorilla in the center of the room, trying to find a substitute for race without admitting they are trying to find a substitute for race in order to avoid being accused of trying to find a substitute for race.
>
> —*Bob Laird, director of undergraduate admissions, UC Berkeley, 1994–1999*

Following the clampdown on race-based affirmative action in the 1990s, American universities began to seek alternative approaches that did not explicitly take race into consideration. Among the ostensibly race-neutral admissions plans that emerged were preferences for students from lower socioeconomic brackets, which we have already considered, and percent plans, also called class rank plans. These plans, which are in effect in Texas, California, and Florida, provide for the automatic admission of students who are in the top tier of their high school class in terms of grades. All three state programs require applicants to complete certain high school courses and to take the SAT or ACT, but test scores are not considered in the admissions decisions. Because they draw top students from all high schools, including high-poverty schools and those with large percentages of students of color, these percent plans were expected to increase socioeconomic and racial diversity.

An overlapping development has been the adoption of "test-optional" admissions programs, which reduce or eliminate the use of standardized test scores as admissions criteria but may otherwise operate in fairly traditional ways. Because Black, Latino, and low-SES students perform more poorly, on average, on standardized admissions tests, the test-optional admissions policies have been promoted as a way to increase campus diversity.[1] In the introduction to his recent book on this topic, Joseph Soares of Wake Forest University contends that at his institution, "as for many other colleges, there is an inverse relationship between the weight placed on high-stakes test scores and the diversity of an applicant pool and matriculating class."[2]

What are the pros and cons of the percent plans and test-optional admissions policies? Do these programs achieve their intended goals? Are they race-neutral? Are they fair?

## The Percent Plans

The first of the class rank plans, the Texas Top Ten Percent Plan, was a direct response to the 1996 *Hopwood* decision, which banned affirmative action admissions in Texas, Louisiana, and Mississippi. Under the Texas plan, as originally implemented, Texas students in the top 10% of their high school class were automatically admitted to any public Texas university they chose. The policy was enacted by the Texas legislature and signed into law by Governor George W. Bush in 1997. Not surprisingly, many eligible high school students chose one of the two flagship universities—Texas A&M and the University of Texas at Austin. UT Austin later obtained an exception to the policy that allowed it to reject some ten percenters.[3] The original University of California percent plan, initiated in 1999, guaranteed that California students in the top 4% of their high schools would be admitted to UC, though not necessarily to the campus of their choice. The plan, formally called "eligibility in the local context" or ELC, was expanded from 4% to 9% in 2012. Florida's Talented 20 program was adopted in 2000 as part of Governor Jeb Bush's One Florida initiative, described in a press release as "an innovative plan to increase opportunity and diversity while ending racial preferences and set-asides in state contracting and university admissions."[4] Under the Talented 20 plan, students in the top 20% of each of the state's public high schools are guaranteed admission to one of the campuses of the state university system, "within space and fiscal limitations."[5] The Florida plan differs from its Texas and California counterparts in that recruitment, retention, and financial aid programs may still target underrepresented racial groups, even though race cannot be used in the admissions decision itself.[6] Another difference among the plans is that whereas the California plan was enacted by the university, the Florida and Texas plans were imposed by the state.

Even before the first results were in, the percent plans met with criticism from both the right and the left. Conservatives feared that the plans would admit unqualified students, exclude talented students whose schools were "too good," and ultimately diminish the quality of top-notch state universities. Some in the civil rights community, including the U.S. Civil Rights Commission itself, decried the fact that the plans depend for their success on the existence of racially segregated and underperforming schools. Critics from all sides argued that class rank plans could encourage students to attend inferior high schools and avoid challenging courses. Proponents, however, have continued to promote these plans as a race-neutral route to campus diversity.

## Test-Optional Admissions

According to Robert Schaeffer, public education director of FairTest, "educators and policymakers . . . increasingly . . . identify standardized admissions tests as significant barriers to entry for thousands of academically qualified minority, first-generation, and low-income applicants. . . . By turning away from reliance on test scores, . . . institutions are promoting equity and excellence."[7] FairTest maintains a list of roughly 850 "colleges and universities that do not use SAT / ACT scores to admit substantial numbers of students into bachelor degree programs." FairTest previously referred to this list as the "test-optional admissions list." The carefully reworded title reflects the fact that some of these institutions merely "deemphasize" tests rather than making them optional.[8]

The policies of the listed institutions vary widely. Two schools, Sarah Lawrence College and Hampshire College, recently enforced a "test-blind" policy—they announced that they would ignore standardized test scores even if students submitted them. However, Sarah Lawrence now has a conventional test-optional policy, meaning that scores will be considered if students wish to provide them.[9] Other schools on the FairTest list require test scores, but not necessarily the ACT or SAT. For example, instead of submitting SAT or ACT scores, applicants to Hamilton College may submit any three exam scores from a menu of options, provided that a quantitative test and a verbal or writing test are among them.[10] The inclusion of certain schools on the FairTest list is a bit of a mystery. In 2014, I picked a school from my home state to examine further: San Jose State University. On the

SJSU website, I found the following information for 2014 applicants: "Submit SAT or ACT test scores by Friday, December 20, 2013.... Freshman applicants are required to submit ... scores from a test taken no later than November 2013. No exceptions! Submit your official scores by the deadline. Failure to do so will result in your application being withdrawn.... Your admission to SJSU is based on a combination of the grades you earned in the approved courses ... and your official SAT / ACT scores." Similar information, without the dire warnings, appears on SJSU's site in 2016.[11]

But even if some schools may have landed on the list by mistake, it's clear that at least among liberal arts schools, there has been a slow but steady move to drop admissions test requirements. During the past decade, more than 50 highly selective liberal arts colleges have adopted test-optional policies.[12] Here, we examine what is known about the impact of percent plans and test-optional admissions programs, beginning with diversity outcomes.

## Diversity Outcomes of Percent Plans and Test-Optional Admissions

We can consider two types of data on the impact of these nominally race-neutral admissions programs on campus diversity: First, simulations that apply admissions rules mimicking these policies to data from actual applicants can offer some insight into the likely results of applying the policies in a systematic way. Second, data from schools that have actually implemented these programs can, of course, be analyzed. As we will see, both simulation data and findings from Texas, California, and Florida show the percent plans to be largely ineffective in increasing ethnic and socioeconomic diversity. In the case of test-optional programs, simulation data show some favorable impact on diversity, while research results from schools that have implemented the programs show mixed results.

### Percent Plans

Because the ELS data do not contain information about participants' high school rank, I was not able to conduct any simulations of the effects of percent plans. However, some earlier simulation results, based on applicants to elite colleges in the 1990s, are available. Using these data, economists Anthony P. Carnevale and Stephen J. Rose concluded that 10% and 20% plans led to a substantial increase in the admission of "qualified" low-SES students in the entering class. (According to the authors' definition, qualified students are those with SAT scores of at least 1000 on a 200-to-1600 scale or equivalent ACT scores.) However, the percent plans had little impact on the percentage of qualified Black and Hispanic students. In addition, Carnevale and Rose predicted low graduation rates under these plans. Modified class rank plans that required a minimum SAT score of 1000 (verbal and math scores combined) were found to produce lower percentages of Black and Hispanic students than had actually enrolled in the schools in question.[13]

A more recent study by Carnevale, Rose, and Jeff Strohl led to different results. They used ELS data to simulate "10 percent models in which the criterion is relative performance in each of the nation's high schools" and concluded that these plans had a favorable impact on diversity. However, their results cannot be compared to the findings of other percent plan research. First, the students selected were those with the best admissions test scores in their high schools, rather than the best grades.[14] In addition, technical factors complicated the implementation: Because only a small number of students in any one high school participate in ELS (an average of 20 per participating school), it is impossible to use the ELS database to determine if an ELS participant is in the top 10% of his or her senior class. The authors therefore had to use approximations in attempting to make these determinations.[15] Finally, two of the three percent plans they investigated also included socioeconomic or racial preferences.

In their book on admissions, Thomas Espenshade and Alexandra Walton Radford conducted a simulation study of two alternative versions of a top ten percent plan, using applicant data from several selective public institutions. In one version, only in-state students were eligible for the percent plan; in the other, all applicants were allowed to benefit from the plan. In both cases, ten percenters were admitted first; then typical admissions criteria (with no affirmative action) were applied to fill the remaining spaces. Both versions led to a reduction in the percentage of Black students from 7.8% (the actual percent of Black students admitted to these schools) to 4.4%. The percentage of White students increased by 3.3%, and the percentages of Hispanic and Asian students were unaffected.[16] The likely reason for this pattern of results is that the actual admissions process included some form of affirmative action that benefited Black students; the percent plan was not able to compensate for the elimination of that preference.

What can be learned from the three states that have percent plans in place? In a 2012 review of the impact on diversity of the percent plans in California,

Florida, and Texas, researcher Catherine Horn concluded that "although varying in scope and rigor, the majority of findings related to racial/ethnic representation among admitted and enrolled students indicate that such policies did little to enhance diversity."[17] Here we consider the research on these three state plans.

Determining the success of percent plans in fostering diversity is not entirely straightforward. Often overlooked is the fact that percent plans constitute only one of several possible pathways to participating institutions and that some students admitted through a percent plan would have been accepted even in its absence. At the University of California, for example, state residents can become eligible for admission not only through the ELC program, but through a "statewide path," which requires that candidates' admissions index values, based on their test scores and grades, be among the top students statewide, irrespective of which high school they attended.[18] There is likely to be a substantial overlap between this pool of applicants and the ELC pool. In fact, according to UC researchers William Kidder and Patricia Gándara, the 4% plan did not have a "discernible" effect on the diversity of UC's entering classes because most of the eligible students would have been eligible for UC anyway.[19] In short, simply looking at the ethnic-group composition of UC's entering classes tells us little about the effectiveness of the ELC program. Proper evaluation requires not only separate demographic data for the ELC admits, but information about which of these students would have been admitted through some alternative path—information that is not easily obtained.

A small analysis I conducted years ago illustrates the phenomenon of overlapping admissions paths. Out of 34,000 applicants to UC Santa Barbara in 2001, more than 3,300 were eligible for UC admission under the 4% plan, including more than 700 from underrepresented ethnic groups (American Indians, Alaskan Natives, African Americans, Chicanos, and Latinos). But of these 3,300, all but 77 (including 37 from underrepresented groups) would have been eligible for UC admission even without the 4% plan. Ultimately, none of the 77 were admitted to UCSB.[20] And yet it could have been truthfully claimed that the ELC program yielded more than 3,000 eligible applicants, about 20% of whom were from underrepresented groups.

Beginning with the class entering in 2012, the University of California ELC plan was modified to accept the top 9% of each high school. According to Kidder and Gándara, the students applying through this program in 2012 were slightly less likely to be underrepresented minorities than the overall pool of UC applicants. Why would this be the case? The researchers note that "many of the schools from which UC would hope to draw a more diverse pool of students neither prepare nor encourage their students to apply to the university, and most of these students have never known anyone who has attended UC."[21] At the flagship campuses, UC Berkeley and UC Los Angeles, the percentage of Black students enrolled in 2013 was considerably lower than in 1995 (3.4% versus 5.7% for Berkeley; 3.9% versus 6% for UCLA) and the percentage of Chicano / Latino students was about the same as in 1995 (13% for Berkeley, 17% for UCLA) despite the statewide increase in the Chicano / Latino population.[22]

A 2003 study of Florida's Talented 20 Plan by the Harvard Civil Rights Project pronounced the supposed successes of the program to be illusory. The researchers concluded that in 2000 and 2001, the program had influenced enrollment of underrepresented minorities to only a trivial degree because "the overwhelming majority of students designated as Talented 20" would have been admitted even without the program.[23] In addition, Black and Hispanic students were found to be less likely to have completed the high school credits necessary to qualify for the Talented 20 program.[24]

A later study by researchers from the University of Pennsylvania used data from 1995 through 2005 to examine whether Hispanics were well represented in Florida and Texas public universities relative to their inclusion among the state's high school graduates. These states were selected for study in part because of their implementation of percent plans. If the percentage of Hispanics was found to be the same among the enrolled college students as among the high school graduates, this would constitute "equity" according to the researchers. Not surprisingly, the study found that Hispanics were far above equity among first-time full-time college enrollments at institutions designated as "Hispanic-serving" in both states, but results were much less favorable at other kinds of schools. At four-year public institutions (considered as a whole), they were somewhat above equity in Florida and somewhat below in Texas. Hispanics were found to be "substantially below equity" at four-year predominantly White institutions and public flagship universities in both Florida and Texas.[25]

Findings on the impact of the Texas plan have been mixed. In 2010 the percentage of Top Ten Percent–eligible students enrolling in the state's elite institutions varied substantially among ethnic groups. Only 44% of eligible Hispanic students and 34% of Black students enrolled, compared to 60% of White and 69% of Asian students.[26] Although the number of Hispanics in Texas higher education institutions has increased in recent years, their representation has actually decreased as a percentage of the Hispanic population in Texas, which has been growing substantially.[27] At the state's most selective institutions, Texas A&M and UT Austin, Hispanic students constitute a smaller percentage of enrollments than during the affirmative action era.[28] This is particularly notable because UT Austin (but not A&M) reinstated racial preferences in admissions following the *Grutter* ruling.[29] It was these racial preferences, employed along with the Ten Percent Plan, that were challenged and ultimately upheld in *Fisher*. That these preferences survived four federal court decisions (two each by the Fifth Circuit Court and the U.S. Supreme Court) could be seen as an acknowledgment by the courts that the Ten Percent Plan is not fully effective in achieving its diversity goals, at least at UT Austin.

## Test-Optional Admissions

Does selecting students based on high school grades alone yield an entering class with a higher percentage of URMs (Black, Hispanic, and Native American) and lower-income students than a selection procedure based solely on test scores? Simulation results appear to support this claim by proponents of test-optional admissions. My analyses of ELS data presented in Chapter 2 showed that selecting students based on high school GPA alone (with a 41% selection rate) resulted in a class with about 10% URM representation, compared to roughly 7% for selection based on admissions test scores alone. Among the actual enrollees, about 12% were URMs. The percentage of students from the lower two socioeconomic quartiles was about 19% for the GPA-based selection rule, 12% for the test-score-based rule, and 16% for the actual enrollees. The demographic differences between the class selected via the GPA rule and the one resulting from the test-score rule were even greater when only the top 10% of applicants were chosen. Overall, despite having considerably lower average admissions test scores, the two entering classes selected using GPA only tended to perform better in college than the two classes chosen using test scores only.

In their more elaborate simulation, Thomas Espenshade and Chang Young Chung used as a starting point the prediction models of the admissions process that they had developed based on data from eight elite schools. Prediction was based on multiple factors, including academic characteristics, social class, and participation in extracurricular activities. Separate models were created for private and public colleges. To simulate the effects of a test-optional policy, they modified their models so that low SAT and ACT scores would be treated the same way as middling scores; high scores retained their original value. The goal was to represent a system in which low scores would not be a disadvantage, but high scores would remain advantageous. In addition, Espenshade and Chung increased the importance assigned to high school grades and other factors and attempted to simulate changes in the applicant pool resulting from the initiation of the test-optional policy. Results for private universities showed that under the assumption that Black and Hispanic applications would increase by 30%, the percentages of Black and Hispanic applicants selected would each increase from about 8% (the actual percentage admitted to these schools) to about 11%. The proportion of Whites, and to a lesser degree Asians, would decrease. The socioeconomic distribution would shift somewhat toward lower income groups as well. Projected changes in the entering class were smaller for other types of applicant pools and for the public universities.[30]

But what have studies of actual test-optional schools shown? One of the first schools to go test-optional was Bates College in Maine, which dropped its SAT requirement in 1984 and eliminated all admissions test requirements in 1990. In 2014 Bates's former admissions director William Hiss and researcher Valerie Franks published a report on the results of test-optional admissions at 33 schools they selected from 120 institutions they originally contacted. The authors did not identify the schools or reveal how they were selected for inclusion, but noted that 20 private colleges and universities, six public state universities, five minority-serving institutions, and two art institutions participated in the study.

The researchers' conclusion about the impact of test-optional policies, in a nutshell: "non-submitters are out-performing their standardized testing."[31] But what does this mean? Did nonsubmitters perform better than their test scores would have predicted? The study does not shed any light on that question. The authors did find, however, that for all the schools combined, submitters and nonsubmitters differed by only 0.05 points in terms of cumulative college GPA (2.88 versus 2.83) and by only 0.6% in graduation rates (64.5% versus 63.9%).[32] Overall, about 30% of students were nonsubmitters; these were "more likely [than submitters] to be first-generation-to-college enrollees, . . . minority students, women, Pell Grant recipients, and students with Learning Differences."[33]

The results of the Hiss and Franks study are not as straightforward as they might seem at first. For one thing, the college GPA findings need to be considered in light of the fact that nonsubmitters differed from submitters in terms of their chosen fields of study: Nonsubmitters were much less likely than submitters to major in science, technology, engineering, or math (STEM) fields, a pattern that held for the private, public, and minority-serving institutions.[34] Results are further complicated by substantial differences among the participating schools in their populations and missions and in the specifics of the test-optional programs themselves. Even the definitions of submitters and nonsubmitters were less than straightforward. Some private schools never saw the test results of nonsubmitters; in other cases, "nonsubmitters" were asked to produce test scores to be used for research purposes. All six public universities in the study required all applicants to submit scores, but used percent plans to select a portion of their students. If an applicant's high school class rank qualified him for automatic admission, his test scores were not considered, and he was labeled a nonsubmitter for purposes of the Hiss and Franks study. However, some of these "nonsubmitters"—those who had above-average test scores—were excluded from certain analyses so as to avoid artificially boosting the performance data for nonsubmitters.[35]

Further clouding the picture, the 33 participating schools submitted data from as many as eight entry years, though "institutions normally submitted two graduated class cohorts and two currently enrolled cohorts."[36] The data were then combined across these varying numbers of entry years, obscuring any possible changes over time. Many of the reported results are combined across institutions as well, but fortunately some disaggregated results are reported. The results tell a subtly different story when they are examined separately by institution. For example, we can see that at 13 of the 15 private schools that provided graduation data, submitters were more likely to graduate than nonsubmitters, and at 15 of the 18 private schools providing relevant data, submitters had higher final college GPAs.[37] Submitters had higher graduation rates at all five minority institutions participating in the study, though they had higher final GPAs at only two of these.[38] Only a narrative description is given for the two participating art institutions; no formal statistics are included. At the single art institution that provided graduation data, submitters reportedly had a higher graduation rate. Cumulative GPAs are stated to be similar for submitters and nonsubmitters at one art institution and higher for nonsubmitters at the other.[39]

It is at the six public institutions, all of which had percent plans, that the authors' claims about the academic advantages of test-optional policies are best supported. Here, "nonsubmitters" (those whose test scores were not used in admissions decisions) did have higher final GPAs at all six universities and higher graduation rates at the five schools for which results were available. Nonsubmitters also entered college with substantially better high school GPAs and SAT scores, but the superior outcomes for nonsubmitters held up even when those with high test scores were removed from the analysis.[40]

The impact of the test-optional policies on campus diversity is another story. Although the authors claimed that "optional testing seems to work as an affirmative action device,"[41] their findings neither support nor contradict the claim that test-optional policies serve to increase minority enrollment: No information is provided as to the demographic composition of the admitted or enrolled students either before or after the implementation of test-optional admissions. The results do indicate that, if the results from all 33 schools are combined, nonsubmitters were more likely than submitters to be ethnic minorities, but this pattern did not hold true for the public universities, where nonsubmitters and submitters included identical percentages of URMs (15%); nonsubmitters also had a trivially higher average family income.[42] At the public institutions, White students were slightly more likely to be nonsubmitters than Hispanic, Black, or Asian students (only American Indians had a higher rate), whereas White students were least likely of all ethnic groups to be nonsubmitters at private schools.[43]

In a study published after the Hiss and Franks report (but, surprisingly, making no mention of it), Andrew Belasco, Kelly Rosinger, and James Hearn of the University of Georgia examined the effects of test-optional admissions policies between 1992 and 2010. They used data from 180 selective liberal arts colleges, 32 of which had adopted test-optional admissions. The researchers provide a harsh evaluation of these policies, claiming that they "have done little to meet their manifest goals of expanding educational opportunity for low-income and minority students." The proportions of Pell Grant recipients and underrepresented minorities were found to be lower at test-optional than at test-requiring institutions, and these rates failed to increase following the introduction of test-optional policies. Test-optional schools did, however, receive larger numbers of applications than their test-requiring counterparts (net of other factors), and also reported higher SAT scores, allowing them to "enhance the appearance of selectivity." The gaps between test-optional and test-requiring institutions in terms of reported SAT scores and number of applications was found to increase over time, leading Belasco and his colleagues to argue that test-optional admissions "may serve to reproduce and maintain the current social structure—and its inequalities."[44]

Belasco's findings about institutional SAT scores are not surprising. It has long been observed that test-optional policies are likely to discourage those with low scores from submitting test results, thus raising an institution's average test score and possibly its ranking. Furthermore, if test-optional policies increase the number of applications, as has typically been found, the admission rate will drop, making the school appear more selective.[45] However, Belasco's determination that test-optional admissions fails to increase the percentage of underrepresented minorities is at odds with simulation-based results. What could account for this discrepancy? One important difference is that Belasco and his colleagues studied the demographic makeup of students who actually enrolled in schools that had implemented test-optional admissions, while the simulations described here (mine included) examined only the impact of these selection rules on the makeup of the "admitted" students.[46] It is possible that despite being admitted at higher rates under test-optional policies, students of color are less likely to actually enroll, perhaps for financial reasons. In addition, the Belasco results may be specific to liberal arts schools, which were the focus of the research.

## Other Outcomes of Percent Plans and Test-Optional Admissions

Apart from their impact on diversity and college outcomes, what are the demonstrated effects of percent plans and test-optional admissions programs? In particular, how do they affect high school students' academic preparation, college aspirations, and application patterns?

A recent study of a large urban school district in Texas considered the question of whether the Texas Ten Percent Plan encouraged attendance at high-quality postsecondary institutions. The study, which found that the district's students in the top 10% were "more likely to be white and female and less likely to be low income than the typical student,"[47] focused on a comparison between students who barely exceeded the cutoff for the Ten Percent Plan to those who "just missed." The eligible students were much more likely than the ineligible students to enroll at one of the two Texas flagships, but this effect was concentrated in schools with high college-sending rates. There was little or no effect at the most disadvantaged schools, a finding that mirrors earlier research on the Ten Percent Plan.[48] Furthermore, many of those who narrowly missed being in the top 10% enrolled in selective private schools outside Texas, leading the authors to conclude that the "increase in flagship enrollment . . . therefore has no effect on overall college enrollment or on the quality of college attended."[49] On the plus side, they found no evidence that Top Ten Percent students were attending colleges that were too challenging for them. Being in the top 10% was not associated with dropping out of college or transferring to a less selective school, as some critics had feared.[50]

Researchers have pointed out several other positive effects of percent plans, noting that they may increase student engagement and college aspirations, improve links between high schools and universities, and give high schools an incentive to improve the availability of college preparatory courses.[51] Similarly, test-optional admissions might make the prospect of applying to college less daunting for some potential applicants, particularly students of color and those from lower socioeconomic brackets. Test-optional admissions has been found to increase the number of applications and, at least in some cases, the diversity of the applicant pool.[52]

## Are These Alternative Admissions Policies Fair?

Both percent plans and test-optional admissions have been touted as race-neutral alternatives to affirmative action. If indeed these policies increased the enrollment of underrepresented minorities and low-income students without using racial criteria, they might actually satisfy the fairness requirements of both sides of the political spectrum. Ironically, however, percent plans in particular have been criticized by both left and right: Even as their effectiveness in promoting diversity has been questioned, these policies have been challenged for failing to qualify as "race-neutral." As we have seen, Justice Ruth Bader Ginsburg has said that only an ostrich would describe percent plans in this way, and, demonstrating that politics does indeed make strange bedfellows, similar doubts have been expressed by Ward Connerly, one of the country's staunchest foes of affirmative action. Commenting on Florida's calculation, following preliminary studies, that 20% of students, not 15% or 10%, should be guaranteed admission under the state's plan, Connerly said, "If you're picking a number because you know that number is going to favor one group or another based on race, that's no different than a system of explicit preferences."[53]

So what exactly does "race-neutral" mean? The answer is not always obvious. To start with a somewhat preposterous example, suppose a university asks applicants not for their own racial identity, but for their mothers' race. Suppose the university then grants admissions preferences to applicants whose mothers are members of underrepresented racial groups. Because the applicant's own racial status is never requested, can the school claim this is a race-neutral admissions policy? The answer is probably no. But what if the university instead uses information about the racial makeup of the applicant's high school or the community he lives in? Or what if the university tries to infer the applicant's race by combining the characteristics of her high school with her family's education, occupation, and income? How accurate would such an attempt be, and would it be legal in a state where affirmative action is banned? Would it be fair?

The accuracy side of this intriguing question was investigated by researcher Mark C. Long of the University of Washington. Using the ELS data for more than 15,000 10th-graders, he was able to identify underrepresented minorities (defined in his research as Black, Hispanic, or Native American) with a fairly high degree of accuracy. To do this, he constructed prediction equations based on 195 pieces of data, including information about students' friends, high school, family situation, and test scores. Of the students tagged as URMs, 82% were, in fact, URMs; 18% of URM students were missed.[54] Remarkably, Long could identify URMs almost as well using just four pieces of information—whether each of the student's three best friends were URMs and whether the student was a native Spanish speaker.

Returning to the legal question, if race can be accurately "predicted," can this proxy be used in the admissions process without violating an affirmative action ban? Guidelines authored by experts in education law and published by the College Board note that intent may be relevant. A policy that is "facially race-neutral" may be considered "race-conscious" from a legal perspective if race-neutral criteria are deliberately used as a proxy for race: "If race is a motivation behind a facially race-neutral alternative, then it is *possible* that the alternative is not truly race-neutral."[55] Universities attempting a covert form of racial affirmative action, it seems, are faced with a catch-22: If a particular factor—say, socioeconomic status—is a poor proxy for race, an admissions policy based on that factor will not have the desired result. However, if the proxy works too well or the intention is too obvious, the policy may be doomed from a legal point of view and would presumably be viewed as unfair by opponents of affirmative action.

Apart from the legalities, policies that use supposedly race-neutral methods for purposes of boosting racial diversity are violating the transparency principle of fairness: For example, although the percent plans' primary purpose is to promote racial and possibly socioeconomic diversity, they do not use explicit preferences that are comprehensible to applicants. A student who attends a poor Black high school will face a less stringent eligibility criterion than a student attending a wealthy White high school, but neither student is likely to know what the applicable GPA cutoff is. More generally, because the GPA an applicant must attain to qualify for a percent plan varies across high schools, changes every year, and depends on the performance of other students, it is nearly impossible for a candidate to know how high his grades will need to be in order to make the cut.

Test-optional admissions programs present somewhat different transparency issues. Enrollment management experts Don Hossler and David Kalsbeek argue that "doing away with standardized tests may actually make the admissions system less transparent and fair and could negatively affect equality of access." They predict that selective colleges that eliminate admissions test requirements will develop ever more sophisticated ways of evaluating the rigor of applicants' high schools. This method of calibrating the strength of applications would be entirely opaque to candidates.[56]

A separate transparency issue arising from test-optional policies is that applicants typically lack the information they need to decide whether it is to their advantage to submit their test scores. The schools' admissions websites provide little guidance. Bryn Mawr, a newcomer to test-optional admissions, says simply that "SAT I or ACT scores are optional for US citizens and US permanent residents." Wake Forest gives the following advice to candidates: "If you feel that your SAT or ACT with writing scores are a good indicator of your abilities, you may submit them and they will be considered in your admissions decision. If, however, you do not feel that your scores accurately represent your academic abilities, you do not need to submit them until after you have been accepted and choose to enroll." But how are applicants to know whether or not it's advantageous to submit their scores? It may be an easy decision for those with very high or very low scores, but it is likely to pose a challenge for the majority of applicants. From this perspective, the test-blind policy adopted by Hampshire College is a fairer one. Making the familiar claim that the SAT and ACT "more accurately reflect family economic status than potential for college success," the college stated in 2014 that it would "no longer consider SAT or ACT scores in any way as part of admissions and financial aid decisions."[57] This rule at least provides a clear instruction to candidates.

In reality, however, test scores are not unique in their association with socioeconomic status or ethnicity. In explaining their finding that test-optional admissions policies did not improve diversity, Belasco and colleagues noted that academically rigorous high school programs, AP and honors courses, and extracurricular activities are more easily accessible in wealthier schools and that relying more heavily on these factors rather than on test scores may actually "perpetuate stratification within the post-secondary sector."[58] I reported on some related findings in 1999, during a wave of strong opposition to the SAT at the University of California. According to popular wisdom, the SAT was responsible for excluding low-income and minority students from UC, but data analyses conducted by the California Postsecondary Education Commission and the UC Office of the President showed that the primary reason for ineligibility for UC admission was failure to complete the required high school coursework. Only 2.5% of California public high school students were ruled out solely because of inadequate test scores. Eliminating the SAT was expected to produce an increase of two percentage points in the eligibility rate for Whites, from roughly 13% to 15%, and very little change for other ethnic groups.[59]

One possible outcome of deemphasizing tests in the admissions process is that the value and meaning of high school grades may change. If tests play a role in "keeping grades honest," as some educators believe, their elimination may exacerbate grade inflation and decrease the usefulness of grades as predictors of college achievement. Under the percent plans, teachers can alter a borderline student's eligibility for college by boosting a single grade, which may contribute to an upward drift. In a recent opinion piece, Calvin Wolf, a high school teacher, made the further argument that eliminating admissions tests would lead to increased gaming of high school grades and would ultimately benefit the rich. As he put it, "wealthier parents have the time and money to spend all day 'networking' for their kids' GPA advantage. . . . The GPAs of rich kids applying to test-optional colleges and universities will inflate, but the GPAs of poor and minority kids . . . will not."[60]

In short, the socioeconomic disadvantages that depress test scores also affect other aspects of academic performance. This includes not only grades, but completion of required college preparatory courses, participation in extracurricular activities, and other résumé-enhancing pursuits. In addition, the achievements of Asian-American and White students in these areas tend to exceed those of Black, Latino, and Native American students. These patterns of academic accomplishment limit the degree to which percent plans or test-optional admissions programs can increase the admission rates of students from underrepresented groups or lower socioeconomic brackets. With regard to their potential role in increasing the enrollment of students of color, these programs are both less effective and less honest than racial preferences. They are a prime example of the attempts that educational institutions must now make to boost diversity while staying on the right side of the law.

Perhaps the greatest contribution of percent plans and test-optional admissions is their apparent role in encouraging high school students who might be intimidated by test-score requirements to apply to college. Encouraging these less confident and often less prepared applicants to actually enroll and helping them to succeed may require much more.

# CHAPTER SIX

# Noncognitive Attributes: A New Frontier in College Admissions?

As entrance requirements in the older sense have diminished in importance, efforts have increased to select students on broad grounds of intellectual promise and aptitude, to understand the dynamics of personality as it affects motives and energy, and to trace the dimensions of human excellence beyond such deceptively simple, unidimensional quantities as school marks and test scores.

—B. *Alden Thresher*

Grit is everywhere these days, showing up at business conventions and academic conferences, in *Forbes Magazine*, in Wikipedia, and—soon—in the congressionally mandated National Assessment of Educational Progress.[1] Grit, which encompasses such "noncognitive" characteristics as perseverance, determination, conscientiousness, and ability to delay gratification, has become so popular a theme in the education world that you now can test your own grittiness via an online questionnaire.[2] And according to some researchers, grit may be the secret to college success.

In recent years there has been a resurgence of interest in personal characteristics and talents outside the cognitive domain. According to one article, the attempt to use "noncognitive measures" to improve the prediction of success in higher education is "the next frontier in college admissions."[3] But the idea of using noncognitive measures to predict college performance is not new. In the early 1960s, both the College Board and ETS issued lengthy monographs on the use of personality measures to predict college performance; the College Board also issued a policy statement on "nonintellective factors that affect college guidance and admission."[4] All three of these documents sounded a cautionary note and advised that more research was

143

needed in this area. More than 20 years later, in his book *Success in College*, ETS researcher Warren Willingham identified a characteristic he called "productive follow-through," defined as "persistent and successful extracurricular accomplishment" in high school. Productive follow-through proved to be a poor substitute for high school grades and admissions test scores in predicting which students would be identified as most successful by their colleges, but taking this quality into account along with traditional academic qualifications substantially improved the prediction of success.[5]

Noncognitive measures have been promoted as a means of acquiring a richer and more complete picture of college applicants than can be obtained through test scores and high school grades alone. However, the literature on noncognitive factors is controversial, starting with the inconsistency in the way the term "noncognitive" is used. Tasks that are noncognitive in the eyes of one researcher are sometimes considered cognitive by another (as I will discuss later in this chapter). Furthermore, the label "noncognitive" can seemingly be stretched to encompass almost any kind of student data. Factors that have been labeled noncognitive in the educational literature include routine descriptive information like work history and geographical origin, effort-related qualities like self-control, study habits, and study motivation, and personality characteristics like extroversion and "agreeableness."[6] One "noncognitive" admissions task that raised eyebrows 15 years ago required groups of applicants to construct a Lego robot that matched a model robot located in an adjacent room. Along with an interview, this task was intended to assess applicants' "adaptability."[7] This approach is among those touted by Harvard Law School professor Lani Guinier. In selecting students for college, Guinier would like to replace "testocratic merit" with "democratic merit," which includes collaborative skills, "optimistic perseverance," and grit.[8]

A pervasive claim about the potential advantages of noncognitive measures is the assertion that they are more fair than "academic" measures by virtue of their smaller differences across ethnic groups. (Here again, as in the grades-versus-tests comparison, the equal performance model of fairness is implicitly invoked.) In fact, the use of noncognitive admissions measures has become linked in theory, if not always in fact, with the goal of providing more accurate assessments of ethnic minorities, presumably leading to an increase in campus diversity. Psychologist Neal Schmitt, who has conducted extensive research on college admissions, has noted that "as opposed to cognitive measures, noncognitive measures usually display minimal subgroup differences; their use to make admissions decisions should increase the probability of admission of members of subgroups whose scores on the SAT/ACT tend to be lower."[9] Similarly, intelligence theorist Robert Sternberg stated that one important goal of his research on broadening admissions criteria "is enhancing ethnic diversity in colleges and universities by reducing ethnic-group differences on tests."[10] And according to William E. Sedlacek, a well-known researcher in this area, "noncognitive variables are useful for all students [but] are particularly critical for nontraditional students, because standardized tests and prior grades may provide only a limited view of their potential."[11] Sedlacek uses the term "nontraditional" to include "various racial-cultural groups, international students, women, gay-lesbian and bisexual students, athletes, students with learning disabilities or physical disabilities and older students."[12]

If incorporating noncognitive factors leads to a more comprehensive assessment of college candidates and holds the promise of increasing campus diversity, why don't we see colleges routinely assessing these factors as part of the admissions process? Of course, many schools do attempt to get at these qualities informally through student essays, letters of recommendation, and interviews, as well as the information applicants provide about their work experience, extracurricular activities, and community involvement. But measuring noncognitive factors in a more formal and systematic way is challenging. Even if we agree that, say, grit is an important characteristic for college students, measuring it is not straightforward, especially in the admissions context. Should a questionnaire be developed, and if so, what should be on it? Should admissions staff try to glean the information from student records? What activities should be considered evidence of a candidate's grittiness? Can one student's record be fairly compared to another's? Collecting and processing data of this kind can be time-consuming and expensive, and, as we will see, there is disagreement about the likely payoff. Also, surveying the candidates themselves about noncognitive characteristics and accomplishments can be problematic because the desired answers are often glaringly obvious. When asked to respond to a true/false question like "I want a chance to prove myself academically," it is the rare applicant who will answer "false."

Surprisingly, this true/false item comes from a questionnaire that has been widely used to measure noncognitive characteristics for at least 30 years—the Non-Cognitive Questionnaire (NCQ), developed by William Sedlacek, now an emeritus professor of education at the University of Maryland.[13] The NCQ has been used in admissions at several institutions and has served as a criterion for selecting Gates Millennium Scholars—minority students who receive scholarships from the Bill and Melinda Gates Foundation.[14] The NCQ is intended to assess such factors as positive self-concept, the ability to deal with racism, and the availability of social support. It is claimed to be useful for predicting college GPA and college persistence, particularly for candidates of color and other "nontraditional" students.[15]

In his work on noncognitive factors, Schmitt has developed questionnaires to measure various student "performance dimensions." In addition, both Schmitt and Sternberg have administered so-called situational judgment tasks, which evaluate candidates' skills in a somewhat less transparent fashion. Schmitt's tasks require applicants to select the best of several possible responses to a particular situation that is relevant to college life. The "correct" answers were determined by polling a separate group of college juniors and seniors, considered to be "experts." One of Schmitt's situations is as follows: "You are assigned to a group to work on a particular project. When you sit down together as a group, no one says anything." The response that yields the highest score is, "Get to know everyone first and see what they are thinking about the project to make sure the project's goals are clear to everyone." A student who picks a different response—for example, "Start the conversation yourself by introducing yourself"—receives a lower score.[16]

Sternberg and his colleagues developed a measure called the Everyday Situational Judgment Inventory. Students are shown video vignettes portraying situations they might encounter in everyday life and are asked to rate six options on a scale ranging from "a very bad course of action" to "an extremely good course of action." According to Sternberg, a "typical practical item would show a movie in which a student has received a low test grade. His roommate experienced a health crisis the previous night, and the student had stayed up all night to help his roommate. His professor handed him back his test, with a look of disappointment on her face. She suggested to the student that he study harder next time. The movie then stopped. The student was asked to characterize how he or she would respond to the situation."[17] Whereas Schmitt's situational judgment tasks are scored with reference to the responses of a separate panel of college students, Sternberg's are scored "in reference to the average, or consensual responses of the sample." That is, the more a student's response resembles the average response of the other test-takers, the higher a score he receives.[18]

Sternberg's group has also tried out other possible admissions criteria intended to measure "creative, analytical, practical, and wisdom-based skills" that are not tapped by standardized admissions tests. The tasks include composing short stories, captioning cartoons (purchased from the *New Yorker* archives), and answering navigation questions based on a map.[19] Interestingly, although Sternberg's tasks clearly share some common ground with the measures developed by Schmitt and other "noncognitive" researchers, Sternberg views the required skills as aspects of "successful intelligence"—the ability to succeed in life—and thus a part of the cognitive realm. As Angela Duckworth, a pioneering researcher on grit, and her coauthor, David Scott Yeager, pointed out in a recent essay, "every facet of psychological functioning, from perception to personality, is inherently 'cognitive' insofar as processing of information is involved."[20] For simplicity, I use the term "noncognitive" in this book to refer collectively to these alternative admissions criteria, in keeping with the majority of the literature.

## Recent Research on Noncognitive Factors

What do we know about the association between noncognitive measures and college success? In evaluating the findings in this area, the first point to note is that most published research has not actually involved the use of noncognitive measures in admissions decisions. Typically studies have involved students who have already been accepted to college, rather than applicants. For example, in two studies in 1984 and 1985 that continue to be cited as evidence for the validity of the NCQ, Sedlacek and his colleague Terence J. Tracey concluded that the NCQ was useful for predicting college grades and persistence—sometimes more useful than the SAT. But the NCQ wasn't used in admissions; it was administered to incoming freshmen.[21] The results reported for Sternberg's Rainbow Project, one of the most highly publicized studies of alternative admissions measures, are based on about 800 students who had already been admitted to college.[22] Another Sternberg project, called Kaleidoscope, involved actual applicants to Tufts University, but the noncognitive measures were an optional feature of the application.[23] Of the three large studies conducted by Schmitt and his colleagues and described in a 2012 review paper, two involved students who had already been admitted. The third study involved applicants who were asked to complete nontraditional measures for research purposes and were assured that their responses would not be used in making admissions decisions. Similarly, the 109 studies included in a 2004 meta-analysis of the effects of "psychosocial and study skill" factors on college success were all based on enrolled students, rather than applicants.[24]

Why is it important to consider the fact that much of the research in this area has involved admitted students? After all, the same is true for research on the predictive value of high school grades and admissions test scores. But in the case of research on noncognitive factors, the implications are different. The admitted students have typically been chosen using test scores and grades (along with other factors). Therefore, among this already select group of students, these traditional academic measures won't vary much and may therefore appear to be less useful than they really are for predicting college outcomes. For research on grades and test scores, then, studying admitted students generally leads to an underestimation of the effectiveness of these predictors. In research on noncognitive factors, however, the use of admitted students can make the alternative measures look strong by comparison, simply because the admitted students have not already been screened using these factors. Whether the findings obtained using admitted students would hold up in an actual admissions situation is not clear.

Also, research based on "low-stakes" uses of noncognitive measures cannot address the concern that widespread "faking"—giving the presumably desired response even if it's false—would occur if these factors actually played a key role in admissions decisions. Wouldn't savvy applicants simply supply the desired answers to questionnaire items? Wouldn't wealthier applicants consider seeking coaches or consultants?[25] Couldn't noncognitive criteria be just another hurdle that affluent students are taught to jump? And if fears about fakeability and coachability were realized, not only the fairness of these measures, but their predictive value, would be compromised: If everyone knows the right answers, no one will get low scores. As Schmitt notes, "the possibility that students may fake these measures remains an important concern about their implementation and may suggest their use in a counseling or guidance as opposed to in an admissions context."[26] Of course, even if students don't fake their answers, they may simply be poor judges of themselves or may give responses that are heavily influenced by a passing mood.

Despite its limitations, the existing research provides some indication of the likely utility of alternative admissions measures. In the case of the NCQ, the literature is decidedly mixed. Sedlacek cites dozens of articles in support of the utility of the NCQ, but many of these show equivocal results.[27] As one example, the oft-cited 1984 study by Tracey and Sedlacek compares the predictive value of the SAT and the NCQ for freshmen in 1979 and 1980. In both student cohorts, the SAT was a better predictor of FGPA for Black students, but the NCQ was a better predictor of college GPA and enrollment after three semesters (which was investigated only for the 1979 cohort).[28] In 2007 three psychologists published a meta-analysis of NCQ studies—a statistical summary of research based on more than 9,000 students from 47 datasets. They found NCQ scores to be "largely unrelated to college performance as measured by GPA, college persistence, and credits earned" and concluded that "the NCQ should not be used for admissions decisions."[29] In a rather mild-mannered rebuttal, Sedlacek told the *Chronicle of Higher Education* that past studies "show lots of indication that these methods work. . . . They show correlation with grades and retention." He also noted that all of his measures are available at no cost and that he's "not trying to sell anything to anybody." Instead, he is "trying to encourage people to think differently and study differently about . . . how to evaluate people, especially people of color."[30]

The 2007 critique of the NCQ was supported by the College Board, sponsor of the SAT, which could lead readers to view it with a skeptical eye. The College Board, however, was also the sponsor of some of the best-known explorations of alternative admissions criteria—Sternberg's Rainbow Project and the recent investigations by Schmitt.

The purpose of the Rainbow Project was to "augment" the SAT with admissions criteria based on Sternberg's triarchic theory of successful intelligence, which stipulates that there are three aspects of intelligence: analytic, practical, and creative. Conventional admissions measures—grades and test scores—are thought to tap mainly analytic aspects and ignore the practical and creative dimensions. Although Sternberg and his coauthors have stated that the "Rainbow measures enhanced predictive validity for college GPA relative to high school grade point average . . . and the SAT and also reduced ethnic group differences,"[31] the results are somewhat less clear-cut.

Reports of the Rainbow Project are based on data collected in 2001 from about 800 students at 13 undergraduate institutions.[32] To avoid overburdening the participants, researchers gave each student only a subset of the Rainbow measures. This feature, as well as some technical problems with computer administration, resulted in a large amount of missing data and complicated the statistical analysis. Perhaps for this reason the analysis results are somewhat inconsistent. It seems clear, however, that the best predictors of college grades were high school grades and two of the Rainbow measures: a multiple-choice creativity measure, and a test of students' ability to compose oral stories.[33] On the creativity test, as well as two "practical performance" measures, White students scored substantially higher than Black students, with differences in average scores at least as large as the Black–White difference on the verbal portion of the SAT. In fact, White students scored higher, on average, than Black and Latino students on all nine Rainbow measures. The differences between the average scores of White and Latino test takers, however, tended to be substantially smaller than those observed on the SAT.[34] (As is typical, the ethnic-group disparities were compared in terms of standard deviation units so that gaps could be compared for measures that have different scales.)[35]

In the Kaleidoscope Project, Sternberg implemented some of the Rainbow Project ideas at Tufts University. Supplementary questions intended to assess wisdom, as well as analytical, practical, and creative intelligence, were included in the Tufts applications between 2006 and 2010. One task, for example, was as follows: "Using an 8.5 × 11-inch sheet of paper, illustrate an ad for a movie, design a house, make an object better, or illustrate an ad for an object of your choice."[36] Other questions required essays or stories as responses. The Kaleidoscope measures were optional; therefore, project participants were likely to have been the most motivated candidates. So that they would not be overloaded, applicants were encouraged to complete only a single task out of eight to ten options. Applicants could also receive a "Kaleidoscope rating" by submitting portfolios of work or evidence of having won prizes or awards.[37]

Sternberg observed that concurrent with the implementation of Kaleidoscope, the academic quality of the Tufts applicant pool increased and speculated that this occurred because low-achieving students "appear to have decided not to bother to apply."[38] The percentage of applications from underrepresented minorities also increased, as did the percentage of African-American applicants who were admitted. No "meaningful differences" among ethnic groups were found on the Kaleidoscope measures, nor did these measures predict academic performance in college. According to Sternberg, "top Kaleidoscope scorers performed equally to other students academically but better in active citizenship and leadership activities in their first year of university."[39]

In three recent studies, Neal Schmitt and his colleagues identified 12 dimensions of college performance and used them to develop both college admissions criteria and measures of subsequent college success. Among the dimensions identified were leadership, perseverance, multicultural appreciation, and interpersonal skills. The first study involved 654 students at a single university, the second was based on more than 2,800 students at 10 institutions, and the third, begun in 2007, involved more than 2,000 applicants to 12 colleges. (As noted earlier, the candidates were aware that the experimental measures would not actually be used in making admissions decisions.)

In all three studies, Schmitt's team found that the best predictors of college grades were high school GPA and scores on the SAT or ACT. The newly developed measures, even when all were considered collectively, added little to the prediction of college grades once test scores and high school GPA were taken into account.[40] The new measures were often more useful than test scores and high school GPA in predicting students' absenteeism and students' self-rated behavior in several areas, including citizenship. (The outcome data were collected at least a year after the predictor data.)

Schmitt reports that differences in ethnic-group scores on the predictors were much smaller on the new measures than on the SAT or ACT.[41] Using data from his 10-institution study, Schmitt sought to investigate the demographic impact of including noncognitive factors in admissions decisions. (Recall that participants in the study were not actually applicants, but admitted students.) Implementing an approach similar to my ELS analyses, he rank-ordered the students in two different ways: One ranking was based solely on cognitive criteria (SAT or ACT scores and high school GPA), and another was based on the cognitive criteria plus 12 noncognitive measures. The two ranking methods were compared under three selection rules that varied in stringency. When students were "admitted" by picking the top 50% or 85% of "applicants," the two ranking methods led to similar results. However, when only the top 15% were selected, including the noncognitive criteria increased the percentages of African-American and Hispanic students by two to three percentage points (relative to the percentages obtained using cognitive measures alone) and decreased the percentages of White and Asian students by the same amount, resulting in a (hypothetical) student body that was about 6% Hispanic, 15% Asian, 4% African-American, and 75% White.[42] Under the 15% rule, those admitted using only cognitive factors were slightly more likely to graduate and had slightly higher college GPAs than those accepted using the ranking that included noncognitive factors.[43]

## Noncognitive Measures and Campus Diversity

It is ironic that the use of noncognitive measures in admissions, now thought to confer the flexibility needed to enact a socially responsible admissions policy, was at one time viewed as a tool that facilitated the exclusion of undesirables—Jews. In his 1977 history of higher education admissions, which focuses heavily on Columbia University, Harold Wechsler argues that Columbia's attempt to limit the number of Jewish students during the 1930s led it to expand its selection criteria beyond strictly academic factors. Applications were modified to include religious affiliation, place of birth, participation in extracurricular activities, and leadership potential, as well as the name, place of birth, and occupation of the applicant's father. Columbia's president approved "the tendency to put more and more stress on personal and family background, character and personality, and not to depend exclusively upon the results of formal examination tests." The goal, according to Wechsler, was to craft an admissions policy that would stop "the Jewish "invasion."[44] In his 2005 book, *The Chosen,* Berkeley professor Jerome Karabel describes how Harvard, Princeton, and Yale also invoked "personality" and "character" so as to "admit the dull sons of major donors and . . . exclude the brilliant but unpolished children of immigrants."[45]

Some commentators have argued that the "holistic" or "comprehensive" review processes used at many elite schools have a (possibly unintended) exclusionary effect on Asian-American applicants. Asians, who usually have higher average test scores and high school grades than other student groups, have been labeled the "new Jews" on campus in recent years.[46] But these concerns are not new. According to the author of a 1989 article on Asian-American admissions, "critics . . . contend that public institutions, like the [University of California] campuses have secretly, without adequate public and legislative discussion, deviated from their long-standing academic, merit-based admissions policies by giving weight to a variety of subjective criteria in the selection process."[47] And of course, a similar argument was made by the chair of the UC Regents, John Moores, who claimed in 2003 that Berkeley's comprehensive review process discriminated against Asian Americans. Although rigid admissions rules based solely on grades and test scores are often viewed as restricting the opportunities of ethnic minorities, flexible criteria that permit special exceptions can also have a dark side.

Is there a legitimate basis for expecting noncognitive measures to boost ethnic diversity? Under certain circumstances, the answer is yes. As a somewhat simplistic example, suppose that a college decides on two equally important criteria for selecting its students: It wants to admit those who have good academic skills and who are also highly motivated to succeed. Suppose that, on average, students from underrepresented groups (say, Black, Hispanic, and American Indian) are not as well prepared academically as other groups, but that they tend to be equally motivated. If the college ignores motivation in selecting students and chooses them only on the basis of academic factors, it is treating Black, Hispanic, and American Indian candidates unfairly under its own definition of important student attributes: A key characteristic that would have boosted these applicants' chances of admission has been omitted. Under a scenario of this kind (which, in the psychometric world, is called "construct underrepresentation"), adding a measure of motivation to the selection criteria (assuming that a good one existed) would be expected to increase the admission of Black, Hispanic, and American Indian students.[48]

However, the typical argument in favor of noncognitive measures is both more pragmatic and less complex: Because noncognitive measures often have smaller ethnic-group disparities than grades or test scores, they are thought to allow schools to achieve affirmative action goals without explicitly using race in admissions decisions. For example, in explaining the goal of her Lego-based admissions task, Deborah Bial said in 1999 that she hoped it could "help universities all over the country continue to admit diverse students," despite the uncertain future of affirmative action.[49] Similarly, Sedlacek advises that using noncognitive variables allows a school to "achieve increased diversity in a more sophisticated way," "by not directly selecting on aspects of diversity."[50]

A rarely mentioned technical issue that is relevant to the smaller group differences often observed in noncognitive measures is the fact that these measures are typically less precise, or reliable, than test scores. This is because they typically involve fewer questions or tasks than conventional tests (thus producing less information) and because the tasks themselves are often more susceptible to differing interpretations. Some kinds of noncognitive data require scoring by raters, which may introduce further inconsistencies. If group differences do, in fact, exist, "noisier," or less reliable, measures will be less able to detect them than more precise assessments. Sternberg seems to acknowledge this phenomenon in one publication on the Rainbow Project, where he notes that "mean differences between groups are a function of score reliabilities" and cautions that "the levels of reliabilities of the Rainbow scores should be kept in mind and . . . group results should be interpreted with caution."[51] However, in a later publication he dismisses the idea, noting that "one reviewer suggested that the reduced ethnic-group differences on our tests relative to the SAT may be a result of the low reliability of the Rainbow measures. We believe this to be unlikely . . . low reliability does not appear to have been a serious limiting factor."[52]

It is worthwhile to note that although some noncognitive measures improve the prediction of college success and some show smaller ethnic-group differences than traditional admissions criteria, it may be difficult to find noncognitive measures that have both of these sought-after features. In discussing Sternberg's Rainbow Project, Schmitt notes that the measures on which Sternberg observed the largest reduction in ethnic-group differences tended not to be predictive of college performance.[53] In the case of the NCQ, the authors of the critical review article mentioned earlier noted that African-American students tended to score higher than White students. Therefore, if used to make admissions decisions, the NCQ could indeed increase the enrollment of Black students. However, the NCQ was found to have a negligible association with college grades or persistence, leading the authors to conclude that the use of the NCQ in admissions "approximates near-random assignment of bonus points for race in an admissions decision."[54]

## Using the ELS Data to Study Noncognitive Factors

The ELS survey included several questionnaire items that are consistent with the kinds of noncognitive variables championed by researchers in this field. I selected three of these, all of which involve students' aspirations in their senior year of high school, and created a selection procedure that included them. The first question captured students' occupational goals: ELS participants were asked what occupation they "expect or plan to have" at age 30. The occupations named by participants were later coded in terms of their prestige. They ranged from "laborer" (not selected by any of the applicants to the competitive colleges) to professional occupations requiring an advanced degree, including clergyman, dentist, physician, lawyer, scientist, and college professor. The second question I used asked about students' immediate plans for post-high-school education, ranging from "don't plan to continue" to "four-year college or university," and the third asked what educational level students expected to eventually attain, ranging from "less than high school graduation" to "obtain PhD, MD, or other advanced degree." (A question essentially the same as the third one is included in Sedlacek's Non-Cognitive Questionnaire.) Higher occupational and educational aspirations corresponded to higher scores.

I combined the responses to these questions with the GPA–test-score composite so that, collectively, the aspiration questions had the same weight as each of the two academic factors, high school GPA and test score.[55] Then I applied two selection rules—a broad rule that involved choosing the top 41% of applicants on this newly created composite and a narrow rule in which the top 10% were accepted. Results for both rules appear in Tables 6-1 through 6-5.[56] Results for the enrollees and for the original GPA–test-score composite are repeated here for comparison.

Compared to the enrollees, the entering classes selected using the noncognitive factors had larger percentages of women (Table 6-1) and smaller percentages of underrepresented minorities (Table 6-2). The composite that included the noncognitive factors did, however, lead to greater ethnic diversity than the original GPA–test-score composite. For the broad noncognitive rule, the percentage of URMs was roughly 10%, compared to 8% for the original composite. The narrow rule yielded about 6% URMs, compared to less than 3% for the original composite. Most of the URMs selected via the noncognitive rules were Hispanic; very few were Black or American Indian. Like the narrow rule based on the original composite, the narrow noncognitive rule yielded a class with a large percentage of Asian students (Table 6-2). The class selected using the broad noncognitive rule had a socioeconomic distribution similar to that of the enrollees, whereas the narrow rule produced a class with about 71% at the highest SES level (Table 6-3). The noncognitive rules did result in a somewhat greater percentage of students in the bottom half of the SES distribution than the rules based on the original composite.

Average admissions test score—and, for the narrow rule, average high school GPA—were slightly lower for the classes selected using the noncognitive composite than for the classes selected with the original composite. However, the average test scores and grades exceeded those of the enrollees (Table 6-4). Table 6-5 shows that college grades and graduation rates for the noncognitive rules were very similar to those produced by the corresponding (broad or narrow) GPA–test-score composite rule. However, the students selected by the narrow noncognitive rule had an unusually high level of postbaccalaureate attainment—about 41%, perhaps reflecting the high aspirations of these students. Interestingly, this percentage is nearly identical to the rate of postcollege attainment obtained with the narrow GPA rule presented in Chapter 2.

Although some aspects of the results are encouraging, these analyses clearly demonstrate that including noncognitive factors in the admissions process does not necessarily produce meaningful increases in ethnic and socioeconomic diversity. The use of the aspiration questions in an actual admissions procedure would also raise a fairness issue: Should low expectations be punished in selecting students for college? High schoolers may have low expectations simply because no one in their family has ever attended college. Aren't these the very students who need more encouragement? Also, the fakeability problem would undoubtedly rear its head. Before long, all college applicants would aspire to be neurosurgeons, Supreme Court justices, and rocket scientists.

Of course, the noncognitive factors I selected were of a particular type, consisting of students' own reports of their educational and occupational aspirations. A different choice of noncognitive measures could have yielded entirely different findings.

## Conclusions

In the world of college admissions today, there is a renewed interest in noncognitive measures, a term that has been applied to a vast array of personal characteristics and background data. Recognizing that high school grades and admissions test scores provide only a narrow view of applicants' potential contributions, researchers and college officials alike have expressed the hope that including noncognitive attributes in admissions decisions can both improve the prediction of college success and boost the admission of underrepresented minorities. Research evidence suggests that the noncognitive factors that are most likely to improve the prediction of college performance involve characteristics that are directly relevant to academic performance and under the candidate's own control, such as persistence, motivation, and study habits. These characteristics also have the advantage of being translatable into concrete evidence, such as completion of long-term research or writing projects or ongoing participation in school-related extracurricular activities. The way the information is to be used in the admissions decision should be made transparent to applicants. To avoid the problems of coaching and faking, however, the relevant data are best collected from sources other than the candidates themselves.

It is not a foregone conclusion that deemphasizing traditional admissions criteria will help disadvantaged or underrepresented groups. In fact, a recent move to broaden college admissions criteria in China has led some educators to express the concern that this change would benefit the elite. Currently admission is based on scores on China's infamous admissions test—the *gao-kao*—but under proposed changes, extracurricular activities would be counted as well. The fear is that this "reform" will disadvantage children from poor areas, who have limited access to these activities.[57]

Similar concerns arise in the United States. In 2016, controversy arose over a report from Harvard's Graduate School of Education that recommended a greater focus on student character in the admissions process. The report, *Turning the Tide: Inspiring Concern for Others and the Common Good through College Admissions*, advised that college admissions offices place a high value on sustained community service (at least a year in duration) and put less emphasis on such factors as Advanced Placement courses. It further suggested that colleges assess whether service (which could include family care) has "enhanced students' understanding of their own ethical strengths, flaws, and blind spots, generated in them greater humility, or deepened their understanding and respect for those who are vulnerable or simply different from them."[58] In addition to the daunting technical challenges that measuring these characteristics would present, the proposed heavier emphasis on service could actually disadvantage low-SES students. Low-income high school students are less likely to have the time and resources that would allow them to work without pay and less likely to have the skills needed to describe service work with the proper spin. At the same time, affluent candidates—and those who coach them—would soon become experts in gaming the system. As an independent college counselor told the *Chronicle of Higher Education*, "smart, rich kids are always going to figure out a way to look the way colleges want them to look."[59] Although the project's goals are laudable—to "deflate undue academic performance pressure and redefine achievement in ways that create greater equity and access for economically diverse students,"[60] the effect could be quite the opposite.

In the same vein, a recent opinion piece pointed out that "poor and minority kids are disadvantaged compared to rich kids when it comes to creating good extracurricular resumes," which are likely to take on greater importance if tests are deemphasized. Mitchell Stevens provides a compelling description of the ways in which even "individualized" reviews of candidates' qualifications favor wealthier students in subtle ways. He argues that differences in the quantity and quality of information available about candidates produce "peculiar and heretofore unacknowledged forms of class bias in selective college admissions."[61] When candidates are able to provide detail about interesting volunteer jobs and extracurricular activities, recommendations from high school counselors known to the committee, and endorsements from people of importance in their communities, their advocates on the admissions committee can use this rich material to craft a story—in effect, to argue their case before the committee. If the candidates have visited the campus and participated in interviews, so much the better—this can be another source of engaging anecdotes. As Stevens notes, the applications from socioeconomically privileged candidates "come loaded with lots of the raw materials evaluators need to tell individually compelling stories." In the meantime, applicants from lower socioeconomic ranks lack "the necessary infrastructure to get word of themselves across."[62]

A study from the United Kingdom provides a vivid illustration of the phenomenon Stevens describes. Educational researcher Steven Jones compared the personal statements of more than 300 applicants to an unidentified university in 2010. Applicants had been asked to explain why they were well suited to the course of study they had selected, to demonstrate enthusiasm and commitment, and to make sure they "stood out from the crowd." Although the candidates studied by Jones were equivalent in academic performance in terms of their exam scores, the quality of their personal statements varied substantially with the socioeconomic level of the secondary schools they had attended.[63] Students who attended higher-SES schools not only had fewer grammar, punctuation, and spelling errors than those who attended lower-SES schools; they also had a much richer set of work experiences and extracurricular activities to draw on in crafting their statements. Students from low-SES schools were more likely to mention unexceptional jobs or hobbies and to describe activities that would be of no value (or perhaps negative value) in the admissions process, such as television watching or "reading up on the latest fashion." Jones contrasts a low-SES student who describes "a part time job as a waitress at a local pub" with a private-school student who mentions "a work experience placement to shadow the Pakistani Ambassador to the United Nations."[64] Jones concludes that, although they are often assumed to enhance fairness, "nonacademic indicators, such as the personal statement, may disfavor young people from certain educational backgrounds."[65] Although they did not have superior exam scores, the higher-SES candidates in the study clearly had better raw material to use in presenting themselves and had a better sense of how to speak the language of the admissions process.

Obtaining a broader picture of applicants' talents is a worthy goal, but the legitimacy and fairness of using noncognitive measures in admissions decisions is, in some cases, highly questionable. For example, on the NCQ, students receive higher scores if they answer yes to the item, "If I run into problems concerning school, I have someone who would listen to me and help me."[66] But even if the availability of a support person is predictive of success in college, is it fair to perpetuate the disadvantage by assigning a lower score to an applicant who is on his own? As another example, one of Schmitt's "multicultural appreciation" questions asks, "If given a choice at a restaurant, would you order any food with which you are unfamiliar?" The most "multicultural"—and thus highest-scoring—answer is, "If given a chance, I will always order a new food and try it."[67] But is it fair to allocate college spaces on the basis of students' food preferences? Should candidates be admitted to college based on their expectations about racism, their ability to caption cartoons, or their health? All have been investigated as part of research on noncognitive factors. And what about situational judgment tasks on which it is an advantage to give the same answers as other students or test takers? Couldn't this be considered rewarding conformity?

Some proponents of using noncognitive measures to select students of color argue that these students don't "show their abilities" on grades or tests.[68] It is obviously true that high school GPA and test scores do not reflect the entirety of anyone's capabilities, and there is some evidence from research pioneered by psychologist Claude Steele that minority students' scores may be depressed by certain features of the testing situation. According to Steele, merely asking test takers to state their ethnic group can detract from their test performance. This inquiry triggers stereotype threat—"the threat of being viewed through the lens of a negative stereotype, or the fear of doing something that would inadvertently confirm that stereotype." The resulting stress ultimately leads the test takers to perform more poorly.[69] Some noncognitive measures have been found to yield smaller disparities among ethnic groups than admissions tests do, but small group differences do not, in and of themselves, imply greater fairness. And isn't it painfully condescending to propose that the selection criteria for people of color should be "noncognitive" but that White students can presumably be selected using cognitive factors? One person who took issue with the use of the NCQ to select the Gates Millennium Scholars in 2000 was Shelby Steele, a scholar at the Hoover Institution (and, intriguingly, the twin brother of Claude). "Don't excuse them from tests," he pleaded. "For God's sake, have some faith in their minds."[70]

So by all means, let's continue exploring noncognitive attributes. But we shouldn't make the mistake of assuming that any admissions requirement that's not a standardized test is by definition a more equitable and benevolent alternative. Remember what Columbia called "character."

*Table 6-1.* Percentages of Women and Men for Enrollees and Four Admissions Models

| | | Broad Selection Rules | | Narrow Selection Rules | |
| | | GPA–Test-Score Composite | Composite Plus Noncognitive | GPA–Test-Score Composite | Composite Plus Noncognitive |
| Gender | Enrollees | | | | |
|---|---|---|---|---|---|
| Women (%) | 53.4 | 57.2 | 57.8 | 53.5 | 58.8 |
| Men (%) | 46.6 | 42.8 | 42.2 | 46.5 | 41.2 |

*Table 6-2.* Percentages of Students in Each Ethnic Group for Enrollees and Four Admissions Models

| | | Broad Selection Rules | | Narrow Selection Rules | |
| | | GPA–Test-Score Composite | Composite Plus Noncognitive | GPA–Test-Score Composite | Composite Plus Noncognitive |
| Ethnic Group | Enrollees | | | | |
|---|---|---|---|---|---|
| Asian (%) | 12.1 | 12.3 | 11.5 | 15.6 | 16.5 |
| Underrepresented minority (%) | 12.4 | 7.9 | 9.8 | 2.5 | 6.3 |
| More than one race (%) | 3.8 | 2.0 | 2.8 | 1.5 | 1.8 |
| White (%) | 71.7 | 77.8 | 76.0 | 80.4 | 75.4 |

*Note:* Some column totals are not exactly 100% because of rounding. Results for Black, Hispanic, and American Indian students were combined to conform with Institute of Education Sciences data security requirements.

*Table 6-3.* Percentages of Students in Each of Four Socioeconomic Categories for Enrollees and Four Admissions Models

| | | Broad Selection Rules | | Narrow Selection Rules | |
| | | GPA–Test-Score Composite | Composite Plus Noncognitive | GPA–Test-Score Composite | Composite Plus Noncognitive |
| Socioeconomic Status (SES) | Enrollees | | | | |
|---|---|---|---|---|---|
| Highest (%) | 63.6 | 64.0 | 63.2 | 70.4 | 70.7 |
| Second highest (%) | 20.8 | 22.4 | 21.6 | 21.8 | 17.9 |
| Second lowest (%) | 11.4 | 9.5 | 10.5 | 4.7 | 8.7 |
| Lowest (%) | 4.2 | 4.1 | 4.7 | 3.0 | 2.8 |

*Note:* Some column totals are not exactly 100% because of rounding.

*Table 6-4.* High School GPA and Test-Score Data for Enrollees and Four Admissions Models

|  | Enrollees | Broad Selection Rules | | Narrow Selection Rules | |
|---|---|---|---|---|---|
|  |  | GPA–Test-Score Composite | Composite Plus Noncognitive | GPA–Test-Score Composite | Composite Plus Noncognitive |
| High school GPA |  |  |  |  |  |
| Average | 3.5 | 3.7 | 3.7 | 3.9 | 3.8 |
| Standard deviation | 0.4 | 0.2 | 0.3 | 0.1 | 0.2 |
| Test Score |  |  |  |  |  |
| Average | 1245 | 1303 | 1289 | 1431 | 1395 |
| Standard deviation | 150 | 111 | 122 | 68 | 92 |

*Table 6-5.* College First-Year Grade-Point Average (FGPA), Graduation Rates, and Postbaccalaureate Attainment Rate for Enrollees and Four Admissions Models

|  | Enrollees | Broad Selection Rules | | Narrow Selection Rules | |
|---|---|---|---|---|---|
|  |  | GPA–Test-Score Composite | Composite Plus Noncognitive | GPA–Test-Score Composite | Composite Plus Noncognitive |
| College FGPA |  |  |  |  |  |
| Average | 3.2 | 3.4 | 3.4 | 3.6 | 3.5 |
| Standard deviation | 0.6 | 0.5 | 0.5 | 0.4 | 0.5 |
| College Graduation |  |  |  |  |  |
| 4-year graduation rate | 64.3 % | 64.7 % | 63.4% | 69.6 % | 69.8 % |
| 6-year graduation rate | 83.7 % | 85.4 % | 84.3% | 88.2 % | 88.1 % |
| Postbaccalaureate attainment rate | 28.0 % | 33.2 % | 34.9% | 33.8 % | 41.3 % |

# CHAPTER SEVEN

# Casting Lots for College

Perhaps it's time for a radical idea: a lottery [admissions] system.
Besides reducing some of the inequities (not to mention the
craziness), a lottery would single-handedly end debates over
affirmative action, legacy admissions, and preference for
student-athletes.

—*Dalton Conley*

Every few years an exasperated educator proposes a revolutionary new idea
for college admissions: How about drawing names out of a hat? Just in the
last 10 years, academics from Berkeley, Columbia, Swarthmore, and New
York University have floated the idea of lottery admissions in the pages of
the *New York Times, Atlantic,* and *Chronicle of Higher Education*.[1] At each of its
rebirths, the lottery is proposed as a solution to the perplexing problem of
how to equitably admit students to schools of higher learning when places
are limited. As far as I can determine, the first to propose lottery admissions
for American colleges was Alexander Astin, an esteemed higher education
researcher then at the American Council on Education. In a 1969 letter to the
editor of *Science,* Astin suggested that a lottery could help to boost minority
enrollment. "In the interests of putting the concept of 'equality of educational
opportunity' into practice," he said, colleges "might want to consider abandoning altogether the use of grades and tests in admissions, and instituting
instead a lottery system."[2]

What are the arguments for and against admissions lotteries in higher education, and what do we know about how well they work in practice? What
does the court of public opinion have to say about this idea? Is admission by
lottery the pinnacle of fairness because it does not differentiate among candidates, or is it unfair precisely because it fails to reward excellence?

Like Astin, most lottery proponents mention the broadening of educational opportunity as the primary rationale. Advocates also claim that random selection would reduce extreme competition—among both students and schools—and eliminate the need to base admissions decisions on razor-thin test-score advantages. In the eyes of some proponents, lotteries can be declared fair on principle. According to Stanford Law professor Hank Greely, "random selection is the only allocative method which honestly can claim the objective equality of opportunity from which the satisfaction of equality of expectation springs. It is the allocative method which maximizes the goal of equality."[3]

Lotteries are assumed to free the decision process from any personal biases of the decision makers and thus "disable bad reasons" for selection.[4] Racial and class biases are not the only ones to fear: Some lottery proponents raise the concern that selectivity in university admissions encourages institutions to devote their energies to choosing the applicants who will be the easiest (and cheapest) to educate, rather than focusing their energies on actually providing an education. Astin suggested that selective admissions was the "surest way for colleges to avoid any responsibility for *educating* the student."[5]

## Previous Findings on Lottery Admissions

Around the time that Astin suggested lottery admissions, it was, in fact, being used in the United States in two cases that generally go unmentioned by lottery advocates. In 1968, Federal City College, a brand-new urban land grant college in Washington, D.C., admitted its entire freshman class of 2,400 using a lottery, in keeping with its intended role as an open-admissions college, primarily serving the local Black community. And in 1970 the College of Liberal Arts and Sciences of the University of Illinois admitted a portion of its freshman class using a lottery. How did these experiments turn out? The Federal City lottery is difficult to evaluate. Many students dropped out during the school's turbulent early years. As described in a 1969 article, the college was contending with numerous problems, including "a warring faculty ... an administration that deliberately provided little traditional leadership ... a potentially repressive Congress," and students seeking degrees who, as "typical products of a typical urban school system, [were] poorly equipped to earn them."[6] Would Federal City have had an easier time and a lower dropout rate if it had used a more selective admissions procedure? Given the complex challenges faced by the institution, it's impossible to know. The lottery at the University of Illinois, however, can be declared an unambiguous failure. More than 800 applicants were rejected as a result of the lottery, including "some of the best students in the state," according to the *New York Times*. A public uproar forced the chancellor to backpedal and admit 839 previously rejected students. He explained the reversal by noting that "some hardships have resulted from the necessity for students denied admission to make other plans."[7]

Similarly, a medical school admissions lottery in the Netherlands (in which selection probabilities varied with grade-point average) was curtailed in 2000 after a public outcry about "the threefold rejection of a highly talented student" and is scheduled to be eliminated entirely by the 2017–2018 academic year.[8] In a 1975 letter to *Science*, critics of the Dutch admissions lottery declared that it was "immoral to have a system in which the future of human beings is decided by a game of chance."[9] Immorality was also a factor in Ricks College's decision to discontinue the lottery admissions procedure it had used to select a portion of its 1996 entering class. The Idaho college, a Mormon institution, decided that lottery-based admission could be viewed as gambling, which is opposed by the Church of Jesus Christ of Latter-day Saints.[10]

Why does the lottery, viewed as the epitome of fairness by some, often evoke strong negative reactions in practice? Probably because the results of an actual random drawing—say, a brilliant and hardworking candidate is rejected in favor of a dim-witted slacker—provide a more vivid display of a lottery's downsides than any abstract description could. The public—particularly the parents of the stellar applicant—are likely to regard an outcome like this as unfair (and a poor use of resources). Although admissions lotteries ignore wealth, celebrity, and political connections—a plus—they are also blind to both talent and accomplishment.

Lotteries are likely to be perceived as a reasonable means of distribution when all contenders are seen as having equal claims to the benefits that are being distributed. Participants who compete for cash prizes in state lotteries generally accept that the results are a matter of luck. Also relatively uncontentious, at least in principle, is the use of lotteries to allocate places in some elementary and secondary schools in the United States and elsewhere.[11] In the United States, this practice is common at charter schools. At these lower levels of schooling, it seems reasonable to regard the candidates as having equal claims to places in a school with limited space. (In fact, conflicts have arisen, as a result of *departures* from random selection, such as the use of weights to benefit disadvantaged students and the use of preliminary screening to weed out "undesirable" candidates.)[12] The equal-claims rationale seems far less palatable at the college level, when the candidates under consideration may differ widely in both their talents and their efforts.

Selection solely via lottery rules out any kind of conscientious individualized evaluation of applications. It is this feature that the led the *Grutter* court to dismiss lotteries as a valid means of increasing campus diversity. According to Justice Sandra Day O'Connor, the University of Michigan Law School, whose policies were being challenged, "considers race as one factor among many, in an effort to assemble a student body that is diverse in ways broader than race. Because a lottery would make that kind of nuanced judgment impossible, it would effectively sacrifice all other educational values, not to mention every other kind of diversity."[13]

Public policy expert Dael Wolfle went so far as to label the allocation of benefits via lottery "a denial of man's humanity." When lotteries are used in this way, said Wolfle, "each man is reduced to a cipher, distinguished from other ciphers only by the uniqueness of the combination of digits that identify his records in a growing number of office files."[14] This is an eerie echo of standard criticisms of the use of test scores in admissions, such as math professor Julian Weissglass's assertion that "no person's understanding or potential can be reduced to a number, and it is disrespectful to do so."[15] Interestingly, Wolfle suggested that lotteries are disrespectful to potential decision makers as well as the candidates for selection: "To choose students by a random process is to deny the ability of the faculty to select those applicants who show greatest promise or who appear most likely to benefit from higher education."[16] Perversely, some may regard this feature as an advantage: A lottery can serve to absolve the putative decision makers of any responsibility for the choices that are made.

A fascinating aspect of the lottery literature is the fact that, having used egalitarian philosophy to make the case for lotteries in public life, many proponents then proceed to alter the proposed lottery, sometimes beyond recognition. Thresholds are added, along with unequal weights, exclusions, and even protections against the vagaries of chance. Let's begin with thresholds. Seemingly every lottery admissions proposal offered during the last 20 years has specified that in order to be eligible for the lottery, applicants would have to exceed a threshold—often a minimum SAT score.[17] Presumably the basis for this policy is that candidates above the threshold can assert equal claims to a college education. Indeed, the argument is often made that there are sure to be groups of applicants who are so similar that no trustworthy method can distinguish among them.[18]

One staunch supporter of admissions lotteries with thresholds is Harvard Law professor Lani Guinier, who has proposed that a minimum SAT score be imposed.[19] It is ironic that as fierce an SAT opponent as Guinier has promoted this idea. In a sense, a lottery admissions process with a test-score threshold relies more heavily on test results than a traditional admissions process does. In this version of the lottery, the test is the sole measure on which admission depends. If a candidate's score is below the threshold, he will certainly be rejected. A score above the threshold buys the candidate a lottery ticket, but he may or may not gain admission. This is similar to what could occur if a very imprecise test were used. In other words, it's test-based admissions at its worst. Using a test in this way also seems inconsistent with the *Standards for Educational and Psychological Testing*, which states that "in educational settings, a decision or characterization that will have major impact on a student should take into consideration not just scores from a single test but other relevant information."[20]

Guinier also suggests the possibility of a weighted lottery: "Concerns about a lottery's insensitivity to an institution's particular needs or values could be dealt with by increasing the selection prospects of applicants with the skills, abilities, or backgrounds that are valued by the institution. For example, a weighted lottery could enhance the chances that certain students will be selected by putting their names in two or three times."[21]

Others have suggested that certain desirable candidates be excluded from the lottery and be guaranteed admission or that the lottery pool be stratified (with random draws taking place within each stratum) to ensure that some groups are not excluded entirely. Most startling is the suggestion that lotteries should come with guarantees against undesirable results. Professor of politics Barbara Goodwin, a lottery advocate, acknowledges that "the lottery has two major disadvantages—uncertainty, and the possibility of a run of losing tickets for some individuals." She suggests modifying lotteries so as to make sure that "no draw would reduce individuals below the social minimum." "The problem of a run of winning or losing tickets, she says, "could be solved by devising a system which guaranteed that nobody would draw a 'losing' ticket more than twice, say, in a row."[22]

The impulse to add thresholds, weights, strata, exceptions, and protections against extreme outcomes suggests that some lottery aficionados are less enamored of the random draw than they claim to be. In commenting on Guinier's proposals, philosophers Robert Fullinwider and Judith Lichtenberg suggest—facetiously—that by weighting applications by such factors as GPA, class rank, and standardized test scores, an elite college could devise a lottery that would produce much the same entering class as its current admissions procedures.[23]

What do we know about the effects of lottery-based admissions on diversity? Of course, a "pure" lottery with equal selection probabilities will result in an entering class that reflects the applicant pool. But how about a lottery with a threshold? At least two previous studies have investigated this issue. Political scientists Bernard Grofman and Samuel Merrill conducted a theoretical analysis of three different selection processes. The situation they considered involved two groups of applicants, one of which was assumed to be disadvantaged. It was of interest to mitigate the exclusionary effects of a purely test-based admissions process on the disadvantaged group, which was assumed to perform more poorly on the selection test. A lottery with a threshold was compared to a test-based admissions procedure with a single standard for both groups and a *group-norming* approach in which the top-scoring applicants within each group were selected.[24] The authors concluded that the likely consequences of a lottery-with-threshold admissions process are "not nearly as attractive as they might first appear to reformers."[25] Realistic thresholds did not yield a substantial improvement in the representation of the lower-scoring group. The authors gave an illustration using 1997 SAT results for Black and White students. They showed that in this instance, "a lottery-based system with a realistic minimum threshold will result in only a minuscule rate of minority acceptance compared to that of whites." Furthermore, they noted that "lottery-based schemes (with minimum thresholds) . . . may lead to a severe drop in mean test scores of the [selected] applicants as compared to either test-based rules or group-norming."[26]

This theoretical result was supported by the simulation-based findings of economists Anthony Carnevale and Stephen Rose, who studied nationally representative data from the 1990s, focusing on applicants to elite colleges. They found that selecting students using a lottery with an SAT threshold of 900 (for verbal and math scores combined) would increase the percentage of low-SES students, but would produce smaller percentages of Black and Hispanic students than actually enrolled at these schools at the time. They noted that the "low shares of minorities in the qualified pool reflect the fact that Blacks and Hispanics are much less likely than Whites to take the SAT or ACT or to score above 900." Carnevale and Rose also concluded that the lottery-with-threshold policy "would likely result in dramatically reduced graduation rates or lowered standards in selective colleges."[27]

## Using the ELS Data to Study Lottery Admissions

In my own ELS analyses, I first considered the effects of implementing an admissions lottery with a test-score threshold equivalent to an SAT score of 1000 for verbal and math score combined, slightly below the national average for the year when these students would have taken the test.[28] About 80% of the ELS applicants to elite colleges satisfied this criterion. Implementing a lottery of this kind in practice would involve randomly choosing students from among these 80% until the desired number had been selected. In using the ELS data to determine the expected result, the number to be chosen is irrelevant. Because selection would be random, we need only examine the characteristics of the students who satisfy the minimum test-score requirement.[29]

As shown in the third column of Tables 7-1 and 7-2, this group of students had a male–female ratio and ethnic composition similar to those of the enrollees. The percentages of Black, Hispanic, and American Indian students were virtually identical, the percentage of White students was slightly higher, and the percentage of Asians slightly lower. In terms of SES, Table 7-3 shows that this lottery scenario led to a decrease of nearly four points in the percentage of students in the highest SES category, relative to the enrollees. The academic performance of those admitted by lottery, however, was somewhat worse than that of the enrolled students. Table 7-4 shows that their average high school GPA was slightly lower and their average admissions test score was lower by 23 points. More significantly, Table 7-5 shows that the difference in four-year college graduation rates was substantial: 55% for those admitted by lottery compared to 64% for the enrollees.

Although those who recommend or study lotteries with thresholds ordinarily define the thresholds in terms of SAT scores, I also evaluated the impact of a lottery with a high school GPA threshold. In order to make the process equal in stringency to my lottery with a test-score threshold (a threshold exceeded by 80% of the applicants), I determined what GPA value was exceeded by 80%. This turned out to be 2.8—a B. The rightmost columns of Tables 7-1 through 7-5 contain the results of this lottery. Compared to the lottery with a test-score minimum, this lottery resulted in somewhat higher percentages of women and URMs. The percentage of students in the highest SES category was about 57%, compared to 60% for the lottery with a test-score threshold. The percentage in the bottom half of the SES distribution was 19%. In terms of diversity, then, the results of this lottery were quite favorable. In fact, the percentage of Black students exceeded the percentage for both race-based affirmative action rules. However, the academic results were poor. This entering class had the same average high school GPA as the enrollees but had an average admissions test score nearly 50 points lower—the lowest of any selection method considered in this book. Like the lottery with a test-score threshold, the lottery with a GPA threshold had a very low four-year college graduation rate—56%.[30] Other than the two lottery procedures, no admissions rule produced a graduation rate below 60%. The six-year graduation rates, average FGPAs, and postbaccalaureate attainment rates were also lower for the lotteries than for any of the other admissions models.

Of course, a lottery is one possible device for allocating goods when demand exceeds supply. But in the case of college admissions, a lottery is unlikely to yield the benefits described by advocates. At top colleges, a lottery with a threshold designed to weed out the bottom 20% appears to carry with it a risk of substantially reduced four-year graduation rates. And even with a lenient threshold like this one, the lottery led, at best, to modest increases over more conventional admissions procedures in the representation of URMs and low-income students. Despite the leniency of the thresholds, the lottery-based entering classes were far less diverse than the applicant pool, which had 21% URMs and 22% in the lower half of the SES distribution.

Compounding these disappointing findings is the considerable public resistance to higher education lotteries. A nationwide survey of 2,100 U.S. adults conducted in 1999 found that 83% opposed the use of lotteries for college admissions.[31] In the Netherlands, a survey of 540 individuals registered as medical school candidates in 1989 showed that only 1% identified the lottery as the preferred admissions mechanism.[32] Public opposition to actual instances of lottery admissions to universities has been strong.

Although a lottery might reduce certain anxieties among applicants—perhaps diminishing obsessive test cramming and résumé building—it would certainly raise other concerns: Even the most qualified candidate might be rejected, just by the luck of the draw. Deciding where to apply, already a complex task, would become even more challenging. And what about the signaling effect of lottery admissions? According to longtime lottery fan Barry Schwartz of Swarthmore, a college admissions lottery with a threshold means that "instead of having to be better than anyone else, [applicants] will just have to be good enough—and lucky."[33] But is this the ideal message to send to high school students? Why try to excel at academics or extracurricular pursuits if no value is placed on excellence? The random aspect of the lottery may even undermine the satisfaction of those who are selected. As philosopher Alan Goldman notes, "dignity, or a sense of personal worth . . . derives from a sense of having accomplished, not won by chance."[34]

Finally, the lottery does not actually resolve the dilemma of how to fairly admit students to college. As political scientist Peter Stone argues, "the random allocation of goods must always be justified in terms of a specific conception of justice. This conception would spell out precisely what gives a person a claim to a good, and what makes one claim stronger or better than another. A lottery would then make sense whenever the conception does not provide a basis for distinguishing between the members of a group of claimants."[35]

But to achieve a situation in which there were no reliable distinctions among applicants would require an extremely high threshold. And in that situation, the lottery would not achieve any substantial reduction in competition, nor would it serve to broaden educational opportunity. For example, suppose we considered only those with test scores in the top 10% to be eligible for the lottery. Based on the data for the ELS applicants to selective schools, we would expect that group to include only 2.5% who were URMs and 6.6% who were in the bottom half of the SES distribution. Also, conducting a lottery with a very high threshold would amount to choosing the easiest students to educate, the very outcome that Astin hoped lotteries could avert.

College admissions lotteries with low thresholds, however, are a recipe for controversy: A low-threshold lottery will include a wide range of students in the selection pool and will inevitably lead to the rejection of some candidates who are seemingly far more qualified than certain admitted students. Outcomes of this kind are likely to spark public protest because of perceived unfairness: A lottery is not impartial, Stone points out, if "there are relevant differences between claimants to a good."[36]

This, of course, takes us back to the question of what constitutes a claim to a place in an institution of higher education—academic talent, hard work in the face of overwhelming obstacles, or perhaps just playing the bassoon.

*Table 7-1.* Percentages of Women and Men for Enrollees and Two Lottery Models

|  | Enrollees | Lottery with Test-Score Threshold of 1000 | Lottery with High-School-GPA Threshold of 2.8 |
|---|---|---|---|
| Women (%) | 53.4 | 51.6 | 56.1 |
| Men (%) | 46.6 | 48.4 | 43.9 |

*Table 7-2.* Percentages of Students in Each Ethnic Group for Enrollees and Two Lottery Models

| Ethnic Group | Enrollees | Lottery with Test-Score Threshold of 1000 | Lottery with High-School-GPA Threshold of 2.8 |
|---|---|---|---|
| Asian (%) | 12.1 | 10.7 | 10.6 |
| Underrepresented minority (%) | 12.4 | 12.3 | 14.5 |
| More than one race (%) | 3.8 | 3.9 | 3.5 |
| White (%) | 71.7 | 73.1 | 71.4 |

*Note:* Results for Black, Hispanic, and American Indian students were combined to conform with Institute of Education Sciences data security requirements.

*Table 7-3.* Percentages of Students in Each of Four Socioeconomic Categories for Enrollees and Two Lottery Models

| Socioeconomic Status (SES) | Enrollees | Lottery with Test-Score Threshold of 1000 | Lottery with High-School-GPA Threshold of 2.8 |
|---|---|---|---|
| Highest (%) | 63.6 | 59.7 | 56.7 |
| Second highest (%) | 20.8 | 23.8 | 24.0 |
| Second lowest (%) | 11.4 | 11.2 | 12.3 |
| Lowest (%) | 4.2 | 5.4 | 7.0 |

*Note:* Some column totals are not exactly 100% because of rounding.

*Table 7-4.* High School GPA and Test-Score Data for Enrollees and Two Lottery
Models

|  | Enrollees | Lottery with Test-Score Threshold of 1000 | Lottery with High-School-GPA Threshold of 2.8 |
|---|---|---|---|
| High school GPA |  |  |  |
| Average | 3.5 | 3.4 | 3.5 |
| Standard deviation | 0.4 | 0.5 | 0.3 |
| Test Score |  |  |  |
| Average | 1245 | 1222 | 1197 |
| Standard deviation | 150 | 130 | 158 |

*Table 7-5.* College First-Year Grade-Point Average (FGPA), Graduation Rates, and
Postbaccalaureate Attainment Rate for Enrollees and Two Lottery Models

|  | Enrollees | Lottery with Test-Score Threshold of 1000 | Lottery with High-School-GPA Threshold of 2.8 |
|---|---|---|---|
| College FGPA |  |  |  |
| Average | 3.2 | 3.1 | 3.2 |
| Standard deviation | 0.6 | 0.7 | 0.6 |
| College Graduation |  |  |  |
| 4-year graduation rate | 64.3 % | 55.1% | 55.8% |
| 6-year graduation rate | 83.7 % | 79.3% | 80.3% |
| Postbaccalaureate attainment rate | 28.0 % | 26.5% | 27.5% |

# CHAPTER EIGHT

# Crafting a Class

> Selective institutions in the United States aim to "create a class" where the admitted "class" has a range of features that meets a range of institutional objectives in different ways.
> —*Anna Mountford Zimdars*

What if a college admissions officer could say, "I want to admit 100 students, including at least 50 from inside the state and at least 30 from disadvantaged or underrepresented groups. Also, I don't want more than 10 students whose GPAs are below the average for their high school class. Given those conditions, I want to admit the applicants with the highest possible admissions test scores."

In striving to create the ideal incoming class, admissions committees are called upon to make countless decisions about which applicants are preferable to others. A host of factors may be considered—high school record, test scores, special talents, an application essay, and perhaps a recommendation letter from a teacher or counselor. And in many cases, membership in an underrepresented ethnic or socioeconomic group will also be taken into account. The deliberations of the committee will often lead to a ranking of the candidates, or at least a partial ranking into "yes," "maybe," and "no" categories. But a ranking process might not be ideal for achieving the complex goals of the typical admissions process. Could our hypothetical 100 students be assembled through ranking? It might be possible to create an index value for each applicant, starting with the applicant's test score and then adjusting it as needed. Candidates from inside the state and those from disadvantaged or underrepresented groups would have their index values augmented; those with low high school GPAs would be docked a certain number of points. But this would by no means be a straightforward process. First, decisions would be needed on exactly how to incorporate each factor. Which is more important, recruiting an applicant who resides within the state or avoiding one with a low high school GPA? Which characteristic is more significant, in-state status or membership in a disadvantaged group? A more serious problem is that even if an acceptable means of combining all these pieces of information could be found and the applicants could ultimately be ranked, there is no assurance that the top 100 would reflect the target proportions of disadvantaged, underrepresented, and in-state students—or would include fewer than 10 students with low GPAs.

But what if the focus were on the properties of the class as a whole, rather than on the individual students? What if the desired characteristics of the student body could be fed into a computer algorithm that would then recommend a full-blown admit pool? In fact, methods of this kind, based on well-established techniques from operations research, have already been spelled out in statistical detail, tested in simulation studies, and even used to admit graduate students. The general approach, called constrained optimization (CO), allows an educational criterion, such as grades or test scores, to be maximized while imposing constraints on class composition.

Under the constrained optimization approach, our applicants would not be ranked. It would not be the individual candidates that would be evaluated, but sets of 100 candidates. The set that yielded the best average test score, given the specified constraints, would be selected. Constrained optimization techniques are therefore ideally suited to the incorporation of academic requirements along with diversity goals. How do these group-based computerized admissions systems work, and what are their pros and cons?

Peter J. Pashley and Andrea E. Thornton, authors of a 1999 report, *Crafting an Incoming Law School Class*, were apparently the first researchers to apply CO methods to admissions problems.[1] To illustrate their method, Pashley and Thornton, researchers at the Law School Admission Council, which is the creator of the Law School Admission Test (LSAT), tried to mimic the results obtained through the actual admissions process at an unidentified law school. They constructed a mission statement that was intended to be consistent with the actual goals of the institution and included the following specifications: "We give consideration to those less-than-privileged individuals who have had to overcome personal, educational, or environmental adversity. Within the above constraints, we also strive to ensure that the group of applicants we admit exhibit as high academic potential as possible, in terms of undergraduate credentials and standardized test scores."[2]

Pashley and Thornton applied their algorithm to information submitted by the actual applicants, supplemented by data from the College Board and the U.S. Census. One of the challenges they set for themselves was to produce an ethnically diverse admit pool without using the applicant's race as a criterion. Toward this end they included such factors as the percentage of minorities within the applicant's area of residency and at the applicant's undergraduate school. They also incorporated other constraints involving the applicants' age, community, in-state status, and undergraduate institution. Given that all constraints were met, an index combining LSAT scores and undergraduate grades was to be maximized. The results showed that there was an overlap of about 75% between the applicants selected using the computerized approach and those who had actually been admitted, and the ethnic composition of the two (overlapping) groups of students was quite similar. In a 2005 publication, the researchers noted that in the course of their research, "this approach ha[d] been applied to admission data from a large number of law schools with very good success."[3]

In its basic form, the CO procedure does not explicitly take into account the fact that some candidates will choose not to attend (a weakness shared by most selection procedures). However, modifications of the basic approach have been developed that take into account the expected yield from an admit pool by incorporating an estimated probability that candidates with various characteristics will accept admission offers. Targets can be then be formulated with respect to the matriculants rather than the admit pool.[4] Other modifications allow for the possibility that applications are evaluated continuously, as they arrive (rolling admissions), and provide for the creation of a waiting list.[5]

A few researchers have followed in the footsteps of Pashley and Thornton. Clarence D. Kreiter and his colleagues at the University of Iowa College of Medicine considered the application of CO to medical school admissions. Like Pashley and Thornton, Kreiter's main motivation in exploring these techniques was to develop admissions models that would facilitate diversity while maintaining academic excellence. In a 2002 article Kreiter illustrated his approach with an artificial example in which the data for each "applicant" consisted of a score on the Medical College Admission Test (MCAT), an undergraduate GPA, a diversity rating (hypothetically assigned by faculty), and an indication of whether the applicant came from a suburban, urban, or rural background. The admissions goal was to select 10 of the 25 applicants, maximizing the average MCAT score while enforcing various combinations of three different constraints on class composition. One constraint was that at least three students with a high diversity rating be included, the second was that at least three students with rural backgrounds and at least two each from suburban and urban backgrounds be selected, and the third was that no more than three students with GPAs in the bottom third of the applicant pool be accepted. Kreiter used this small simulation to illustrate the impact of each of the constraints. The constraint involving suburban, urban, or rural background was found to be the most influential in limiting the average MCAT score that could be achieved. The author concluded that the use of CO "to aid admission decisions provides a method for the accurate translation of class composition goals while also optimizing applicant attributes."[6]

In a subsequent study Kreiter and his colleagues applied CO techniques to actual data from medical school applicants to an institution in the Midwest. Their goal was "to select 80 students [from a pool of 409 applicants] with academic scores as high as possible while accepting a representative number of minority applicants," and they wanted to do so without explicitly using applicant race in the admissions process.[7] The only information to be used for selection was the applicants' MCAT scores and their own indication of whether they were economically disadvantaged—information that was already being collected as part of the medical school application process. The average MCAT score of the entering class was to be maximized under the constraint that at least 15 selected students be disadvantaged. This approach generated a class with 12 ethnic minorities and an acceptably high average MCAT score. Interestingly, the resulting class was identical to the one attained through a much more laborious ranking procedure that involved the creation of weighted composites of MCAT scores and disadvantage status.

In what appears to be the only documented application to an actual admissions process, the University of Chile's Department of Industrial Engineering used CO in 2007, 2008, and 2009 to select entering classes of roughly 50 students for a special master's degree program in globalization management.[8] To further its goal of increasing educational opportunity, the department imposed constraints on the composition of the entering classes in terms of gender, regional origin, and socioeconomic background. Specifically, the intent was to encourage the participation of women, low-SES students, and those from outside the Santiago region. In 2009 a constraint was added to facilitate the participation of non-engineers. Curiously, the authors, Guillermo Durán and Rodrigo Wolf-Yadlin, seemed unaware of the earlier research on the use of CO as a means of promoting campus diversity.[9]

The admissions procedure used by Durán and Wolf-Yadlin was more complex than the processes described in the earlier studies, which were purely illustrative. Each year, the university used stringent preliminary requirements to trim the applicant pools from roughly 600 to 85 before the optimization procedure was applied. In this preliminary screening, applicants were assigned scores that summarized their qualifications, and they were ranked based on these scores. (In this case, then, optimization techniques were used to supplement, rather than replace, the ranking of applicants.) The authors then tried three selection models that shared the same constraints on the composition of the class but differed in terms of the quantity that was to be optimized. In one model, the sum of the applicants' scores was to be maximized, in the second, the sum of the applicants' ranks was to be minimized, and in the third, the rank assigned to the last candidate chosen was to be minimized. (Minimization, rather than maximization, was involved in the second two models because low ranks corresponded to high performance.) The best three solutions (sets of students) for each of the three models were then obtained, and a complex process was used to combine these top nine solutions to obtain the final admissions decisions. In general, the more solutions an applicant appeared in, the greater his chances of admission. Applicants who were included in the best solution for all three models were admitted immediately.

Durán and Wolf-Yadlin conducted post hoc analyses to determine the *robustness* of the admissions decisions: Would the same students be chosen if slight changes were made in the selection criteria? The analyses were used to assess the effect of each individual constraint and to determine the number of students who were admitted only because of the class composition constraints. According to administrators of the program, "having this information allows the decision makers to feel more certain they are making the right admission choices." Administrators praised the CO approach for its robustness and transparency and for facilitating high-quality admissions decisions that would have been virtually impossible to achieve manually.[10]

## Application of Constrained Optimization to ELS Data

Apparently no previous research has been conducted on the use of CO to promote diversity in undergraduate admissions. I tried out the method on the ELS applicant data, with the goal of maximizing the academic credentials of the entering class while ensuring its diversity. In my initial application, I set a few simple goals: The GPA–test-score composite was to be maximized, subject to the constraints that the number of admits be exactly the same as the real-life number of enrollees (970) and that the percentage of underrepresented minorities be at least as large as the actual percentage enrolled (12.6%). The columns labeled "CO (Match diversity)" in Tables 8-1 through 8-5 contain these results, which can be compared to those for the enrollees. Then I tried a version of the CO approach that had more ambitious goals. I wanted at least 20% of the entering class to be underrepresented minorities and at least 20% to be from the lower half of the SES distribution. The results for this version appear in the columns labeled "CO (Exceed diversity)." The rightmost column in each table shows the outcome of unconstrained optimization. To obtain these results, I selected the top 970 students on the GPA–test-score composite without regard to demographics.

It turns out that, mathematically speaking, the CO approach becomes unwieldy if sampling weights are included in the analysis.[11] So, to demonstrate the method, I omitted the weights. The analyses still tell us how well the method worked as an admissions model, but unlike the other analysis results in this book, the outcomes in Tables 8-1 to 8-5 are not representative of the high school seniors of 2004. (To allow for legitimate comparisons, I omitted the weights in calculating results for the enrollees and for the unconstrained optimization procedure as well. That is why the enrollee results in this chapter look different from those elsewhere in this book.) Of course, this technical complication would never occur in an actual college admissions situation—it's a problem tied to the use of weighted survey data.

Both CO procedures yielded a slightly higher percentage of women than were present among the enrollees (Table 8-1) and yielded the target percentages of URMs (Table 8-2). For the "exceed diversity" version, the percentage of White students was 56.5%, notably lower than the corresponding percentage for the enrollees (61.1%). Table 8-3 shows that the "match diversity" procedure, which did not include any socioeconomic constraints, produced an SES distribution very similar to that of the enrollees, whereas the "exceed diversity" method yielded the targeted 20% representation of students from the bottom half of the SES distribution. (In the "exceed diversity" analysis, 7% of accepted students met both criteria—they were URMs from the lower half of the SES distribution.) The class selected using unconstrained optimization was similar to the enrollees in terms of socioeconomic characteristics, but contained only 7.5% URMs (Table 8-2).

The more interesting aspect of the results is the academic performance of the entering classes selected via constrained optimization. Table 8-4 shows that both CO procedures yielded classes with higher average high school GPAs and admissions test scores than the enrollees. For example, the "match diversity" version produced an average test score of 1307, compared to 1250 for the enrollees. Table 8-5 shows that for both CO classes, average college grades were slightly higher than those of the enrollees, while college graduation rates resembled the enrollee rates. Remarkably, the CO classes had a much higher rate of postbaccalaureate accomplishment, with at least 34% completing some kind of postcollege credential, compared to only about 24% for enrollees. Overall, the findings are striking: The CO entering classes are more diverse than the enrollees and their academic performance is superior.[12] Even more intriguing was the finding that the high school and college performance results for "match diversity" were almost identical to those for unconstrained optimization, and results for "exceed" diversity were nearly as good. This means that imposing constraints on class composition had very little impact on the academic quality of the incoming class.

## Advantages and Disadvantages of the Constrained Optimization Approach

An advantage of the CO approach is that it exploits the superior ability of computers to maximize the academic accomplishments of the selected group while enforcing certain requirements on its composition. Except at the tiniest institutions, implementing a similar process "by hand" would be an impossible task. Also, in applying a CO procedure, there is no need to assign points or weights to various applicant attributes, nor is it necessary to combine disparate characteristics, like test scores, race, grades, and income, into a single composite. The need to rank candidates is completely eliminated. But as in the case of statistical prediction, these advantages have a dark side: To some, a selection procedure like this one looks like just another instance of mindless computerization of a complex process. It's important, then, to keep in mind that even when this kind of algorithmic approach is used, human judgment continues to play a key role. Consider the use of CO to admit students to the globalization management program in Chile. Program administrators had to determine what factors were to be considered in the admissions decisions and how to assess them. They elected to use an elaborate initial screening process, including an evaluation of the candidates' academic and work backgrounds and the administration of aptitude tests, a psychological evaluation, and (in two of the three years) an English test. Program organizers used all of these results to determine a short list of candidates, which was then used as the basis for the CO procedure. They also determined what demographic requirements were to be imposed and how they were to be measured. For example, how, precisely, was "low-income" to be defined? The developers of the computer algorithms, also humans, determined exactly what criterion was to be optimized in each of the three selection methods they applied and devised a way to combine the results of these methods to arrive at a final list of students. They also collaborated with program administrators in studying the impact of the selection procedure.

If constrained optimization were to be adopted for U.S. college admissions, human involvement would be no less essential than in many existing admissions procedures. Applications would still need to be read, of course. Along with academic and demographic characteristics, ratings of personal qualities, as reflected in letters of recommendation and personal statements, could be taken into account, as they are in more conventional selection methods. Admissions policy makers would also need to establish target values for each admissions criterion: What is the minimum acceptable percentage of students from disadvantaged backgrounds? What is the desired percentage of students from within the state? Finally, admissions personnel would, of course, have the opportunity to review and modify the initial selections. Pashley and Thornton note that CO could be combined with traditional admissions methods in several ways: It could be used as a first step, to winnow the applicant pool so that admissions staff could focus their attention on a smaller set of candidates. It could also be used as a supplement to a traditional admissions process, to identify promising candidates that could help to fulfill diversity goals.

In any case, those who object to the computerization of admissions processes have already lost the battle. Elaborate computer algorithms are already widely used in admissions, though not ordinarily for diversity-enhancing purposes. Large institutions routinely use software focused on "enrollment management," which encompasses such activities as recruitment; marketing; prediction of yield, performance, and attrition; and allocation of financial aid. The *Atlantic* described the financial aid component of enrollment management like this: "Using the logic of the Saturday-night stay and the fourteen-day advance purchase, advanced financial-aid leveraging . . . forecast[s] how much each student is willing to pay, and guarantee[s] the best class at the lowest price."[13] A subsequent academic journal article on the topic used strikingly similar language, referring unapologetically to the "going rate" for particular students and remarking approvingly on the similarity between a university's enrollment management activities and efforts by airlines and hotels to collect "the best price possible for each seat / resource."[14]

In a 2013 report, Jerome A. Lucido, executive director of the University of Southern California's Center for Enrollment, Research, Policy, and Practice, lamented the fact that typical enrollment management strategies "operate to place inexperienced and less wealthy students at a disadvantage in negotiating the system."[15] According to Lucido, the main goal of enrollment managers is to "identify and enroll the students who can pay the level of tuition needed to cover campus revenue requirements," while simultaneously producing results that will allow their institutions to "leapfrog each other in college rankings or in other measures of prestige." "Broader social missions," Lucido continues, "are achieved to the extent that they are done under these constraints."[16]

By contrast, Pashley and Thornton, Kreiter and colleagues, and Durán and Wolf-Yadlin used the CO methods for the purpose of enhancing the diversity of entering classes. Pashley and Thornton and Kreiter sought to achieve racial diversity without explicitly using race in the selection process and succeeded in doing so by using factors such as the candidate's self-reported disadvantage status and the degree of minority representation in the candidate's community and undergraduate institution. Enrollment management tools could also be used to maximize diversity, but they are usually applied for other purposes—often, financial ones.

Another computerized approach to admissions, called Applications Quest, does have campus diversity as its goal. The software was developed by Juan Gilbert, a professor at the University of Florida who is the recipient of several awards, including the 2011 Presidential Award for Excellence in Science, Mathematics, and Engineering Mentoring. According to the product's website, Applications Quest "recommends a diverse group of applicants . . . without giving preferences to any race, ethnicity or any other specific attribute" using a process that is "free of human error and / or bias."[17] Applications Quest uses a numerical method called cluster analysis to group similar applicants together based on user-specified factors, such as grades, test scores, gender, and race / ethnicity. The cluster analysis technique ensures that the differences *among* these internally homogeneous groups are maximized. The software then recommends for admission the "most unique" applicants from each cluster, ideally resulting in a more diverse student body. According to its developer, Applications Quest "includes race / ethnicity as one of the factors considered, but does not assign a numerical value to it and thus complies with the Supreme Court [*Gratz*] decision [on the use of race in admissions]."[18]

Applications Quest differs from the CO approach in that it is not geared toward maximizing the academic accomplishments of the admit pool. An "automatic admit" phase that takes place before software implementation is used to accept "privileged students that get immediate acceptance" and further screening is then conducted to eliminate applicants deemed to lack minimal academic qualifications. At this point in the process, "there is no notion of one student being more qualified than another. If such a notion exists, the admissions committee will simply move the bar or set the minimum qualifications requirements higher."[19] Also, although diversity is the goal, the method is not guaranteed to produce any particular level of diversity. In fact, there is no way to determine in advance the demographic composition of the admit pool that will result. Gilbert told the *Chronicle of Higher Education* in 2013 that only Clemson's School of Nursing had used the method to screen applicants.[20]

I found three published studies of Applications Quest. In two of these studies, the software was not used to make actual admissions decisions. Instead, hypothetical entering classes were selected based on applicant data and compared to the classes that had been chosen in practice. In these two studies, published in 2008 and 2013, Applications Quest produced hypothetical entering classes that were more diverse than those resulting from the actual admissions processes but had generally inferior academic credentials. In the 2013 study, which involved choosing 434 students out of 2,550 university candidates, a more stringent pre-screening process was applied in a second phase of research in an attempt to improve the academic quality of the selected applicants.[21] In a third study, which appeared in 2008, a "major research institution in the Southeast" used Applications Quest for two years in a row to select 50 students from over a hundred applicants to a summer research program in science, technology, engineering, and mathematics. In each year, the average GPA for the selected students was slightly lower than the average GPA for the applicants, but the entering class was judged to be more diverse than the applicant pool.[22]

A disadvantage that the CO approach shares with Applications Quest is technical complexity. The unfamiliar mathematical approach could well appear to be a "black box" and might be distrusted for this reason. A further limitation of the CO approach is that it is not always possible to find a solution—an entering class—that meets all constraints. An obvious example of this problem would occur if, say, the target number of low-income admits was 100 and there were fewer than 100 low-income applicants. Solutions can also be impossible when there is a large number of constraints. When this situation occurs, it may be possible to achieve a solution by gradually loosening constraints.[23]

Another point to note is that, in the current legal climate, the particular version of CO implemented here, like the race-based affirmative action rule considered earlier, would not pass muster. The Supreme Court has ruled that "narrowly tailored" policies to promote racial diversity are permissible if race-neutral polices are unavailable; neither fixed quotas nor processes that automatically award extra points to certain ethnic groups are allowed. A modified approach that did not explicitly use race would be needed.

Is admissions via constrained optimization fair? Impossible to say: CO is a process and not an admissions policy. But for those who favor taking steps to enhance the opportunities of underrepresented ethnic and socioeconomic groups, CO provides a sound way to do so.

Despite its complexity, the CO approach is in some ways remarkably transparent, as the administrators of the Chilean graduate program noted. The method requires that the goals of the admissions procedure be spelled out in detail, and these goals can then be made public. In fact, a key advantage of the CO approach is that it forces admissions policy makers to formalize both the academic and the nonacademic aims of the admissions process. The CO method is also reproducible in a way that many admissions processes are not. Run the algorithm twice and you'll get the same answer. The approach can be used to easily address "what if" questions: If the potential effects of a proposed admissions policy need to be investigated, the selection process can easily be redone with a new set of constraints. In short, constrained optimization can provide a flexible means of translating policy into practice and could serve as a valuable tool for admissions policy makers who wish to maximize academic excellence while increasing the diversity of the student body.

*Table 8-1.* Unweighted Percentages of Women and Men for Enrollees and Three
Optimization Models

| Gender | Enrollees | CO (Match diversity) | CO (Exceed diversity) | Unconstrained Optimization |
|---|---|---|---|---|
| Women (%) | 55.1 | 57.2 | 57.4 | 56.7 |
| Men (%) | 44.9 | 42.8 | 42.6 | 43.3 |

*Note:* Because sampling weights are not incorporated, results for enrollees differ from
those in previous chapters.

*Table 8-2.* Unweighted Percentages of Students in Each Ethnic Group for Enrollees
and Three Optimization Models

| Ethnic Group | Enrollees | CO (Match diversity) | CO (Exceed diversity) | Unconstrained Optimization |
|---|---|---|---|---|
| Asian (%) | 22.3 | 21.5 | 21.2 | 22.6 |
| Underrepresented minorities (%) | 12.6 | 12.6 | 20.1 | 7.5 |
| More than one race (%) | 3.9 | 2.6 | 2.3 | 2.8 |
| White (%) | 61.1 | 63.4 | 56.5 | 67.1 |

*Note:* Some column totals are not exactly 100% because of rounding. Because sampling
weights are not incorporated, results for enrollees differ from those in previous chapters.
Results for Black, Hispanic, and American Indian students were combined to conform with
Institute of Education Sciences data security requirements.

*Table 8-3.* Unweighted Percentages of Students in Each of Four Socioeconomic
Categories for Enrollees and Three Optimization Models

| Socioeconomic Status (SES) | Enrollees | CO (Match diversity) | CO (Exceed diversity) | Unconstrained Optimization |
|---|---|---|---|---|
| Highest (%) | 68.2 | 67.9 | 63.0 | 68.2 |
| Second highest (%) | 18.3 | 18.6 | 17.0 | 19.2 |
| Second lowest (%) | 8.9 | 8.5 | 12.7 | 8.3 |
| Lowest (%) | 4.6 | 4.9 | 7.4 | 4.2 |

*Note:* Some column totals are not exactly 100% because of rounding. Because sampling
weights are not incorporated, results for enrollees differ from those in previous chapters.

*Table 8-4.* Unweighted High School GPA and Test-Score Data for Enrollees and Three Optimization Models

|  | Enrollees | CO (Match diversity) | CO (Exceed diversity) | Unconstrained Optimization |
|---|---|---|---|---|
| High school GPA |  |  |  |  |
| Mean | 3.5 | 3.7 | 3.7 | 3.7 |
| Standard deviation | 0.4 | 0.3 | 0.3 | 0.3 |
| Test score |  |  |  |  |
| Mean | 1250 | 1307 | 1291 | 1310 |
| Standard deviation | 153 | 116 | 137 | 112 |

*Note:* Because sampling weights are not incorporated, results for enrollees differ from those in previous chapters.

*Table 8-5.* Unweighted College First-Year Grade-Point Average (FGPA), Graduation Rates, and Postbaccalaureate Attainment Rate for Enrollees and Three Optimization Models

|  | Enrollees | CO (Match diversity) | CO (Exceed diversity) | Unconstrained Optimization |
|---|---|---|---|---|
| College FGPA |  |  |  |  |
| Average | 3.2 | 3.4 | 3.3 | 3.4 |
| Standard deviation | 0.6 | 0.5 | 0.5 | 0.5 |
| College Graduation |  |  |  |  |
| 4-year graduation rate | 65.6% | 66.4% | 65.0% | 66.3% |
| 6-year graduation rate | 84.2% | 85.6% | 84.7% | 85.4% |
| Postbaccalaureate attainment rate | 24.3% | 34.6% | 34.0% | 34.1% |

*Note:* Because sampling weights are not incorporated, results for enrollees differ from those in previous chapters.

# CHAPTER NINE

# Conclusions

> The natural distribution [of talent] is neither just nor unjust;
> nor is it unjust that persons are born into society at some particular
> position. These are simply natural facts. What is just and unjust is the
> way that institutions deal with these facts.
>
> —*John Rawls*

Studying the economic benefits of college has emerged as a major focus of public policy research during the last few years. Although there are some naysayers, a flurry of reports—from the U.S. Treasury Department, the Census Bureau, the Brookings Institution, the Georgetown Center on Education and the Workforce, the College Board, and the State Higher Education Executive Officers—have all reached essentially the same conclusion: College pays.[1]

According to the College Board, "the evidence is overwhelming that for most people, education beyond high school is a prerequisite for a secure lifestyle and significantly improves the probabilities of employment and a stable career with a positive earnings trajectory."[2] College graduates earn far more than high school graduates, and the college premium has increased over time. As of 2011 the median income for individuals aged 25 to 34 who had at least a bachelor's degree was about 70% higher than the median income for those in the same age group with only a high school degree. College graduates are more likely to receive health insurance and pensions from their employers and are only half as likely to be unemployed as individuals with only a high school diploma.

But the advantages are not only financial. College-educated adults live healthier lives—they are more likely to exercise and less likely to smoke or to be obese. They are more involved in civic life and more likely to report being "very satisfied" with their jobs.[3] Although it can't be proven that all these differences are actually *caused* by the completion of a bachelor's degree, these findings contribute to the public perception that a college degree paves the way to the good life. It's no wonder, then, that college admission seems to be something of a national obsession in recent years. And today, many students and their families are convinced that the most selective colleges provide the most direct route to a lifetime of success. Consider the fact that Stanford alone attracted nearly 44,000 applicants in 2016.[4]

But as significant as the income differential might be, the current notion of a college degree as a ticket to higher earnings and a more comfortable life is troubling. First, the disproportionate emphasis on the economic and lifestyle benefits of higher education detracts attention from more fundamental questions. What about the quality of the education itself? How much do students learn in college? Does the college experience help them develop their intellectual capacities? Do they gain a deeper understanding of the world and its people? These questions tend to fade into the background when we focus instead on the college wage premium.

Second, the obsession with the most prestigious colleges and universities perpetuates the distorted perception that a good education can be had at only a few top-ranked schools—excellence has come to be defined in terms of exclusiveness. A prominent example is the ubiquitous *US News & World Report* college ranking, in which an institution's position is affected by its selectivity: The lower its acceptance rate and the higher the admissions test scores and high school standing of its past freshmen, the higher its rank.[5] A higher rank, in turn, leads to an increase in demand, which further boosts the college's status. This phenomenon seems to transform the college into a mere collector of talented students, recalling B. Alden Thresher's remark, "If Satan tempts the professor, it is in offering him an opportunity to eliminate all but the ablest 10 percent—or 1 percent—of potential students." The professor can still "have a good conscience, since it is all done in the name of high standards."[6]

Another disturbing but unavoidable conclusion is that gaining access to the intellectual as well as the economic benefits of a college education is much more difficult for some high school students than for others. As my analyses of Education Longitudinal Study data and countless other studies show, students from poor families are much less likely to be ready for the academic challenges of college than are students from upper-class families, and a large gap exists among ethnic groups as well. On average, American

Indian, Black, Hispanic, and low-income students have much lower high school grades and admissions test scores than their White, Asian, and high-income counterparts. Throughout their schooling, these students have been more likely to attend poorly funded and ineffective schools that did not allow them to fully develop their academic skills, and they have had fewer chances to compensate for these limitations through out-of-school enrichment activities.

Relatively few students from socioeconomically disadvantaged groups or students of color even apply to the most competitive colleges. The ELS data illustrate the striking scarcity of low-SES students. Only about 8% of the high school seniors who applied to colleges designated as "most competitive" or "highly competitive" in 2004 were from the bottom SES quartile; 54% were from the top quartile. This is quite consistent with the pattern observed by William Bowen, Martin Kurzweil, and Eugene Tobin, who found that "the [chances] of getting into the pool of credible candidates for admission to a selective college or university are six times higher for a child from a high-income family than for a child from a poor family."[7] And whereas 28% of the ELS senior cohort were American Indian, Black, or Hispanic—groups that are routinely underrepresented in selective institutions—only 21% of the applicants to elite schools were members of these groups. Among the students who enrolled in these top schools in 2004, the percentage fell to 12%. In terms of socioeconomic status, 64% of the enrollees were from the top quartile.

These grimly reliable ethnic and socioeconomic patterns in college application and enrollment rates attest to the need for a wide range of interventions, from the most sweeping programs—combating poverty and equalizing educational opportunities beginning in early childhood—to more focused outreach programs, like those that help high school students plan and complete college preparatory coursework, assist them with the application process, and help to arrange financial aid. Surprisingly, even some narrowly targeted efforts that help high school seniors and their families apply for admission and financial aid have been found to increase college enrollment.[8]

But what about the students who are, to borrow Mitchell Stevens's phrase, "delivered to the point of application"?[9] What properties characterize the most equitable and effective admissions systems? Here we consider what principles can be distilled from the findings and deliberations in this book, beginning with a second look at my analyses of high school seniors who took part in the Education Longitudinal Study of 2002.

## Comparing College Admissions Models for the ELS Applicants to Selective Colleges

What conclusions can be gleaned from my comparisons of 16 competing admissions models? First I will consider the 12 rules that were based on a rank-ordering of the applicants. Six of the ranking methods involved grades or test scores only; the other six included racial preferences, socioeconomic preferences, or noncognitive factors as well.

Which admissions models led to the best college performance? Models that selected 10% of applicants (the narrow rules) yielded better college graduation rates and first-year college GPAs than those that selected 41% (the broad rules), presumably reflecting the fact that students accepted under the more stringent rules were better prepared: Average admissions test scores and high school grades were, of course, higher under the narrow selection models.

Admissions rules based on high school GPA or on a composite of GPA and test score yielded higher graduation rates and college grades than models based solely on test score, supporting the prevailing belief that GPA reflects characteristics like willpower and diligence. The apparent role of grades as indirect measures of these attributes confirms the advice perennially offered by testing companies that admissions test scores be used in combination with high school grades. Among the narrow selection rules, using the GPA–test-score composite (with or without other factors) produced better graduation rates than using GPA alone.

For the most part, the admissions rules that augmented the academic composite to incorporate affirmative action policies or to include noncognitive measures produced college grades, graduation rates, and postcollege accomplishments similar to those obtained using the unvarnished composite and better than the results for the enrollees. There were two notable exceptions: First, students who were selected using the narrow GPA rule or the narrow noncognitive rule were much more likely to have obtained a postbaccalaureate credential (typically a master's degree or professional doctorate) within nine years of high school graduation than any of the other entering classes. This finding suggests that both GPA and the occupational and educational aspirations included in the noncognitive rule served as measures of students' motivation and perseverance. A second exception was the four-year graduation rate of 75.4% for the narrow race-based affirmative action rule—about 6 percentage points higher than that of the corresponding rule based on the original composite. This disparity is particularly interesting because these two classes resembled each other in terms of gender, SES, college selectivity, and field of study. (The broad race-based affirmative action rule, however, did not produce a parallel result.)

Turning to college access, which of the ranking-based selection rules increased ethnic and socioeconomic diversity? The two race-based affirmative action models produced entering classes that had somewhat larger percentages of URMs than the enrollees—and generally had higher average GPAs, test scores, college grades, and postbaccalaureate accomplishments—certainly an encouraging finding. However, even under these models, the percentages of Black and American Indian students were small; Hispanic students were the primary beneficiaries. Given that there were so few American Indians among the applicants, it is not surprising that they were so poorly represented. In the case of Black applicants, the 200-SAT-point boost associated with the affirmative action scenario was not sufficient to bring many into the top ranks. In order to be more effective, the racial preferences would have had to be much larger—perhaps more than just a "thumb on the scale"—or take a different form entirely, such as the constrained optimization approach, which allows academic criteria to be optimized while imposing requirements on the composition of the class.

The effect of admissions policies on Asian applicants has been in the news in recent years, with some advocacy groups raising concerns that Asian Americans are held to a higher standard than other students. How did the representation of Asians vary across the admissions rules? For the broad ranking models, the percentage selected tended to be similar to the percentage of Asians among the enrollees. The percentage varied substantially among the narrow rules, however. When the top 10% of applicants were chosen based on test score, the entering class was about 17% Asian, compared to only about 7% Asian when students were chosen using high school GPA. These results suggest that at selective institutions, deemphasis of test scores in favor of high school grades could lead to lower acceptance rates for Asian applicants.

The ranking rules that produced the highest percentages of students from the lower half of the SES distribution were, not surprisingly, the two SES-based affirmative action models, with the broad GPA-based model coming in third. It is worth noting that the SES-based affirmative action rules did not increase ethnic diversity. In fact, the narrow SES-based rule yielded one of the smallest percentages of URMs of all the admissions rules—under 6%. Similarly, the race-based rules did not increase the representation of low-income applicants. Although race and SES are quite closely related among the applicants considered as a whole, there is almost no correlation between underrepresented minority status and SES among the applicants with the highest academic qualifications.

The six models that used academic factors only—GPA, test scores, or a combination—produced classes that were roughly 80% White, with 7% to 19% of students coming from the bottom half of the SES distribution. The smallest percentage of low-SES students among these six models occurred for the narrow rules based on test score and on the composite; the highest percentages emerged from the two GPA-based rules.

The selection procedures that included measures of students' aspirations yielded greater percentages of URMs and students from the bottom half of the SES spectrum than the rules based on the original GPA–test-score composite. However, these percentages were below the rates observed for the enrollees, demonstrating that the inclusion of noncognitive factors is not guaranteed to substantially affect diversity. Other kinds of noncognitive factors, such as demonstrated evidence of perseverance in the academic realm, may produce quite a different result.

Some intriguing patterns occurred in the percentages of women for the 12 rank-based admissions models. The percentage was highest for the narrow GPA rule, where it came in at an astonishing 65%, and it was nearly that high for the broad GPA model. The percentage of women was smallest for the two test-score-based models, falling to about 45% for the narrow version.

Clearly the weights attached to high school grades and admissions test scores, the additional factors considered, and the stringency of the selection rules substantially affected the entering classes that were "admitted." Overall, my ELS analyses suggest that a modified composite that gives more weight to GPA than to test score may yield acceptable proportions of URMs, Asians, low-SES students, and women. In fact, many composites now being used in college admissions do weight GPA more heavily than test scores.[10] In the interest of furthering ethnic and socioeconomic diversity, substantial preferences for underrepresented groups would need to be incorporated in the admissions process as well. Alternatively, a composite of grades and test scores could be maximized, using the constrained optimization procedure, subject to requirements for the representation of targeted student groups.

The first of two constrained optimization procedures I tried produced exactly as many URMs as were present among the enrollees, as intended, and led to a similar SES distribution. A more ambitious version of this approach resulted in an entering class with 20% URMs and a 20% representation of students from the bottom half of the SES distribution, far exceeding the corresponding percentages among the enrollees. The high school GPA, test score, FGPA, and postbaccalaureate attainment rate for these entering classes were notably superior to those of the enrollees, affirming the potential of this selection method.[11]

In addition to the 12 admissions models based on ranking and the two constrained optimization methods, I applied two lottery models. The lottery with a high school GPA threshold of 2.8 produced almost as high a proportion of URMs as the race-based affirmative action rules and included the highest proportion of Black students. It also yielded one of the highest percentages of low-SES students. From a diversity standpoint, in fact, it was the best of all the admissions rules. But its four-year graduation rate of 56% was substantially below the rate for competing models, and the average FGPA and postcollege attainment rate were low as well. The lottery with an SAT threshold of 1000 produced similar academic results, although with somewhat fewer URMs, low-SES students, and women. In any event, admission lotteries cannot be regarded as fair unless there is a sound basis for considering all candidates to be equivalent. Setting a threshold high enough to make this assumption plausible would vitiate any diversity-enhancing effects of the lottery. In addition, both past experience and polling results suggest that the use of lotteries at the university level would be highly controversial.

## Principles for College Admissions Policies

Of course, a series of "what if" analyses can, at best, provide some rough guidance as to how selection rules should be crafted. My findings are merely tentative for a number of reasons, chief among them the fact that I treated 2,000 applicants to elite colleges as though they were applicants to a single university and treated the college results for the hypothetical entering classes as though they came from a single institution as well. In fact, these high school seniors had applied to many institutions, and their college grades and graduation rates also came from multiple schools. And although the applicants I studied are nationally representative of high school seniors who applied to selective institutions in 2004, the characteristics of college applicants have undoubtedly changed to some degree since then. In addition, my

16 selection rules were intentionally very simple, shorn of the intricacies of actual admissions processes. Real-life admissions procedures take into account many factors that are not encompassed by the simplified rules illustrated here, such as applicants' unusual talents, accomplishments, and experiences—and possibly, their roles as legacies, athletes, or celebrities.

In any case, an admissions policy is not merely a set of selection rules, and statistics can't tell us what student characteristics to value. What precepts should shape the development of the admissions policy itself? Here, I lay out seven key principles and then elaborate on each one:

- Admissions policies and criteria should emerge from the institutional mission.
- There is no universal definition of "merit." Whether an applicant is entitled to be selected is entirely contingent on the school's admissions policy.
- Schools should be free to incorporate socioeconomic and racial preferences. The strongest justification for these preferences is that they address a social problem—the exclusion of people of color and low-income individuals from many sources of well-being in our society.
- Applicants should not be denied admission because they need financial aid, nor should they be admitted because of their parents' alumni status or donor potential. Athletes who fall short of an institution's academic standards should not be recruited.
- High school grades should continue to play a key role in admissions, particularly because of their apparent value in measuring students' tenacity and commitment. Test scores can be useful in identifying talented students who have so far been unsuccessful in school and in facilitating the comparison of candidates from very different academic backgrounds, including home-schooled students and those from outside the United States.
- Nontraditional admissions criteria and holistic evaluations are not always helpful to those they are intended to support. The less clear the admissions criteria, the more likely they are to benefit the wealthier, more savvy candidates.
- Admissions policies should be transparent. Applicants are entitled to know the rules of the game so that they can make their best case for admission. And because of the central role of education in society,

institutions have an obligation to inform the public of their admissions priorities. As part of their accountability responsibilities, institutions should conduct and report research on the impact of their admissions policies and procedures.

Now, let's consider each of these points in detail. First, the goals of the admissions policy and criteria should flow from the mission of the institution. Bob Laird, Berkeley's former admissions director, recommends that each institution have "a clear statement of purpose for its admissions policy." He offers some examples: "to enroll a freshman class with the most distinguished high school academic records," "to enroll a freshman class that will have the highest 4-year ... graduation rate," or, in a different vein, "to enroll a class that will reflect the racial and ethnic diversity of the state."[12]

Whether a student is entitled to admission depends entirely on the purpose and rules of the school's admissions system. Each policy has implications for the demographic and academic characteristics of the entering class, the resources they will need, and the likelihood that they will succeed. On the one hand, a class selected to maximize high school academic record will typically be less diverse, ethnically and socioeconomically, than a class selected to reflect the demographic composition of the state or the neighboring community. On the other hand, such a class might require less academic support and have higher graduation rates. An institution is not obliged to select the students who are deemed most likely to earn high grades or graduate. Indeed, if an institution's mission is to educate the least prepared, it may choose its students accordingly. There is no all-purpose blanket "entitlement" to be admitted to college—"no combination of abilities and skills and traits that constitutes 'merit' in the abstract," as the legal scholar Ronald Dworkin put it.[13]

Why should preferences for certain racial and socioeconomic characteristics be allowed in admissions? One argument is that race-based affirmative action is necessary to compensate for America's shameful legacy of slaveholding. But this argument weakens over time and does not apply in any obvious way to applicants who are not African-American. A more broadly applicable justification is based on the idea that less stringent admissions criteria should be applied to candidates who have withstood some kind of disadvantage—racism, poverty, a childhood illness, or a difficult family situation. A third rationale focuses on the importance of maintaining diversity in educational settings, and indeed, some studies have shown that more diverse college classrooms lead to improved cognitive, interpersonal, and psycho-social development, greater commitment to social justice, and higher minority student retention.[14]

But the most compelling arguments look to the future. According to Dworkin, "affirmative action [as practiced by universities] is a forward-looking, not a backward-looking, enterprise, and the minority students whom it benefits have not necessarily been victims, as individuals, of any distinct injustice in the past." Affirmative action is intended to solve a societal problem—"the de facto racial stratification that has largely excluded blacks and other minorities from the highest ranks of power, wealth and prestige."[15] Even in today's America, where a Black president recently occupied the White House, Dworkin's description still holds. His characterization could be further expanded to include members of low-income families, who are much less likely than their wealthier counterparts to complete a college education and reap its benefits. According to an ELS report about the high school sophomores of 2002, 61% of those in the top income quartile had attained a bachelor's degree 10 years later, compared to 15% in the lowest quartile, illustrating once again the stark educational disparity between the poor and the prosperous.[16]

Race and socioeconomic status should be among the wide array of characteristics that colleges can consider in arriving at an admissions decision. Among the factors that should *not* be considered are how much a candidate's parents earn, whether they're alumni, and whether they're likely to donate a building. These factors are neither related to the educational mission of the institution nor do they support any social justice goal. Applicants should not be denied admission because of their need for financial aid. And athletes should be recruited only if they have satisfactory academic records.

What academic criteria should be used in choosing candidates? High school GPA is important to the admissions process because it provides a summary of students' classroom accomplishments, reflecting both their skills and their studiousness and perseverance. Grading standards, however, are not comparable across schools or teachers. Admissions tests provide a way to compare the academic skills of students who come from a wide range of educational backgrounds and can help to identify promising candidates who have not met with success in high school.

The role of tests in college admissions continues to be controversial, however, partly because of the large score gaps among ethnic and socioeconomic groups. The testing profession has warned against overreliance on test scores. The *Standards for Educational and Psychological Testing* states that "in educational settings, a decision or characterization that will have major impact on a student should take into consideration not just scores from a single test but other relevant information."[17] An ACT document notes that its clients should not "rely on assessment data as the sole criterion for making selection decisions, but [should] consider all available information that addresses additional relevant skills and abilities . . . (e.g., high school grades, supervisors' ratings) and various noncognitive factors (e.g., previous experience, interests, special skills)."[18] And the College Board advises that SAT scores should be used "in conjunction with other indicators, such as the secondary school record (grades and courses), interviews personal statements, writing samples, portfolios, recommendations, etc., in evaluating the applicant's admissibility."[19] It is also important that small score differences not be overinterpreted. Admissions tests primarily assess a specific range of verbal and quantitative skills and do so mostly through the use of multiple-choice questions.[20] In the future, when these tests are administered via computer, more complex and engaging questions that involve a wider variety of cognitive capacities are likely to be included. These could involve multistep math problems or simulated science experiments and might require responses in the form of a paragraph, a drawing, or an equation.

Some commentators and even admissions officers have argued that both high school grades and test scores are undesirable or unnecessary as admissions criteria. Goucher College recently encouraged the submission of two-minute video applications, and Bennington College now allows the submission of "curated" portfolios of student work in place of standard applications. In neither case are high school transcripts or admissions test scores required.[21] But although an unduly heavy emphasis on standard academic selection criteria—grades and test scores—may yield a limited perspective on a candidate's talents, it does not follow that eliminating them entirely is preferable, nor is it the case that measuring criteria outside the traditional cognitive domain—applicants' cartoon-captioning skills or multicultural IQ—will necessarily improve the prediction of college success or enhance fairness. In fact, some nontraditional criteria are likely to be more easily coached than admissions tests. It is particularly disturbing to think that applicants with superior self-marketing abilities may gain an advantage under policies that involve curation and video production.

Whatever the criteria and procedures for evaluating applications may be, candidates should be apprised of the rules of the game. Applicants should not be led to believe that academic credentials are the sole determinants of admission if, as is typical, they are not. Institutions should let candidates know what characteristics and accomplishments are considered valuable and how these factors are weighted and combined in making an admissions decision. It is only through publication of these standards that applicants can determine if they have been treated fairly.

Holistic admissions procedures seem to be particularly remiss in this respect. Opinion pieces by university faculty and admissions personnel at Harvard, Berkeley, and UCLA have called holistic admissions an "excuse for cultural bias," a "fig leaf" that obscures the actual decision process, and a "secretive" system bristling with "unspoken directives" and "through-the-looking-glass moments."[22] And research based on the work of sociologist Pierre Bourdieu suggests that the less specific the demands of university gatekeepers, the more important the role of the candidates' *cultural capital*— in this case, knowledge about the university culture.[23] Thus, the fuzzier the admissions criteria, the greater the disadvantage suffered by those not already steeped in the academic ethos.

If racial preferences for underrepresented minorities are incorporated in the admissions process, this should be made explicit. But in this arena, what's ethical and what's legal are in opposition. Because using automatic racial preferences would risk running afoul of the *Gratz* decision (and sometimes state prohibitions as well), institutions try "to find a substitute for race without admitting they are trying to find a substitute for race," as Laird has pointedly observed.[24] Ideally this would not be so. As Bowen and his colleagues note in this context, "there is much to be said for avoiding charades."[25] But in this case, the admissions officer's hands are tied by the Supreme Court.

A recent series of events revealed the degree to which institutions are resistant to transparency in their admissions policies. In early 2015 an online newsletter, the *Fountain Hopper*, urged Stanford students to request their admission records using the Family Educational Rights and Privacy Act, or FERPA. The *Fountain Hopper* pointed out that, under the FERPA laws, the university was required to produce these materials within 45 days. Reportedly, nearly 3,000 individuals ultimately requested their admission files from Stanford. And the movement spread—other universities started receiving these requests too. According to the *New York Times*, the records received by one Stanford student included "an assessment of a few hundred words" from admissions officers, along with "a set of scores, on a scale of 1 to 5, on criteria like test scores, high school record, personal qualities, and how the student fared in an interview." The disclosed material also included "boxes to check for ethnicity [and] parents who are alumni or big donors." Just 15 days after the floodgates were opened, Stanford slammed them shut, destroying existing files and changing policies that would have kept such files on record. Other elite schools, including Yale, have made similar changes.[26]

To determine whether admissions policies are consistent with the institutional mission in their effects as well as their intent, rigorous research is needed. Is the policy conceptualized and documented in such a way that application evaluators have a common understanding of the goals of the admissions process and the specific criteria that are to be used in selecting students? If the admissions criteria are expected to predict college grades, graduation, citizenship, or any other aspect of college performance, do they in fact do so? If the selection rules are designed to identify talented students that would otherwise be overlooked, do they serve this purpose? Is the ethnic, socioeconomic, and geographic composition of the resulting entering class consistent with the intent of the policy? To the degree possible, the results of this research should be publicly available. Indeed, publishing research on the effects of admissions policies is one of the requisites of both public accountability and transparency. And transparency is much needed in order to tame applicant anxieties, increase public faith in the admissions process, and pave the way for improvements.

The goal of the admissions policies in place at most top colleges—to consider the full range of a candidate's accomplishments, capabilities, and characteristics—is a good one. A narrow and formulaic admissions policy is not an attractive or useful alternative. But in order to judge the fairness and effectiveness of an admissions policy, it's necessary to know what the policy is. This includes both the intent and the outcomes of the policy. Access to America's top universities is a prized good, and the methods of allocating places in these schools will always be the subject of debate. Our public conversation about college admissions needs to be less rancorous and more productive. The first step is for schools to reveal what is behind the curtain.

NOTES

REFERENCES

ACKNOWLEDGMENTS

INDEX

# Notes

## Introduction

*Epigraph:* Klitgaard, 1985, p. 51.

1. *Fisher v. University of Texas at Austin,* 2016.
2. Soares, 2012, p. 6.
3. "Repairing the Rungs on the Ladder," p. 14.
4. Schwartz, 2012.
5. Wechsler, 1977, p. viii.
6. Ibid., p. 17.
7. Ibid., pp. 25–26.
8. The Butler quote appears in ibid., p. 97. Wechsler, p. 99, gives the number of initial Board members as 11, but in his history of the College Board, Fuess (1950, pp. 37–38) lists the 12 charter members: Barnard College, Bryn Mawr College, Columbia University, Cornell University, Johns Hopkins University, New York University, Rutgers College, Swarthmore College, Union College, University of Pennsylvania, Vassar College, and the Woman's College of Baltimore.
9. College Entrance Examination Board, 1905, p. 12.
10. Ibid., p. 39.
11. Wechsler, 1977, p. 4; Zwick, 2002a, pp. 2–3.
12. https://www.collegeboard.org/program-results/participation; http://www.act.org/newsroom/u-s-high-school-graduates-showing-little-progress-in-college-readiness/.
13. National Center for Education Statistics, 2014, Table 305.40. The Universal College Application (www.universalcollegeapp.com/), which includes 46 schools, and the newly initiated Coalition for Access, Affordability, and Success (www.coaltionforaccess.org), with more than 90 institutional members, are alternatives to the Common Application (www.commonapp.org).

14. Clinedinst, Koranteng, & Nicola, 2016, pp. 7–8.
15. Rosen, 2013, p. A13.
16. National Center for Education Statistics, 2015a, pp. 190–192. These statistics are based on degree-granting institutions with first-year undergraduates. Somewhat different institutional counts appear in Table 1 of Ginder, Kelly-Reid, & Mann, 2015, based on the Integrated Postsecondary Education Data System (IPEDS), which collects data from postsecondary institutions in the United States and U.S. jurisdictions.
17. Lorin, March 31, 2015; Anderson, April 1, 2016.
18. Ginder, Kelly-Reid, & Mann, 2015, Table 2.
19. McPherson & Schapiro, 2006.
20. Thresher, 1989, pp. 5–6.
21. Stevens, 2007, p. 161.
22. Jaschik, 2007.
23. See Stevens, 2007, chap. 4.
24. National Center for Education Statistics, 2015b, Table 1. The figures provided are the four-year adjusted cohort graduation rates (ACGR). As explained in the NCES document, "the 4-year ACGR is the number of students who graduate in 4 years with a regular high school diploma divided by the number of students who form the adjusted cohort for the graduating class. From the beginning of 9th grade (or the earliest high school grade), students who are entering that grade for the first time form a cohort that is 'adjusted' by adding any students who subsequently transfer into the cohort and subtracting any students who subsequently transfer out, emigrate to another country, or die."
25. Clinedinst, Koranteng, & Nicola, 2016, pp. 30–31.
26. Ibid., p. 17.
27. Ibid., pp. 18–20; Clinedinst, 2015, p. 28.
28. Klitgaard, 1985, pp. 52–55.
29. Laird, 2005a, p. 121.
30. Thresher, 1989, p. 22.
31. Sander, 2012, p. 1.
32. Sackett, 2005, p. 111.
33. Fremer, 2005, p. ix.
34. Sherley, 2007, pp. 1695–1696.
35. Sternberg, 2010, pp. viii–ix.
36. See Zwick, 2002c, 2013.
37. Sandel, 2009, p. 169.
38. Geiser & Santelices, 2007, p. 27.
39. Zwick, 2002c; Zwick & Green, 2007.
40. Cornwell, Mustard, & Van Parys, 2013; Godfrey, 2011.

41. Atkinson, 2001; Lohman, 2004, p. 41.
42. Organisation for Economic Co-operation and Development, 2010, p. 13. See also Zwick, 2002c.
43. Lawton, 1996; Winerip, 1994.
44. Atkinson, 2001.
45. Evangelauf, 1990.
46. Pitsch, 1990.
47. The *2015 College-Bound Seniors* report (College Board, 2015a, Table 7) shows a mean of 531 for Asian Americans and 513 for White students.
48. E.g., S. Steele, 2001, p. 24.
49. Berry, 2000, p. A48. For a similar view, see "Why the '4 Percent Solution' Won't Restore Racial Diversity," 1999.
50. Cullen, Long, & Reback, 2011, p. 25.
51. See Table 4 in Ginder, Kelly-Reid, & Mann, 2015.
52. D. Carnevale, 1999.
53. Brownstein, 2000.
54. Demick, 2013.
55. General information on ELS:2002 comes from the NCES website (http://nces.ed.gov/surveys/els2002/) and from Ingels, Planty, & Bozick, 2005.
56. Ingels et al., 2015. Additional information about the characterization of the sample was supplied by ELS project officer Elise Christopher via email, July 15, 2015. Analysis details appear in the online appendix.
57. Cohen, 1988, p. 26. See the online appendix for further details on this computation.
58. C. M. Schmitt, 2009.
59. I made two inquiries to the ELS staff asking why the percentages of the senior cohort in each of the SES quartiles were not closer to 25%. An email response I received from Pablo Traverso of NCES (April 2, 2015) showed that the percentages are almost exactly equal to 25 if the analysis is performed using students from the first follow-up, including those who were incapable of completing a questionnaire, along with a different set of sampling weights (F1EXPWT). According to the email message, "percentages are not guaranteed to match when using other weights." In response to my second inquiry, I learned that the SES distribution for the senior cohort seen in Table I-6 (with 58% of students in the top two quartiles) is related to the fact that this ELS sample corresponds to the population of 2004 seniors who attended (but did not necessarily graduate from) a postsecondary institution (email from ELS project officer Elise Christopher, July 15, 2015). Thus, their SES tends to be higher than that of the original senior cohort.

60. These analyses made use of the sampling weights. Students were "admitted" until the weighted admission rate was as close to the target percentage as possible. Departures were trivial. Details are in the online appendix.
61. Toutkoushian & Paulsen, 2016.
62. College Entrance Examination Board, 1999, p. 7.
63. Atkinson & Geiser, 2009, p. 3.
64. Conley, 2012; Schwartz, 2012.
65. Pashley & Thornton, 1999; Pashley, Thornton, & Duffy, 2005.
66. Zwick, 2002b, p. 13.

## 1: Evaluating the Fairness and Effectiveness of an Admissions System

*Epigraph:* Thresher, 1989, p. 56 (a reissue of the original 1966 monograph).
1. University of California, 2001, p. 2.
2. Ibid.
3. Moores, 2003, p. 4.
4. According to UC Berkeley statistics at opa.berkeley.edu/statistics/cds/2002 -2003.pdf, the total number of first-year, first-time admits for that year was 8,710.
5. Moores, 2004.
6. Trounson, 2003.
7. Asian Law Caucus et al., 2003.
8. Schevitz, 2003.
9. University of California, 2001, p. 1.
10. Perry, Brown, & Sawrey, p. 104.
11. M. T. Kane, 2013, p. 1.
12. Voting Rights Act Amendments of 1975 Public Law 94-73.
13. 360 U.S. 45 (1959).
14. 384 U.S. 655 (1966).
15. *Oregon v. Mitchell*, 1970.
16. Soares, 2009.
17. Sacks, n.d.
18. Asian Law Caucus et al., 2003, pp. 22, 25.
19. Ibid., p. 3.
20. University of California Office of the Vice President, 2008, p. 1.
21. Kidder & Rosner, 2002, p. 175; University of California Office of the Vice President, 2008, p. 3; Pernell, 2015, p. 1379. For example, U.S. Department of Education regulations associated with Title VI enforcement state that programs may not "utilize criteria or methods of administration *which have the effect of* subjecting individuals to discrimination because of their race,

color, or national origin." (Italics added.) See U.S. Government Publishing Office, 2005.

22. Pernell, 2015, p. 1376.
23. Gándara, Moran, & Garcia, 2004, pp. 33–34; Kidder & Rosner, 2002, pp. 173–183; Mank, 2008, pp. 34–39.
24. Kidder & Rosner, 2002, pp. 172–173.
25. Ibid., p. 198.
26. Fullinwider & Lichtenberg, 2004, p. 44.
27. Wechsler, 1977, pp. 186–187.
28. Library of Congress, Primary Documents in American History, www.loc.gov/rr/program/bib/ourdocs/Morrill/html; Library of Congress, United States Statues at Large, vol. 12, p. 504. http://memory.loc.gov/cgi-bin/ampage?collId=llsl&fileName=012/llsl012.db&recNum=534.
29. http://www.higher-ed.org/resources/land_grant_colleges.htm.
30. Haycock, Lynch, & Engle, 2010, p. 2.
31. Ibid., p. 11.
32. See, for example, College Entrance Examination Board, 1999, pp. 5–7.
33. http://www.antiochcollege.org/about/mission_and_history.html; www.cca.edu/about/diversity.
34. National Association for College Admission Counseling, 2003, p. x. Because the response rate was low (31% of 1,470 NACAC members who were chief admissions officers; p. ix) and respondents cannot be assumed to be representative of all postsecondary institutions, results should be interpreted with caution.
35. www.howard.edu/president/vision.htm.
36. saas.byu.edu/tools/b4byu/sites/b4/?new-freshman/acceptance-criteria2/.
37. College Entrance Examination Board, 1999, p. 20.
38. Clinedinst, Koranteng, & Nicola, 2016, pp. 21–22. Because the response rate was low and respondents cannot be assumed to be representative of all postsecondary institutions, results should be interpreted with caution.
39. College Entrance Examination Board, 1999, p. 21; Clinedinst, Hurley, & Hawkins, 2012, p. 69.
40. Stevens, 2007, p. 200.
41. Golden, 2003a.
42. Golden, 2003b.
43. www.muhlenberg.edu/main/aboutus/finaid/applyingForAid/merit.html.
44. Fullinwider & Lichtenberg, 2004, p. 30.
45. yalecollege.yale.edu/content/mission-statement-yale-college.
46. Bowen & Bok, 1998, p. 281.
47. www.suny.edu/about_suny/mission.cfm.
48. web.mit.edu/facts/mission.html.

49. Klitgaard, 1985, p. 70.
50. Zwick & Dorans, 2016. See Meyer, 2013, for another discussion of philosophical perspectives on fairness in university admission.
51. See Sandel, 2009, pp. 190–191, for a related discussion.
52. Fullinwider & Lichtenberg, 2004, pp. 11, 13.
53. Ibid., p. 208.
54. Petersen and Novick (1976) provide a detailed review of 10 approaches.
55. E.g., McLoyd, 1998.
56. National Center for Education Statistics, 2014, Table 102.60.
57. Lee & Burkam, 2002, chap. 1.
58. Betts, Rueben, & Danenberg, 2000, pp. 205–207; OECD, 2010, p. 101.
59. American Educational Research Association, American Psychological Association, and National Council on Measurement in Education, 2014, p. 54.
60. www.fairtest.org/act-biased-inaccurate-and-misused.
61. Helms, 2006; see esp. Table 2 and the surrounding discussion.
62. Hughes, 1998.
63. *Statistical Decision Functions,* by Abraham Wald, the first comprehensive treatment of this field, was published in 1950. For applications in the admissions context, see also Gross & Su, 1975, and Petersen, 1976.
64. Petersen, 1976, pp. 349–356.
65. Cronbach, 1976, p. 31.
66. Sackett & Wilk, 1994.
67. See Cleary, 1968, pp. 115. Earlier work by Lloyd Humphreys, 1952, is also relevant. Although the equal prediction perspective is usually interpreted today to mean that a selection rule is fair only if the relationship between the test and the performance is the same for all groups, some earlier researchers interpreted the rule to mean that different prediction equations are acceptable, as long as the appropriate one is used for each student: This interpretation appears in Gross & Su, 1975, p. 350, and Petersen & Novick, 1976, p. 5. Here we assume the equal prediction model requires the same selection procedure to be applied to all candidates.
68. More detail on this finding appears in Chapter 3.
69. American Educational Research Association et al., 2014, p. 51.
70. An early reference on this point is Linn & Werts, 1971. For criticisms of the equal prediction model, see Kane & Mroch, 2010, and Terris, 1997.
71. *DeFunis v. Odegaard,* 1974.
72. Breland & Ironson, 1976, p. 92.
73. Stemler, 2012, p. 6.
74. Ibid., p. 10.
75. Crouse & Trusheim, 1988, p. 6.

76. ACT, Inc., 2014; Robbins, Allen, Casillas, & Le, 2006; Sternberg, 2010.
77. E.g., ACT, Inc., 2014; Burton & Ramist, 2001; Robbins et al., 2006.
78. See Johnson, 1997; Stricker et al., 1994, and Willingham et al., 2002, for reviews.
79. E.g., Burton & Ramist, 2001.
80. Bowen, Chingos, & McPherson, 2009, p. 2.
81. Willingham, 1974, p. 275.
82. See Zwick, 2002a, pp. 94–96, for further discussion.
83. Cronbach, 1976, p. 40; Darlington, 1976, p. 46.
84. Drum, 2007.
85. Zwick, 2016.
86. American Educational Research Association et al., 2014, pp. 134, 131.
87. Pinker, 2014.
88. University of California, 2001.
89. Starkman, 2013.
90. "Complaint against Harvard University," 2015; see also Golden, 2006. A similar complaint was filed in 2016 against Brown, Dartmouth, and Yale (Belkin, 2016).The Harvard complaint was dismissed in July 2015 because the concerns raised were similar to those in a federal lawsuit filed against Harvard in 2014 ("Harvard Bias Complaint Dismissed," 2015). A related suit was filed against the University of North Carolina at Chapel Hill.
91. See https://college.harvard.edu/admissions/application-process/what-we -look.
92. *Grutter v. Bollinger,* 2003.
93. Espinosa, Gaertner, & Orfield, 2015, pp. 28–29. The number of schools whose participation was solicited was 1,562 (p. 9) and the number of respondents was 338 (p. iii), for a response rate of 21.6%. Because of the low response rate and because the responding schools cannot be assumed to be representative of all postsecondary institutions, results should be interpreted with caution.
94. Lewin, 2012.
95. Wildavsky, 2015.
96. Using Table 10 from Hout, 2005, I calculated the ratio of the regression coefficient to its standard error and focused my discussion on the factors for which this ratio exceeded 5 in magnitude. Robert D. Mare came to similar conclusions about the most important admissions factors in his 2012 study of holistic admissions at UCLA.
97. I sent email to Cynthia Schrager on February 14, 2014, and emails to Greg Dubrow on February 14 and 21, and March 6, 2014.
98. Wildavsky, 2015. I emailed Papadopoulos on August 9, 2015, requesting details, but did not receive a response. A UC Berkeley institutional

researcher from whom I sought information let me know only that the Papadopoulos study was "unofficial"; i.e., it was not associated with the institutional research office.

99. Hout, 2005, p. 31.
100. Van Buskirk, 2006.

## 2: Admissions Tests and High School Grades

*Epigraph:* M. Young, 1994, pp. 79, 83.
1. M. Young, 1994, p. 170.
2. ETS, 1950, pp. 9–10.
3. Ibid., p. 14.
4. Lemann, 1999, p. 119.
5. Sacks, 1997, p. 25.
6. https://www.collegeboard.org/program-results/participation; http://www
.act.org/newsroom/u-s-high-school-graduates-showing-little-progress-in
-college-readiness/.
7. Gewertz, 2016.
8. http://www.fairtest.org/university/optional.
9. The 1926 SAT is described in Lawrence et al., 2004. The essay tests
continued to be offered until 1942; see Fuess, 1950, pp. 157–158.
10. Fuess, 1950, p. 102; https://www.collegeboard.org/about.
11. Ibid., p. 103.
12. A reproduction of the particular form of the Army Alpha that contains
this question is at http://arcweb.sos.state.or.us/pages/exhibits/war/ww1
/engineer.html. A similar question appears in Form 8, which appears in
Brigham, 1923, p. 9. The 1926 SAT is from ETS archives.
13. Brigham, 1923, pp. xxi, 190.
14. Downey, 1961, p. 27.
15. Brigham, 1930, p. 165.
16. Downey, 1961, p. 26.
17. Brigham, 1923, pp. xvii, 182–186.
18. Ibid., p. 210.
19. Fuess, 1950, pp. 106–107, 110–111.
20. More precisely, the correlation is an index of the linear relationship
between two quantities, with a positive value indicating that the two
quantities tend to increase together, a negative value indicating that one
tends to increase as the other decreases, and a value of zero indicating that
there is no linear relationship. However, two quantities could have a
nonlinear relationship yet have a correlation of zero. There are various
ways of assessing the correlation between the ACT and the SAT. The

correlation between the ACT composite score and the total SAT score (critical reading + math + writing) was found to be .92 in the most recent large-scale study; see Dorans & Moses, 2008.

21. "President Emeritus Talks about *The Big Test*," 1999.
22. Atkinson, 2001, p. 3.
23. Atkinson, 2004, p. 17.
24. For example, see Weissglass, 1998.
25. Office of Technology Assessment, 1992, p. 111.
26. http://www.pbs.org/wgbh/pages/frontline/shows/sats/where/three.html; also see Lemann, 1999.
27. Atkinson, 2001.
28. Camera, 2015. The number continues to fluctuate.
29. Hoover, 2012; Jaschik, 2013.
30. College Board, 2015b; see also https://collegereadiness.collegeboard.org /sat/inside-the-test/key-changes; https://collegereadiness.collegeboard .org/sat/scores/understanding-scores/structure; https://collegereadiness .collegeboard.org/sat/scores/understanding-scores/new-scores-meaning -for-students.
31. https://collegereadiness.collegeboard.org/educators/higher-ed/scoring -changes/concordance; and https://collegereadiness.collegeboard.org/sat /scores/understanding-scores/sat-score-converter.
32. Anderson, May 11 and 12, 2016.
33. See Lawrence, Rigol, Van Essen, & Jackson, 2004, for a review of content changes from 1926 through 2004.
34. Shaw et al., 2016, pp. 5, 15.
35. ACT, 2009a; https://www.act.org/products/k-12-act-test/.
36. Information was gathered from Hoover, June 6, 2014, and from the following websites: www.act.org/newsroom/fact-sheets/the-act; www .actstudent.org/scores/understand/#multchoice; and http://www.act.org /content/act/en/products-and-services/the-act-educator/about-the-act /continuous-improvement.html.
37. http://www.act.org/actnext/.
38. Godfrey, 2011; Willingham, 2005; Willingham, Pollack, & Lewis, 2002.
39. Downey, 1961, p. 20.
40. Kobrin, Patterson, Shaw, Mattern, & Barbuti, 2008, p. 5.
41. Downey, 1961, p. 20.
42. http://admission.universityofcalifornia.edu/campuses/files/freshman -profiles/freshman_profile_berkeley.pdf.
43. Zwick, 2013; Zwick & Himelfarb, 2011.
44. Downey, 1961, p. 21.
45. See J. W. Young, 1993, for a dated but still useful review.

46. Legislation passed in 2009 allowed the University of Texas at Austin to admit a smaller percentage.

47. Willingham, 2005, pp. 130, 134; Willingham, Pollack, & Lewis, 2002.

48. Malouff, 2008, p. 191.

49. Willingham, Pollack, & Lewis, 2002, p. 10.

50. Landy & Sigall, 1974; Perlmutter, 2004.

51. Cornwell, Mustard, & Van Parys, 2013, p. 251.

52. Rauschenberg, 2014.

53. Saslow, 1989.

54. Brennan, Kim, Wenz-Gross, & Siperstein, 2001, p. 175.

55. Ibid., p. 206.

56. Office of Educational Research and Improvement of the U.S. Department of Education, 1994.

57. Geiser & Santelices, 2007, pp. 2, 27.

58. College Board, 2015a, Table 10. ACT results are based on email from Kenneth Bozer of ACT, September 15, 2015. The average score for an income of more than $150,000 was 24.9; for less than $24,000, it was 17.9. The total-group standard deviation was 5.49.

59. Zwick, 2004, 2012.

60. Bozick, Ingels, & Owings, 2008, pp. 12, 21. The study was based on 9,460 students who had complete data and participated in ELS in 10th and 12th grades (p. 30).

61. Ibid., pp. 12, 18, 21, 33–34, 63. Researchers categorized only 55% of students' course sequences; the remaining ones were placed in an "other" category.

62. ETS, 2009, p. 11.

63. For a more detailed description of this type of analysis, with examples, see Zwick, 2002a, pp. 127–130, 151–156.

64. Camara & Schmidt, 1999; Ingels, Planty, & Bozick, 2005; McLoyd, 1998; Owings, McMillen, & Burkett, 1995; Zwick, 2004, 2012. Literature reviews appear in White, 1982, and Sirin, 2005.

65. See Zwick & Green, 2007, pp. 41–42. We also note that, despite its lesser precision, high school GPA typically has a higher correlation with FGPA than do admissions test scores. This is likely due to the fact that both types of grades (high school and college) measure characteristics that are not reflected in test scores, such as attendance, classroom behavior, and motivation.

66. These data are from www.zillow.com and www.weatherbase.com.

67. Freedman, 2002.

68. A detailed computational example appears in Zwick, 2013. While the concept of within-school and between-school correlations may not be

widely familiar, it is based on the principles of multilevel (or hierarchical) analysis, which is recognized as the optimal analysis method for hierarchical data structures in which individuals are grouped into units (e.g., see Raudenbush & Bryk, 2002). It turns out that in practice, the distinction between student-level and school-level correlations is not that important for high school grades because the *average* GPA for the students in a high school tends to be about the same everywhere—and these high school averages don't tend to vary much with average income. So when we consider the ordinary correlation between high school GPA and income, we're getting at roughly the quantity we're interested in. This isn't so for SAT, where we get a combination of two different relationships—one among high schools, and one among students within high schools.

69. Zwick & Green, 2007, Table 7. Our data did not allow us to identify students or schools. Our findings were replicated by Mattern, Shaw, & Williams, 2008.

70. The FTC later modified its conclusions on coaching effects, having failed to take into account the differences between coached and uncoached students in terms of high school grades and demographic factors. Federal Trade Commission, 1978, 1979; see Zwick, 2002a, p. 161.

71. See Zwick, 2002a, pp. 160–167; Briggs, 2009. Kaplan (2005), who is unrelated to Kaplan Test Prep, reports a larger coaching effect for his own SAT math-coaching courses. In a recent review of multiple studies, Montgomery and Lilly (2012) also obtained higher estimates (23.5 points on the verbal section and 32.7 points on the math section), but their results are highly questionable. Only seven studies were included in their analysis, five of which predate 1987. The authors provided little explanation of their criteria for selecting these seven out of 311 candidate studies, and they excluded the most credible SAT coaching research.

72. See ACT, Inc., 2005; Briggs, 2001, 2009; Moss, Chippendale, Mershon, & Carney, 2012.

73. See http://www.princetonreview.com/college/sat-test-prep.

74. Steinberg, 2009.

75. Waldman, 2014.

76. "Admissions Officers Speak Out on Private Counselors," 2006.

77. Buchmann, Condron, & Roscigno, 2010, p. 435.

78. https://web.archive.org/web/20140103093943/http://www.sylvanlearning.com/.

79. ftp://www.leginfo.ca.gov/pub/97-98/bill/sen/sb_1651-1700/sb_1697_bill_19980824_amended_asm.html.

80. Livestreamed presentation by David Coleman, March 5, 2013; "The College Board Announces Bold Plans," 2014. SAT prep videos are now available at

https://www.khanacademy.org/login?continue=https%3A//www
.khanacademy.org/mission/sat.

81. http://www.act.org/newsroom/act-to-provide-low-income-students
-with-free-access-to-new-version-of-act-online-prep/; Hoover, April 19,
2016.

82. See Gándara, 2004; Laird, 2005a, chap. 9.

83. Using the applicants as a reference population, the test scores and high
school GPAs were standardized by subtracting the weighted mean and
dividing by the weighted standard deviation. Then the two quantities were
added together. See the online technical appendix for details.

84. NCES, 2014, *Digest of Education Statistics*, Table 326.10, at https://nces.ed.gov
/programs/digest/d14/tables/dt14_326.10.asp; Bowen, Chingos, &
McPherson, 2009, chap. 10. Heil, Reisel, & Attewell, 2014, have disputed the
association between selectivity and graduation rate.

85. Bowen, Chingos, & McPherson, 2009, p. 124.

86. Borghans et al., 2011. See also Kautz et al., n.d.

87. Those selected using the narrow GPA rule were less likely to attend "most
competitive" or "highly competitive" schools than those selected by the
other two narrow rules. They were also somewhat less likely to major in
engineering and more likely to major in the social sciences. Further detail
on college competitiveness and field of study appear in the online technical
appendix.

88. Beatty, Greenwood, & Linn, 1999, p. 22. The ACT writing test is optional.
Starting in 2016 the SAT writing test was made optional.

89. National Center for Education Statistics, 2012, p. 2.

90. College Board, 2011, p. 9.

91. Briggs, 2009, pp. 8, 19. Because the response rate was low (23%) and
respondents cannot be assumed to be representative of all postsecondary
institutions, results should be interpreted with caution.

92. National Association for College Admission Counseling, 2008, p. 33.

93. Jencks, 1989, p. 117.

94. Kohn, 2001.

95. Guinier, 2015, p. 29.

## 3: Performance Predictions and Academic Indexes

*Epigraph:* Gough, 1962, p. 527.

1. For example, Dawes, 1971, and Wiggins & Kohen, 1971; see Dawes &
Corrigan, 1974, p. 98. I use "statistical" here to refer to a prescribed numeral
formula for combining data. In the literature, the terms "actuarial" and
"mechanical" are also used.

2. Downey, 1961, p. 20.
3. For example, see Kobrin, Patterson, Shaw, Mattern, & Barbuti, 2008.
4. For example, see Geiser & Studley, 2004.
5. See http://admissions.uiowa.edu/rai and http://www.regents.iowa.gov/RAI /FAQ122607.pdf.
6. Hernández, 1997, p. 59; Pennington, 2011.
7. See http://admission.universityofcalifornia.edu/freshman/California -residents/admissions-index/.
8. The term "multiple regression" is sometimes used when there is more than one predictor.
9. Strictly speaking, this statement requires some qualification: If the true relationship between GPA and SAT is linear, and if the "best weighting" is defined as that which minimizes the sum of the squared differences between actual and predicted grades, the statement is true. Further detail can be found in references on least squares regression, such as Kutner, Nachtsheim, & Neter, 2004. Note also that the size of unstandardized regression weights like those shown here depends in part on how spread out the predictor values are: High school GPA, which ranges from 0 to 4, will have a much larger weight than the two SAT scores, which range from 200 to 800. The additive term, which is equal to 0.82 in the example, represents the predicted FGPA for an applicant whose high school GPA and SAT scores are equal to zero. The term is not meaningful in itself; it serves as a sort of baseline. (Standardized regression coefficients are expressed in standard deviation units, and the corresponding equations do not include an additive term.)
10. The prediction equation will generally be less effective when applied to a new group of applicants than it was for the students used to derive the equation because the initial derivation may capitalize on chance relationships that do not hold in the later sample. In many regression applications, a portion of the initial sample is reserved for *cross-validation*, a procedure in which the prediction equation derived on the main part of the sample is applied to the reserved portion to verify its utility. Unfortunately, cross-validation has not become standard practice in prediction studies of college performance. A separate reason that prediction equations may be less effective when applied to subsequent cohorts is that the new applicants may differ in some systematic way from the students whose data were used to derive the equation.
11. Cohen, 1988, pp. 79–80.
12. ACT, Inc., 2014; Beard & Marini, 2015; Camara & Echternacht, 2000; Kobrin et al., 2008; Westrick et al., 2015.
13. ACT, Inc., 2009b; Kobrin et al., 2008.

14. Roughly 2,000 first-term students at 15 colleges participated in the study in fall 2014. All had taken the pre-2016 SAT previously. To motivate participants, researchers paid them, with larger payments to be awarded to those whose scores equaled or exceeded their previous scores. The multiple correlation between redesigned SAT scores (using both the math and evidence-based reading and writing scores) and FGPA (obtained in 2015) was .35. When both high school GPA and SAT scores were included in the prediction equation, the correlation rose to .40. See Shaw, Marini, Beard, Shmueli, Young, & Ng, 2016, p. 14. (The corresponding correlations for the pre-2016 SAT for pilot study participants were not reported.) Some students with large discrepancies between their pre-2016 SAT scores and their later scores were excluded from the analysis (p. 9), with unknown impact on analysis results.

15. Kobrin et al., 2008.

16. See Ibid. Geiser and Studley (2004, p. 130) found the SAT to be more predictive in one of four entry cohorts studied. Agronow and Studley (2007) found a small advantage for the SAT in one of two cohorts studied.

17. Mattern, Patterson, Shaw, Kobrin, & Barbuti, 2008.

18. See J. W. Young, 2004.

19. Gough, 1962, p. 527.

20. Underwood, 1979, p. 1414; Silver, 2012, p. 112.

21. Sarbin, 1943; see Zwick, 2013. Interestingly, Sarbin (p. 595) also notes that "nonintellective factors" such as vocational aspiration, personal morale, and social adjustment (what we would call noncognitive factors today) were not significantly correlated with college achievement.

22. See Wiggins & Kohen, 1971; Dawes & Corrigan, 1974, pp. 101–102.

23. Kuncel, Klieger, Connelly, & Ones, 2013, pp. 1062–1064.

24. Dawes, 1979, p. 580.

25. Willingham, Pollack, & Lewis, 2002, pp. 17–18.

26. Dawes, 1979, p. 580.

27. See Underwood, 1979, for an interesting discussion of legitimacy of predictors in other contexts.

28. In reality, using race in this way would certainly be found to violate Title VI of the Civil Rights Act of 1964.

29. E.g., see Lauff, Ingels, & Christopher, 2014; Rothstein, 2004.

30. The Hayes segment, which aired March 7, 2014, is available at http://www.msnbc.com/all-in/watch/college-board-announces-sat-overhaul-186505795947. See also Guinier, 2015, p. 11; Sacks, 1997, p. 27; Deresiewicz, 2014, p. 206; Zumbrun, 2014.

31. Geiser & Studley, 2001, p. 9; also see Geiser & Studley, 2004.

32. Hoover, 2004; Rothstein, 2004.

33. Linn, 2009, p. 678.
34. Zwick, Brown, & Sklar, 2004, pp. 8, 25–26.
35. Sackett et al., 2012, pp. 1005, 1006; see also Sackett, Kuncel, Arneson, Cooper, & Waters, 2009.
36. Westrick et al., 2015, p. 39.
37. The analysis appearing on the Web is at http://www.statcrunch.com/5.0 /viewreport.php?reportid=28583. The detailed analysis is by Caruso, Fleming, and Spector, 2014. Thanks to Michael Zieky for suggesting a basketball example.
38. Kobrin et al., 2008, p. 5. Statistical corrections are also sometimes made for the imprecision—or *unreliability*—of the criterion that is being predicted, in this case, FGPA. See the related discussion in Chapter 2. Correlations reported in this book are not corrected except where noted.
39. Taylor & Russell, 1939, p. 566.
40. Ibid., p. 575. Under the assumption that the predictor and criterion are bivariate normal with a correlation of .35, it can be shown that the probability that the criterion variable is above its mean (i.e., in the top 50%), given that the predictor is above the 90th percentile, is equal to .744.
41. Ibid., p. 571.
42. Cleary, 1968; Mattern et al., 2008; J. W. Young, 2004.
43. Bowen & Bok, 1998, p. 262.
44. See Zwick, 2002a, pp. 117–124, for further discussion.
45. Zwick & Himelfarb, 2011. The study was supported by the College Board, which also provided the data. Low-SES schools were defined as schools with SES index values below the median for students in the study. High-SES schools were those above the median.
46. Betts, Rueben, & Danenberg, 2000, pp. 205–207; OECD, 2010, p. 101.
47. Small average prediction errors for White students are expected because of the high proportion of White students in most of the colleges. Under these circumstances, the total-group regression is heavily influenced by the results for White students.
48. Mattern et al., 2008, p. 11; J. W. Young, 2004, p. 296; Zwick, 2002a, pp. 146–151.
49. Details on these analyses appear in the online technical appendix.
50. The regression equation corresponds to a line. Assume that the horizontal axis corresponds to the composite and the vertical axis corresponds to FGPA. The regression line intersects the vertical axis at an FGPA value of 2.99 (the y-intercept). The slope of the line is 0.25. Analysis results indicated that if separate lines had been estimated for the two groups, they would have been parallel (equal slopes), but with different intercept values.

51. If there were equal proportions of men and women, the magnitude of underprediction for women would be exactly equal to the magnitude of overprediction for men. See the online technical appendix.
52. Burton & Ramist, 2001; Radunzel & Noble, 2012b; Westrick et al., 2015.
53. Radunzel & Noble, 2012a, pp. 6, 10, 67.
54. Mattern, Shaw, & Marini, 2013, pp. 3, 7, 9.
55. Adelman, 1999; Astin & Osequera, 2002; Astin, Tsui, & Avalos, 1996; Manski & Wise, 1983; also see Burton & Ramist, 2001. Note that single-institution studies tend to find weaker associations between test scores and graduation than studies based on large national databases. Multi-institution analyses of graduation are usually based on the combined data from all the schools (unlike multi-institution FGPA prediction studies, which typically involve analyses that have been conducted within colleges and then averaged). To some extent, the apparent association between test scores and graduation in these multi-institution studies reflects the fact that some *institutions* have both higher average test scores and higher graduation rates than others: A portion of the relationship is between, rather than within, colleges. This phenomenon was noted by Willingham, 1985, p. 105. See Chapter 2 for a discussion of between-school and within-school associations
56. Geiser & Santelices, 2007, pp. 21–24. Their prediction models also included parents' education, family income, and measure of school quality.
57. Bowen, Chingos, & McPherson, 2009, p. 113.
58. Ibid., pp. 121, 123.
59. Mattern, Patterson, & Wyatt, 2013, p. 12.
60. Ibid., p. 17.
61. Relevant technical details on the Bowen, Chingos, & McPherson, 2009, study appear in their online appendix B, pp. 14, 20–24, available at http://press.princeton.edu/titles/8971.html.
62. Mattern, Patterson, & Wyatt, 2013, pp. 19–20.
63. Bowen, Chingos, & McPherson, 2009, p. 123.
64. Laird, 2005b, p. 23.

## 4: Admissions Preferences

*Epigraph:* Sandel, 2009, p. 19.
1. "Controversial Bake Sale at Berkeley," 2011; Wollan, 2011.
2. Rooney & Schaeffer, 1998. The same title was later used for another FairTest publication (Schaeffer, 2012).
3. Karabel, 2005, p. 5.

4. MacLaury, 2010. Kennedy's speech involved the first use of the term "affirmative action" in the context of racial discrimination. The term had been used in other contexts earlier.
5. Asimov, 2014. In 1995, before the passage of the statewide affirmative action ban, the University of California Regents enacted a ban on racial and gender preferences. This ban was rescinded in 2001, a move that was purely symbolic because the statewide proposition remained in effect.
6. "Affirmative Action: State Action," 2014.
7. *University of California Regents v. Bakke*, 1978.
8. Chapa & Lazaro, 1998, p. 60.
9. *Grutter v. Bollinger*, 2003.
10. Lewin, 2014.
11. *Fisher v. University of Texas at Austin*, 2016, pp. 8–10; Denniston, 2016.
12. *Schuette v. Coalition to Defend Affirmative Action*, 2014, p. 96.
13. President Lyndon B. Johnson's commencement address at Howard University: "To Fulfill These Rights," 1965.
14. Krauthammer, 2001.
15. See Sandra Day O'Connor's ruling in *Grutter v. Bollinger*, 2003.
16. http://www.supremecourt.gov/oral_arguments/argument_transcripts/11-345.pdf; http://www.supremecourt.gov/oral_arguments/argument_transcripts/14-981_p8k0.pdf; *Fisher v. University of Texas at Austin*, 2013; *Fisher v. University of Texas at Austin*, 2016.
17. Goldman, 1976, p. 192, makes this point.
18. Sandel, 2009, p. 154.
19. Rawls, 1999, p. 274.
20. Dworkin, 1977, p. 7.
21. Sandel, 2009, pp. 161, 178.
22. T. J. Kane, 1998, p. 451.
23. Bowen & Bok, 1998, p. 51.
24. Bowen, Kurzweil, & Tobin, 2005, pp. 184. The data were from 18 of the 19 institutions in the Expanded College and Beyond database maintained by the Mellon Foundation.
25. Espenshade & Radford, 2009, p. 350.
26. Gaertner & Hart, 2013; Kahlenberg, 1996, 2012. Gaertner and Hart (2013) acknowledge that the overachievement indexes draw on the work of Roger Studley (e.g., Studley, 2004). These indexes are also similar to those developed by A. P. Carnevale and Haghighat (1998) and by Manning and Wild; see Manning, 1977, p. 54. The rationale for such indexes is questioned by Wainer & Brown, 2007.
27. According to email from Matthew Gaertner, February 28, 2014, the rates that appear in Gaertner & Hart, 2013, p. 392, are in error.

28. This was confirmed in an email from Matthew Gaertner, February 27, 2014.

29. Gaertner & Hart, 2013, p. 398. A. P. Carnevale, Rose, and Strohl (2014) also show some gains in African-American and Hispanic enrollment using socioeconomic preferences along with a test-score-based percent plan; see Chapter 5 for further discussion. A second approach, which added racial preferences, led to further increases in diversity. The authors indicate that a third approach, a "test-based merit" plan that included socioeconomic preferences, "improves Hispanic access but reduces African-American and Asian access below current levels" (p. 191). The results of these three plans are difficult to interpret because of the lack of detail. For example, admission rates are not mentioned and college performance data are not examined.

30. Espenshade & Radford, 2009, pp. 152, 428.

31. Relevant research by Long, 2015, is described in Chapter 5.

32. Gaertner, 2014, pp. 178–179.

33. Gaertner & Hart, 2013, p. 394.

34. Gaertner & Hart, 2015, Tables 5 and 6, pp. 457–458.

35. Ibid., Tables 7 and 8, pp. 459, 461.

36. *Fisher v. University of Texas at Austin*, 2013.

37. Espenshade, Chung, & Walling, 2004, p. 1431.

38. In terms of the selectivity of the colleges they attended and the fields they studied, those chosen by the narrow race-based and SES-based affirmative action rules were very similar to the students selected by the other narrow rules. Those selected using the broad affirmative action rules were similar to those chosen using the other broad rules. See Chapter 2.

39. Similarly, the ELS analyses showed that race-based affirmative action failed to increase socioeconomic diversity.

40. These are phi correlations (i.e., correlations between two dichotomous variables), based on weighted frequencies. See the online technical appendix for details.

41. Golden, 2012, pp. 14–15.

42. Golden, 2006, p. 5.

43. Bowen, Kurzweil, & Tobin, 2005, p. 172; Espenshade & Chung, 2005, p. 294; Golden, 2006, pp. 5–6.

44. Espenshade, Chung, & Walling, 2004, p. 1431; Shyong, 2015. For a similar finding, see Hout, 2005.

45. Espenshade, Chung, & Walling, 2004, p. 1431.

46. Bowen, Kurzweil, & Tobin, 2005, pp. 103–106.

47. Fiske, 2001.

48. Golden, 2006, pp. 261–265.

49. Stewart, 2013; Woodhouse, 2015; "New York Reaches Deal with Cooper Union, Plaintiffs," 2015; http://www.berea.edu/admissions/financial-aid-scholarships/bereas-tuition-scholarship/.
50. Giancola & Kahlenberg, 2016, p. 31.
51. Golden, 2006, p. 125.
52. See http://catalog.gsu.edu/undergraduate20132014/undergraduate-admissions/.
53. They are, however, asked about the importance of extracurricular activities and "portfolios," both of which consistently rank low; see Clinedinst et al., 2012, p. 35.
54. Breland et al., 1995, p. 72. The responding institutions cannot be considered nationally representative.
55. Golden, 2006, pp. 157–159.
56. Bowen, Kurzweil, & Tobin, p. 116.
57. Barrett, 2014; Lyall, 2014.
58. Powell, 2016.
59. Jaschik, 1990; Karabel, 2005, pp. 503–505.
60. "Education Department Challenges Report on Harvard Inquiry," 1991.
61. Schmidt, 2014; Denniston, 2016.
62. Lorin, May 15, 2015. According to the *Los Angeles Times* ("Harvard Bias Complaint Dismissed," 2015), the complaint was dismissed in July 2015 because the concerns were similar to those in the federal lawsuit.
63. Worland, 2011.

## 5: Percent Plans and Other Test-Optional Admissions Programs

*Epigraph:* Laird, 2005a, p. 142.
1. See Long, 2015, pp. 2–3; Zwick, 1999.
2. Soares, 2012, p. 3.
3. UT Austin was concerned that the automatic admission of a large number of ten percenters left the university few additional seats to allocate. In 2009 the Texas legislature passed a law allowing UT Austin to reduce the number of ten percenters it admits to 75% of its "available Texas resident spaces." For students applying in 2014, for example, this requirement implied that applicants needed to be in the top 7% of their high schools to be automatically admitted to UT Austin. See the UT Austin website at http://bealonghorn.utexas.edu/freshmen/decisions/automatic-admission.
4. See http://www.adversity.net/florida/jeb_bush_ends_quotas.htm#press_release.
5. See www.fldoe.org/Talented20/.
6. Colavecchio, 2009; Horn, 2012; Marin & Lee, 2003.

7. Schaeffer, 2012, p. 153.

8. A list dated 2009 is at http://www.fairtest.org/testoptional-admissions-list-tops-815; a list dated 2016 is at http://www.fairtest.org/university/optional.

9. Espenshade & Chung, 2012, p. 187; Hoover, June 18, 2014; https://www.hampshire.edu/admissions/faq-for-prospective-students; https://www.sarahlawrence.edu/admission/apply/first-year.html.

10. https://www.hamilton.edu/admission/apply/requirements.

11. http://info.sjsu.edu/web-dbgen/narr/admission/rec-7327.10786.10787.html; http://info.sjsu.edu/web-dbgen/narr/static/admission/freshman-req.html.

12. Belasco, Rosinger, & Hearn, 2015, p. 209.

13. A. P. Carnevale & Rose, 2003, pp. 50–53.

14. A. P. Carnevale, Rose, & Strohl, 2014, pp. 188, 191.

15. The ELS (base year) sample consists of 15,362 students from 752 high schools (Ingels et al., 2007, p. 50), an average of 20.4 ELS participants per participating high school. According to email messages from Jeff Strohl (June 20, 21, 22, and 27, 2016), the authors used the following procedure to label students as being in the top 10% of their high school classes: First, the authors discarded the data from high schools with very few ELS participants. Within each remaining school, they determined each ELS participant's rank *among the ELS participants at that school* and identified those whose admissions test scores were in the top 10%. Strohl noted that because high schools with too few students were excluded, this procedure resulted in a sample that was "not representative at the school level" (email dated June 22, 2016). Overall, it is impossible to know whether this ranking method produced results similar to those that would have been obtained if data for the entire senior class in each school had been available.

16. Espenshade & Radford, 2009, p. 362–364.

17. Horn, 2012, p. 40.

18. See http://admission.universityofcalifornia.edu/freshman/california-residents/index.html.

19. Kidder & Gándara, 2015, p. 23.

20. This example was originally presented in Zwick, 2002a, pp. 136–137. See also Zwick, 2007b.

21. Kidder & Gándara, 2015, p. 24.

22. University of California Office of the President, 2013; http://legacy-its.ucop.edu/uwnews/stat/enrollment/enr1995/95sst7d.html; http://legacy-its.ucop.edu/uwnews/stat/enrollment/enr1995/95sst7a.html.

23. Marin & Lee, 2003, pp. 22–23.

24. Ibid., p. 25.

25. Perna, Li, Walsh, & Raible, 2010, pp. 155, 162.

26. Flores & Horn, 2015, pp. 9–10.
27. Ibid., pp. 7–9.
28. Ibid., p. 11.
29. *Fisher v. University of Texas at Austin,* 2013.
30. Espenshade & Chung, 2012, pp. 187–193.
31. Hiss & Franks, 2014, p. 2.
32. Ibid., pp. 3, 7, 14. No distinction was made among four-, five-, and six-year graduation rates.
33. Ibid., p. 3. Pell Grants are need-based grants provided by the federal government to low-income students.
34. Ibid., pp. 24, 36, 44.
35. Ibid., pp. 6–8, 12.
36. Ibid., p. 5.
37. Ibid., p. 26.
38. Ibid., p. 46.
39. Ibid., p. 50.
40. Ibid., pp. 35–38. The analysis in which those with high test scores were removed was for all six public universities combined; results of this analysis were not reported separately by institution; see p. 37.
41. Ibid., pp. 20, 30.
42. Ibid., p. 36.
43. Ibid., pp. 21, 30.
44. Belasco, Rosinger, & Hearn, 2015, p. 218. Belasco is also the CEO of a college consulting firm, College Transitions LLC.
45. Hoover & Supiano 2008; Yablon, 2000; Zwick, 2002a, p. 55.
46. Belasco, Rosinger, & Hearn, 2015, p. 209.
47. Daugherty, Martorelli, & McFarlin, 2014, p. 65.
48. Ibid., p. 64; see also Horn, 2012, p. 39.
49. Daugherty, Martorelli, & McFarlin, 2014, p. 64.
50. Ibid., pp. 67–68.
51. Flores & Horn, 2015, p. 16; Horn, 2012, p. 39.
52. Allman, 2012; Belasco, Rosinger, & Hearn, 2015; Espenshade & Chung, 2012.
53. Selingo, 2000. Florida's Talented 20 policy is clearly not race-neutral in any case because it permits race-conscious financial aid, recruiting, and retention programs.
54. Predictions made via probit regression were used to identify the N students most likely to be URMs, where N was equal to the actual number of URMs (Long, 2015, pp. 3–4). It follows that the percentage of URMs that were missed is equal to 100 minus the percentage of those tagged who were, in fact, URMs. Results were less impressive for two other datasets studied by Long.

55. Coleman, Palmer, & Winnick, 2008, pp. 5, 10.
56. Hossler & Kalsbeek, 2009, p. 9. These kinds of adjustments already take place at some colleges, at least informally. See University of California Office of the Vice President, 2008, p. 14, for an example of explicit adjustment of prior GPAs for law school applicants.
57. See https://www.brynmawr.edu/admissions/first-year-students /standardized-testing-policy; http://admissions.wfu.edu/apply/sat.php; and https://www.hampshire.edu/news/2014/06/18/no-to-satsacts-not -even-optional-at-hampshire-college. The term "SAT I" in the Bryn Mawr quotation is an old name for the SAT.
58. Belasco, Rosinger, & Hearn, 2015, p. 218.
59. Zwick, 1999, pp. 323–324.
60. Wolf, 2014.

## 6: Noncognitive Attributes

*Epigraph:* Thresher, 1989 (reissue of a 1966 monograph)
1. Sparks, 2015.
2. For discussions of research on these factors, see, e.g., Kyllonen, 2012; Sedlacek, 1987. The questionnaire, cited by researcher Angela Duckworth on NPR's *TED Radio Hour,* November 13, 2013, is at https://sasupenn .qualtrics.com/SE/?SID=SV_06f6QSOS2pZW9qR.
3. Hoover, January 14, 2013.
4. Stein, 1963; Messick, 1964; College Entrance Examination Board, 1963.
5. Willingham, 1985, p. 184.
6. Kyllonen, 2012; N. Schmitt, 2012, pp. 18–19.
7. Gose, 1999.
8. Guinier, 2015, pp. xi, 79, 106.
9. N. Schmitt, 2012, p. 19.
10. Sternberg, Bonney, Gabora, & Merrifield, 2012, p. 34.
11. Sedlacek, 2005, p. 180.
12. http://williamsedlacek.info/publications/articles/analternative.html.
13. Sedlacek, 1990, item 27.
14. Ramsey, 2008.
15. Sedlacek, 1990, 1998; Tracey & Sedlacek, 1984.
16. N. Schmitt, 2012, p. 23. The information on the scoring of the exemplar task is based on email from Neal Schmitt, November 12, 2013.
17. Sternberg, 2005, p. 167; Sternberg et al., 2012, p. 33.
18. Sternberg & The Rainbow Project Collaborators, 2006, p. 16.
19. Ibid., p. 7; Sternberg et al., 2012.

20. Duckworth & Yeager, 2015, p. 238. This issue is briefly mentioned in Sternberg et al., 2012, p. 37.
21. Tracey & Sedlacek, 1984, 1985.
22. Sternberg & The Rainbow Project Collaborators, 2006; Sternberg, 2010.
23. Sternberg et al., 2012, p. 35.
24. N. Schmitt, 2012, p. 24; Robbins, Lauver, Le, Davis, Langley, & Carlstrom, 2004.
25. See Kyllonen, 2008 and 2012, for a discussion of these issues.
26. N. Schmitt et al., 2009, p. 1494.
27. See the reference list in Sedlacek, 2005.
28. Tracey & Sedlacek, 1984, Table 2.
29. Thomas, Kuncel, & Credé, 2007, p. 648.
30. Glenn, 2004. Sedlacek was reacting to an early version of the research results, which did not appear in a journal until later (Thomas, Kuncel, & Credé, 2007).
31. Sternberg & the Rainbow Project Collaborators, 2006, p. 321.
32. Sternberg, 2005, 2009, 2010; Sternberg & the Rainbow Project Collaborators, 2006; Sternberg et al., 2012.
33. Sternberg & the Rainbow Project Collaborators, 2006, Table 12.
34. Ibid., Table 15.
35. The standard deviation (SD) is a measure of how spread out a set of values is. Roughly speaking, the standard deviation of a set of values is the average distance of a value from its mean. As an example of how scores are translated to standard deviation units, in 2014 the average SAT math score for Asian Americans was 598, the average for Whites was 534, and the overall standard deviation was 120. Therefore, the Asian-American average exceeded the White average by $(598–534)/120=.53$, or slightly more than half a standard deviation unit. (Some minor refinements of this type of computation are sometimes used.)
36. Sternberg, 2010, p. 183.
37. Sternberg et al., 2012, p. 35.
38. Ibid., p. 36.
39. Sternberg, 2009, p. 284.
40. N. Schmitt, 2012, p. 25.
41. Ibid., p. 26.
42. Ibid., Table 5. In this table and in N. Schmitt et al., 2009, Table 7A, it appears that using the noncognitive admissions criteria substantially decreases the percentage of African Americans when a "moderate" selection rule is used. However, in emails dated November 12, 2013, and December 5, 2013, Schmitt explained that these tables contain typographical errors. In the

"Moderate" row, the entries for "African American" should be 8.3 and 10.0. Also, the entries for "Asian" should be 10.5 and 10.1.

43. N. Schmitt et al., 2009, Tables 7B and 7C.

44. Wechsler, 1977, pp. 133, 155–156, 168.

45. Karabel, 2005, p. 2.

46. E.g., Nieli, 2013; Zimmerman, 2012.

47. Nakanishi, 1989, p. 45.

48. See Sackett & Wilk, 1994, pp. 934–935, for a related discussion.

49. Gose, 1999. Deborah Bial founded the Posse program, an innovative effort that "identifies public high school students with extraordinary academic and leadership potential who may be overlooked by traditional college selection processes" (www.possefoundation.org/about-posse). The program uses a nontraditional admissions procedure that includes individual and collaborative interviews and tasks. Selection decisions are made jointly by Posse staff and partner institutions. I asked the Posse Foundation about research on the effectiveness of the admissions process or the program itself. In a February 2, 2016, email, Rassan Salandy, Vice President for External Affairs, said, "To my knowledge, no such independent research on Posse exists."

50. Sedlacek, 2005, p. 189. Although Sedlacek (p. 188) asserts that the court has supported the use of noncognitive variables in admissions, this is somewhat misleading: In the case in question (*Farmer v. Ramsay*, 2001), which involved the University of Maryland School of Medicine, many of the factors that were labeled "noncognitive" were fairly conventional, such as geographical region, work history, and quality of schools attended. Rob Farmer, a White applicant, contended that his application was rejected because the university used these factors as part of a de facto racial quota system favoring minorities. In deciding against Farmer, the court focused, not on the criteria themselves, but on the question of whether a minority applicant with similar qualifications would have been accepted, and whether the university's rejection of the applicant was a pretext for racial discrimination.

51. Sternberg & The Rainbow Project Collaborators, 2006, p. 344.

52. Sternberg et al., 2012, p. 34.

53. N. Schmitt et al., 2009, p. 1481.

54. Thomas, Kuncel, & Credé, 2007, p. 649.

55. Refer to the online technical appendix for details.

56. In terms of the selectivity of the colleges they attended and the fields they studied, those chosen by the broad noncognitive rule were very similar to the students selected by the other broad rules. See Chapter 2. Those selected using the narrow noncognitive rule were somewhat unusual: They were the most likely among my 16 "entering classes" to attend one of the

"most competitive" or "highly competitive" colleges (82.9% did so), were slightly more likely to major in biological sciences (14.6%), and substantially less likely to major in business (4.4%).

57. "Not Educating the Masses," 2014.

58. Weissbourd, n.d., p. 10.

59. Hoover, January 20, 2016.

60. Weissbourd, n.d., p. 1.

61. Wolf, 2014; Stevens, 2007, p. 186.

62. Ibid., p. 226.

63. The exams used to classify students were the A-levels. All applicants included in the study had grades of BBB, i.e., a grade of B in each of three subjects, excluding general studies. The high-SES schools were private or grammar schools. The low-SES schools were comprehensives or sixth-form colleges.

64. Jones, 2013, p. 411.

65. Ibid., p. 419.

66. Sedlacek, 1990.

67. N. Schmitt, 2012, p. 23. Information about the right answer comes from an email from Neal Schmitt, November 12, 2013.

68. E.g., Sedlacek, 1990.

69. C. M. Steele, 1999. The relevant literature is reviewed in Inzlicht & Schmader, 2012.

70. Pulley, 2000.

## 7: Casting Lots for College

*Epigraph:* Conley, 2012.

1. Conley, 2012; Goodman, 2014; Karabel, 2007; Schwartz, 2012.

2. Astin, 1969, 1970. I have discussed lottery admissions previously in Zwick, 2007a, 2007b.

3. Greely, 2011, p. 62.

4. Stone, 2011, p. xxviii.

5. Astin, 1970 (emphasis in original). See also Mead, 2010.

6. Roberts, 1969, p. 45.

7. Reinhold, 1970; "U. of I. Opens Doors for 839 Barred by Admissions Lottery," 1969.

8. Fuller, 1996; Reumer & van der Wende, 2010, p. 2; Stasz & van Stolk, 2007; see also https://equalitybylot.wordpress.com/2014/03/14/lottery-selection -for-medical-students-scrapped-in-the-netherlands/; and http://www .ikwildokterworden.nl/loting. (Thanks to Peter van Rijn for providing a translation.)

9. Meijler & Vreeken, 1975.
10. "Ricks College Decides Not to Use Lottery in Admissions," 1996.
11. Stasz & van Stolk, 2007. Public-school lotteries in the United States tend to be criticized because of the uncertainties and inconveniences involved, rather than because of fundamental fairness issues.
12. Ash, 2014; Phillips, 2011.
13. *Grutter v. Bollinger*, 2003.
14. Wolfle, 2011, p. 32.
15. Weissglass, 1998.
16. Wolfle, 2011, p. 32.
17. Conley, 2012; Karabel, 2007; Matloff, 1995; Schwartz, 2005, 2012; Sturm & Guinier, 2000. See also Jump (1988), who recommended a lottery for "qualified" applicants.
18. E.g., see Stone, 2013.
19. Guinier, 2000, p. 571; Guinier, 1997; Sturm & Guinier, 2000.
20. American Educational Research Association et al., 2014, p. 198.
21. Guinier, 2001, p. B10.
22. Goodwin, 2011, pp. 120–121.
23. Fullinwider & Lichtenberg, 2004, pp. 126–127.
24. In effect, this approach enforces different qualifying scores for each group, which would be unlikely to pass legal muster today. In the employment setting, using test-score cutoffs that differ by race, color, sex, or national origin is prohibited by the Civil Rights Act of 1991. See Sackett and Wilk, 1994.
25. Grofman & Merrill, 2004, p. 1448.
26. Ibid., pp. 1464, 1465.
27. A. P. Carnevale & Rose, 2003, p. 49.
28. In 2003 the nationwide average score was 507 for the verbal section and 519 for the math section (College Board, 2003). In the ELS database, ACT scores have been converted to an SAT equivalent.
29. If a lottery with a threshold were to be conducted in practice, it would involve first identifying the applicants who exceeded the threshold and then randomly sampling among them to obtain the desired number of students. In the present case, in which we are simply trying to characterize the applicants who exceed a threshold, taking a random sample would merely add error to our analyses. A random sample would imperfectly mirror the properties of the population exceeding the threshold. Therefore, to characterize those above the threshold, I merely selected those applicants and then summarized their characteristics.
30. In considering these findings, it is important to note that the lottery admits tended to attend less selective institutions than the other entering classes. Slightly more than half of these students attended institutions from the top

two competitiveness tiers, compared to 63% to 66% of those admitted using the broad selection rules and even larger percentages of those selected using the narrow rules. Attending a less competitive school may be a disadvantage, given that more selective schools tend to have higher graduation rates, all other things being equal. The lottery admits were also slightly less likely to study engineering and more likely to study business than students admitted using the other rules.

31. A. P. Carnevale & Rose, 2003, pp. 26, 49.

32. Hofstee, 2011, pp. 259–260. Another 57% selected "a mixture" of methods. On a second question that asked what the preferred mixture would be, 79% picked "waiting list and selection." "Selection" was intended to refer to achievement or ability testing.

33. Schwartz, 2012.

34. Goldman, 1977, p. 26.

35. Stone, 2011, p. xvii.

36. Ibid.

## 8: Crafting a Class

*Epigraph:* Zimdars, 2016, p. 44.

1. Pashley & Thornton, 1999; Zwick, 2002b.

2. Pashley & Thornton, 1999, p. 7.

3. Pashley, Thornton, & Duffy, 2005, p. 242.

4. Gottlieb 2001; Pashley et al., 2005.

5. Durán & Wolf-Yadlin, 2011; Pashley et al., 2005; Kreiter & Solow, 2002.

6. Kreiter, 2002, p. 151.

7. Kreiter, Stansfield, James, & Solow, 2003, p. 119.

8. In an article about admission to a baccalaureate program in nursing, the authors allude to the use of constrained optimization (Walker, Tilley, Lockwood, & Walker, 2008, p. 348). However, they appear to use the term simply to indicate that they tried to optimize performance, while taking other factors into consideration. No optimization algorithm is mentioned. My email inquiry to one of the authors went unanswered.

9. Durán & Wolf-Yadlin, 2011, p. 280. The only use of constrained optimization in admissions that is cited by these authors is a research application by Gottlieb (2001) that did not involve any demographic factors.

10. Durán & Wolf-Yadlin, 2011, pp. 285, 286, 288.

11. Without the weights, the optimization is achieved through a simple application of linear programming. However, incorporation of the weights would require application of nonlinear integer programming. See the online technical appendix for details.

12. In terms of the selectivity of the colleges they attended and the fields they studied, those chosen by the CO rules were very similar to the students selected by the broad selection rules in Chapter 2.
13. Quirk, 2005.
14. Rebbapragada, Basu, & Semple, 2010, pp. 129, 131.
15. Lucido, 2013, p. 10.
16. Ibid., pp. 5–6.
17. See www.applicationsquest.com/.
18. Gilbert, 2006, p. 100.
19. Gilbert & Johnson, 2013, p. 73.
20. Hoover, April 29, 2013.
21. Gilbert, 2008; Gilbert & Johnson, 2013, pp. 74–78.
22. Gilbert & Lewis, 2008. In this situation, the "more diverse" entering classes had smaller percentages of African Americans than did the applicant pool, which was heavily African-American in both years.
23. The CO procedure can also lead to multiple solutions—e.g., if two or more students have identical data.

## 9: Conclusions

*Epigraph:* Rawls, 1999, pp. 87–88. The work was originally published in 1971.
1. Baum, Ma, & Payea, 2013; DeSantis, 2012; Huckabee, 2012.
2. Baum, Ma, & Payea, 2013, p. 7.
3. Ibid., pp. 5–6, 10, 16,19, 21, 29.
4. Anderson, April 1, 2015.
5. These factors collectively count for 12.5% of the college's ranking. See http://www.usnews.com/education/best-colleges/articles/ranking-criteria -and-weights.
6. Thresher, 1989, p. 19.
7. Bowen, Kurzweil, & Tobin, 2005, p. 248. Emphasis in original. Although the authors use the term "odds," it is clear that they mean "probability."
8. Kautz et al., n.d., pp. 51–52.
9. Stevens, 2007, p. 161.
10. For example, the eligibility index used by the California State University system, described at https://secure.csumentor.edu/planning/high_school /eligibility_index.asp, is obtained by multiplying high school GPA by 800 and then adding total SAT score (on the 200–1600 scale; the essay test is not included). If the goal of the weighting were simply to adjust for the fact that GPA and SAT are measured on very different scales, the weight for GPA would be about 300. One way to obtain weights for GPA and test score that compensates for their different measurement scales is to multiply GPA

by the ratio of the standard deviation of SAT score to the standard deviation of GPA (essentially the method I used in creating my composite). In the case of the ELS data, this was roughly equivalent to multiplying GPA by 330. An approximation to this weighting could be achieved by multiplying GPA by the ratio of the range of SAT scores to the range of GPA, or (1600–400)/(4–0)=300. Assigning a weight of 800 implies that CSU considers GPA significantly more important than SAT scores.

11. No sampling weights were used in the constrained optimization procedure. Therefore, results were compared to unweighted results for enrollees. See Chapter 8.

12. Laird, 2005b, p. 19.

13. Dworkin, 1977, p. 7.

14. See ibid.; Terenzini et al., 2001.

15. Dworkin, 1998.

16. Lauff, Ingels, & Christopher, 2014.

17. American Educational Research Association et al., 2014, p. 198.

18. ACT, Inc., 2011, p. 8.

19. College Board, 2011, p. 9.

20. The ACT also includes a science test, which measures "interpretation, analysis, evaluation, reasoning, and problem-solving skills required in the natural sciences." See http://www.actstudent.org/testprep/descriptions/scidescript.html.

21. See Anderson, 2014; Hoover, September 24, 2014.

22. Harberson, 2015; Pinker, 2014; Starkman, 2013; see Zwick, 2016.

23. See Reumer & van der Wende, 2010; Jones, 2013.

24. Laird, 2005a, p. 142.

25. Bowen, Kurzweil, & Tobin, 2005, p. 151.

26. Pérez-Peña, 2015; Hensley-Clancy, 2015.

# References

ACT, Inc. (2005). *Issues in college readiness: What kind of test preparation is best?* Retrieved from http://www.act.org/research/policymakers/pdf/best_testprep.pdf.

ACT, Inc. (2009a, Autumn). ACT at 50: A mission in progress. *Activity*, 47(3). Retrieved from www.act.org/activity/autumn2009/anniversary.html.

ACT, Inc. (2009b). *The ACT Writing Test technical report*. Iowa City: Author.

ACT, Inc. (2011). *Policies and guidelines for uses of data from ACT-owned assessments*. Iowa City: Author.

ACT, Inc. (2014). *The ACT technical manual*. Iowa City: Author.

Adelman, C. (1999). *Answers in the tool box: Academic intensity, attendance patterns, and bachelor's degree attainment*. Washington, DC: U. S. Department of Education.

Admissions officers speak out on private counselors. (July 7, 2006). *Chronicle of Higher Education*. Retrieved from http://chronicle.com/article/Admissions-Officers-Speak-Out/5848/.

Affirmative action: State action. (2014, February). National Conference of State Legislatures. Retrieved from http://www.ncsl.org/research/education/affirmative-action-state-action.aspx.

Agronow, S., & Studley, R. (2007). *Prediction of college GPA from new SAT test scores: A first look*. Retrieved January 17, 2012, from http://www.cair.org/conferences/CAIR2007/pres/Agronow.pdf.

Allman, M. (2012). Going test-optional: A first year of challenges, surprises, and rewards. In J. A. Soares (Ed.), *SAT wars: The case for test-optional admissions*, pp. 169–176. New York: Teachers College Press.

American Educational Research Association, American Psychological Association, & National Council on Measurement in Education. (2014). *Standards for educational and psychological testing*. Washington, DC: American Educational Research Association.

Anderson, N. (2014, September 3). Goucher College allows video applications, without transcripts or test scores. *Washington Post*. Retrieved from http://www.washingtonpost.com/local/education/goucher-college-allows -video-applications-without-transcripts-or-test-scores/2014/09/03/5e01f512 -3384-11e4-9e92-0899b306bbea_story.html.

Anderson, N. (2016, April 1). Applied to Stanford or Harvard? You probably didn't get in. *Washington Post*. Retrieved from https://www.washingtonpost .com/news/grade-point/wp/2016/04/01/applied-to-stanford-or-harvard-you -probably-didnt-get-in-admit-rates-drop-again/.

Anderson, N. (2016, May 11). Why your new SAT score is not as strong as you think it is. *Washington Post*. Retrieved from https://www.washingtonpost.com /news/grade-point/wp/2016/05/11/why-your-new-sat-score-is-not-as-strong -as-you-think-it-is.

Anderson, N. (2016, May 12). What's a college test score worth? An ACT-vs.-SAT dispute. *Washington Post*. Retrieved from https://www.washingtonpost.com /news/grade-point/wp/2016/05/12/whats-a-college-test-score-worth-an-sat -vs-act-dispute/.

Ash, K. (2014, March 20). Weighted admissions lotteries: Will they reshape charter demographics? *Education Week*. Retrieved from http://www.edweek .org/ew/articles/2014/03/18/26charterlottery.h33.html.

Asian Law Caucus, Barlow, A., Ding, L., Duster, T., Equal Justice Society, Evans, P., . . . Zenone, H. (2003, October 24). *Facts and fantasies about UC Berkeley admissions: A critical evaluation of regent John Moores' report*. Retrieved from http://www.equaljusticesociety.org/UC_Coalition_Report.pdf.

Asimov, N. (2014, March 13). California lawmakers look to change college admission rules. *San Francisco Chronicle*. Retrieved from http://www.sfgate .com/education/article/California-lawmakers-look-to-change-college -5308643.php.

Astin, A. W. (1969, November 21). Total view of campus unrest [Letter to the editor]. *Science*, 945.

Astin, A. W. (1970, February 20). Should college applicants be selected by lottery? [Letter to the editor]. *Science*, 1075–1076.

Astin, A. W., & Osequera, L. (2002). *Degree attainment rates at American colleges and universities*. Los Angeles: Higher Education Research Institute.

Astin, A., Tsui, A., & Avalos, J. (1996). *Degree attainment rates at American colleges and universities: Effects of race, gender, and institutional type*. Los Angeles: University of California, Los Angeles, Higher Education Research Institute.

Atkinson, R. (2001, February). *Standardized tests and access to American universities*. The 2001 Robert H. Atwell Distinguished Lecture, delivered at the annual meeting of the American Council on Education, Washington, DC. Retrieved from http://works.bepress.com/richard_atkinson/36.

Atkinson, R. C. (2004). Achievement versus aptitude in college admissions. In R. Zwick (Ed.), *Rethinking the SAT: The future of standardized testing in university admissions*, pp. 15–23. New York: RoutledgeFalmer.

Atkinson, R. C., & Geiser, S. (2009). Reflections on a century of college admissions tests. *Educational Researcher, 38*(9), 665–676.

Barrett, P. M. (2014, February 27). In fake classes scandal, UNC fails its athletes—and whistle-blower. *BloombergBusinessweek*. Retrieved from http://www.businessweek.com/articles/2014-02-27/in-fake-classes-scandal-unc-fails-its-athletes-whistle-blower#p7.

Baum, S., Ma, J., & Payea, K. (2013). *Education pays 2013*. New York: College Board.

Beard, J., & Marini, J. P. (2015). *Validity of the SAT for predicting first-year grades: 2012 SAT validity sample* (College Board Statistical Report No. 2015-2). New York: College Board.

Beatty, A., Greenwood, M. R. C., & Linn, R. L. (1999). *Myths and tradeoffs: The role of tests in undergraduate admissions*. Washington, DC: National Academy Press.

Belasco, A. S., Rosinger, K. O., & Hearn, J. C. (2015). The test-optional movement at America's selective liberal arts colleges: A boon for equity or something else? *Educational Evaluation and Policy Analysis, 37,* 206–223.

Belkin, D. (2016, May 23). Asian-American groups seek investigation into Ivy League admissions. *Wall Street Journal*. Retrieved from http://www.wsj.com/articles/asian-american-groups-seek-investigation-into-ivy-league-admissions-1464026150.

Berkelaar, M. (2014). *Package lpSolve*. Retrieved from cran.r-project.org.

Berry, M. F. (2000, August 4). How percentage plans keep minority students out of college. *Chronicle of Higher Education*, A48.

Betts, J. R., Rueben, K. S., & Danenberg, A. (2000). *Equal resources, equal outcomes? The distribution of school resources and student achievement in California*. San Francisco: Public Policy Institute of California.

Borghans, L., Golsteyn, B. H. H., Heckman, J., & Humphries, J. E. (2011). Identification problems in personality psychology. *Personality and Individual Differences, 51,* 315–320.

Bowen, W. G., & Bok, D. (1998). *The shape of the river: Long-term consequences of considering race in college and university admissions*. Princeton, NJ: Princeton University Press.

Bowen, W. G., Chingos, M. M., & McPherson, M. S. (2009). *Crossing the finish line: Completing college at America's public universities*. Princeton, NJ: Princeton University Press.

Bowen, W. G., Kurzweil, M. A., & Tobin, E. M. (2005). *Equity and excellence in American higher education*. Charlottesville: University of Virginia Press.

Bozick, R., Ingels, S. J., & Owings, J. A. (2008). *Mathematics coursetaking and achievement at the end of high school: Evidence from the Education Longitudinal Study of 2002* (ELS:2002) (NCES 2008-319). Washington, DC: National Center for Education Statistics.

Breland, H. M., & Ironson, G. H. (1976). DeFunis reconsidered: A comparative analysis of alternative admissions strategies. *Journal of Educational Measurement, 13,* 89–99.

Breland, H. M., Maxey, J., McLure, G. T., Valiga, M. J., Boatwright, M. A., Ganley, V. L., & Jenkins, L. M. (1995). *Challenges in college admissions: A report of a survey of undergraduate admissions policies, practices, and procedures.* American Association of Collegiate Registrars and Admissions Officers, American College Testing, The College Board, Educational Testing Service, and National Association of College Admission Counselors.

Brennan, R. T., Kim, J., Wenz-Gross, M., & Siperstein, G. N. (2001). The relative equitability of high-stakes testing versus teacher-assigned grades: An analysis of the Massachusetts Comprehensive Assessment System (MCAS). *Harvard Educational Review, 17*(2), 173–216.

Briggs, D. C. (2001). The effect of admissions test preparation: Evidence from NELS: 88. *Chance, 14*(1), 10–18.

Briggs, D. C. (2009). *Preparation for college admission exams* (NACAC Discussion Paper). Arlington, VA: National Association for College Admission Counseling.

Brigham, C. C. (1923). *A study of American intelligence.* Princeton, NJ: Princeton University Press.

Brigham, C. C. (1930). Intelligence tests of immigrant groups. *Psychological Review, 37,* 158–165.

Brownstein, A. (2000, October 9). Admissions officers weigh a heretical idea: Affirmative action for men. *Chronicle of Higher Education.* Retrieved from http://chronicle.com/article/Admissions-Officers-Weigh-a/106790/.

Buchmann, C., Condron, D. J., & Roscigno, V. J. (2010). Shadow education, American style: Test preparation, the SAT and college enrollment, *Social Forces 89*(2), 435–462.

Burton, N. W., & Ramist, L. (2001). *Predicting success in college: SAT studies of classes graduating since 1980* (Research Report 2001-2). New York: College Entrance Examination Board.

Butler, C. (2012, September 25). Focus on 7 strategies to get into college. *US News.* Retrieved from http://www.usnews.com/education/best-colleges/articles/2012/09/25/focus-on-7-strategies-to-get-into-college.

Camara, W. J., & Echternacht, G. (2000, July). *The SAT and high school grades: Utility in predicting success in college* (College Board Research Note RN-10). New York: College Entrance Examination Board.

Camara, W. J., & Schmidt, A. E. (1999). *Group differences in standardized testing and social stratification* (College Board Report 99-5). New York: College Entrance Examination Board.

Camera, L. (2015, September 21). As test results trickle in, states still ditching Common Core. *U.S. News & World Report.* Retrieved from http://www.usnews .com/news/articles/2015/09/21/as-test-results-trickle-in-states-still-ditching -common-core.

Carnevale, A. P., & Haghighat, E. (1998). Selecting the strivers: A report on the preliminary results of the ETS "educational strivers" study. In D. Bakst (Ed.), *Hopwood, Bakke, and beyond: Diversity on our nation's campuses,* pp. 122–128. Washington, DC: AACRAO.

Carnevale, A. P., & Rose, S. J. (2003, March). *Socioeconomic status, race / ethnicity, and selective college admissions.* New York: Century Foundation.

Carnevale, A. P., Rose, S. J., & Strohl, J. (2014). Achieving racial and economic diversity with race-blind admissions policy. In R. Kahlenberg (Ed.), *The future of affirmative action: New paths to higher education diversity after Fisher v. University of Texas,* pp. 187–202. Washington, DC: Century Foundation.

Carnevale, D. (1999, September 3). Lawsuit prompts U. of Georgia to end admissions preferences for male applicants. *Chronicle of Higher Education,* A68.

Caruso, D. R., Fleming, K., & Spector, E. D. (2014). Emotional intelligence and leadership. In G. R. Goethals, S. T. Allison, R. M. Kramer, & D. M. Messick (Eds.), *Conceptions of leadership: Enduring ideas and emerging insights,* pp. 93–110. New York: Palgrave Macmillan.

Chapa, J., & Lazaro, V. A. (1998). Hopwood in Texas: The untimely end of affirmative action. In G. Orfield & E. Miller (Eds.), *Chilling admissions: The affirmative action crisis and the search for alternatives,* pp. 51–70. Cambridge, MA: Harvard Education Publishing Group.

Cleary, T. A. (1968). Test bias: Prediction of Negro and White students in integrated colleges. *Journal of Educational Measurement, 5*(2), 115–124.

Clinedinst, M. E. (2015). *2014 State of college admission.* Arlington, VA: National Association for College Admission Counseling.

Clinedinst, M. E., Hurley, S. F., & Hawkins, D. A. (2012). *State of college admission 2012.* Arlington, VA: National Association for College Admission Counseling.

Clinedinst, M. E., Koranteng, A.-M., & Nicola, T. (2016). *2015 State of college admission.* Arlington, VA: National Association for College Admission Counseling.

Cohen, J. (1988). *Statistical power analysis for the behavioral sciences.* (2nd ed.). Hillsdale, NJ: Erlbaum.

Colavecchio, S. (2009, December 13). A decade of Gov. Jeb Bush's One Florida has seen minority college enrollment rise. *Tampa Bay Times.* Retrieved from http://www.tampabay.com/news/politics/legislature/a-decade-of-gov-jeb -bushs-one-florida-has-seen-minority-college-enrollment/1058572.

Coleman, A. L., Palmer, S. R., & Winnick, S. Y. (2008). *Race-neutral policies in higher education: From theory to action.* New York: College Board. Retrieved from

http://diversitycollaborative.collegeboard.org/sites/default/files/document
-library/race-neutral_policies_in_higher_education.pdf.

College Board. (2003). *2003 College-Bound Seniors*. Retrieved from http://media
.collegeboard.com/digitalServices/pdf/research/cb-seniors-2003-TOTALGRP
_PRD.pdf.

College Board. (2011). *Guidelines on the use of College Board test scores and related data*.
Retrieved from https://professionals.collegeboard.com/profdownload
/guidelines-on-uses-of-college-board-test-scores-and-data.pdf.

College Board. (2015a). *2015 College-bound seniors: Total group profile report*. Retrieved from https://secure-media.collegeboard.org/digitalServices/pdf/sat
/TotalGroup-2015.pdf.

College Board. (2015b). *2015–2016 counselor resource guide to the redesigned assessments:
SAT®, PSAT/NMSQT®, PSAT™ 10, and PSAT™ 8/9*. New York: Author.

The College Board announces bold plans to expand access to opportunity,
redesign of the SAT. (2014, March 5). (College Board press release.) Retrieved
from https://www.collegeboard.org/releases/2014/expand-opportunity
-redesign-sat.

College Entrance Examination Board. (1905). *Examination questions in botany,
drawing, chemistry, geography, physics*. New York: College Entrance Examination
Board.

College Entrance Examination Board. (1963). A statement on personality testing.
*College Board Review, 51,* 11–13.

College Entrance Examination Board. (1999). *Toward a taxonomy of the admissions
decision-making process*. New York: Author.

Complaint against Harvard University and the president and fellows of Harvard
College regarding discrimination against Asian-American applicants in
the college admissions processes (executive summary). (2015, May 15).
Retrieved from http://www.asianamericancoalition.org/p17125&g
=4028&tag=892&page=1.

Conley, D. (2012, April 1). Harvard by lottery. *Chronicle of Higher Education*. Retrieved from http://chronicle.com/article/Harvard-by-Lottery/131322/.

Controversial bake sale at Berkeley stirs debate over affirmative action. (2011,
September 27). *Chronicle of Higher Education*. Retrieved from http://chronicle
.com/article/Controversial-Bake-Sale-at/129173/.

Cornwell, C., Mustard, D. B., & Van Parys, J. (2013). Noncognitive skills and the
gender disparities in test scores and teacher assessments: Evidence from
primary school. *Journal of Human Resources, 48,* 236–264.

Cronbach, L. J. (1976). Equity in selection: Where psychometrics and political
philosophy meet. *Journal of Educational Measurement, 13,* 31–42.

Crouse, J., & Trusheim, D. (1988). *The case against the SAT*. Chicago: University of
Chicago Press.

Cullen, J. B., Long, M. C., & Reback, R. (2011). *Jockeying for position: Strategic high school choice under Texas' top ten percent plan.* (NBER Working Paper No. 16663). Cambridge, MA: National Bureau of Economic Research.

Darlington, R. B. (1976). A defense of "rational" personnel selection, and two new methods. *Journal of Educational Measurement, 13,* 43–52.

Daugherty, L., Martorelli, F., & McFarlin, I. (2014, Summer). The Texas Ten Percent Plan's impact on college enrollment. *Education Next,* 63–69.

Dawes, R. M. (1971). A case study of graduate admissions: Application of three principles of human decision making. *American Psychologist, 26,* 180–188.

Dawes, R. M. (1979). The robust beauty of improper linear models in decision making. *American Psychologist, 34*(7), 571–582.

Dawes, R. M., & Corrigan, B. (1974). Linear models in decision making. *Psychological Bulletin, 81*(2), 95–106.

*DeFunis v. Odegaard,* 416 U.S. 312 (1974).

Demick, B. (2013, February 20). China college admissions bias is testing girls' patience. *Los Angeles Times.* Retrieved from http://www.latimes.com/news/nationworld/world/la-fg-china-female-students-20130221,0,3188288.story.

Denniston, L. (2016, June 23). *Opinion analysis: A brief respite for affirmative action?* (Blog post). Retrieved from http://www.scotusblog.com/2016/06/opinion-analysis-a-brief-respite-for-affirmative-action/.

Deresiewicz, W. (2014). *Excellent sheep: The miseducation of the American elite and the way to a meaningful life.* New York: Free Press.

DeSantis, N. (2012, October 5). Benefits of attending college outpace rising costs, report says. *Chronicle of Higher Education.* Retrieved from http://chronicle.com/blogs/ticker/benefits-of-attending-college-outpace-rising-costs-report-says/50104.

Dorans, N., & Moses, T. (2008). *SAT/ACT concordance 2008: Which score pair to concord?* (ETS Statistical Report No. SR 2008-092). Princeton, NJ: Educational Testing Service.

Downey, Matthew T. (1961). *Carl Campbell Brigham: Scientist and educator.* Princeton, NJ: Educational Testing Service.

Drum, K. (2007, May 14). Obama and affirmative action. *Washington Monthly.* Retrieved from http://www.washingtonmonthly.com/archives/individual/2007_05/011305.php.

Duckworth, A. L., & Yeager, D. S. (2015). Measurement matters: Assessing personal qualities other than cognitive ability for educational purposes. *Educational Researcher, 44,* 237–251.

Durán, G., & Wolf-Yadlin, R. (2011). A mathematical programming approach to applicant selection for a degree program based on affirmative action. *Interfaces, 41*(3), 278–288.

Dworkin, R. (1977, November 10). Why Bakke has no case. *New York Review of Books*. Retrieved from http://www.nybooks.com/articles/archives/1977/nov/10/why-bakke-has-no-case/.

Dworkin, R. (1998, November 5). Is affirmative action doomed? *New York Review of Books*. Retrieved from http://www.nybooks.com/articles/archives/1998/nov/05/is-affirmative-action-doomed/.

Education department challenges report on Harvard inquiry. (1991, March 27). *Chronicle of Higher Education*. Retrieved from http://chronicle.com/article/Education-Dept-Challenges/87439/.

Educational Testing Service. (1950). *Annual report to the board of trustees: 1949–1950*. Princeton, NJ: Author.

Educational Testing Service. (2009). *ETS guidelines for fairness review of assessments*. Princeton, NJ: Author.

Espenshade, T. J., & Chung, C. Y. (2005). The opportunity cost of admission preferences at elite universities. *Social Science Quarterly, 86*(2), 293–305.

Espenshade, T. J., & Chung, C. Y. (2012). Diversity outcomes of test-optional policies. In J. A. Soares (Ed.), *SAT wars: The case for test-optional admissions*, pp. 177–200. New York: Teachers College Press.

Espenshade, T. J., Chung, C. Y., & Walling, J. L. (2004). Admission preferences for minority students, athletes, and legacies at elite universities. *Social Science Quarterly, 85*(5), 1422–1446.

Espenshade, T. J., & Radford, A. W. (2009). *No longer separate, not yet equal*. Princeton, NJ: Princeton University Press.

Espinosa, L. L., Gaertner, M. N., & Orfield, G. (2015). *Race, class, and college access: Achieving diversity in a shifting legal landscape* (American Council on Education report). Retrieved from http://www.acenet.edu/news-room/Documents/Race-Class-and-College-Access-Achieving-Diversity-in-a-Shifting-Legal-Landscape.pdf.

Evangelauf, J. (1990, November 7). College Board to introduce new version of entrance exam. *Chronicle of Higher Education*. Retrieved from http://chronicle.com/article/College-Board-to-Introduce-New/86381/.

*Farmer v. Ramsay, et al.*, 159 F. Supp 2d 873 (D. Md. 2001).

Federal Trade Commission. (1978). *The effects of coaching on standardized admission examinations* (Staff memorandum of the Boston Regional Office of the Federal Trade Commission). Washington, DC: Author.

Federal Trade Commission. (1979). *Effects of coaching on standardized admission examinations* (Revised statistical analyses of data gathered by Boston Regional Office of the Federal Trade Commission). Washington, DC: Author.

Finn, C. E. (1999). Foreword. In Phelps, R. P., *Why testing experts hate testing* (Fordham report). Washington, DC: Thomas B. Fordham Foundation.

Fisher v. University of Texas at Austin, 570 U.S. (2013), Docket No. 11-345.

Fisher v. University of Texas at Austin, 579 U.S. (2016), Docket No. 14-981.

Fiske, E. B. (2001, January 7). Gaining admission: Athletes win preference. New York Times. Retrieved from http://www.nytimes.com/2001/01/07/education /gaining-admission-athletes-win-preference.html.

Flores, S. M., & Horn, C. L. (2015). Texas Top Ten Percent Plan: How it works, what are its limits, and recommendations to consider (Educational Testing Service issue brief). Retrieved from http://www.ets.org/Media/Research/pdf/flores_white _paper.pdf.

Freedman, D. A. 2002. The ecological fallacy. Berkeley: University of California. Retrieved from http://www.stat.berkeley.edu/~census/ecofall.txt.

Fremer, J. (2005). Foreword. In R. P. Phelps (Ed.), Defending standardized testing. Mahwah, NJ: Erlbaum.

Fuller, M. (1996, September 27). Lottery costs top medical student university place. TES Newspaper. Retrieved from https://www.tes.co.uk/article.aspx ?storycode=20337.

Fullinwider, R. K., & Lichtenberg, J. (2004). Leveling the playing field: Justice, politics, and college admissions. Lanham, MD: Rowman & Littlefield.

Fuess, C. M. (1950). The College Board: Its first fifty years. New York: Columbia University Press.

Gaertner, M. N. (2014). Advancing college access with class-based affirmative action: The Colorado case. In R. Kahlenberg (Ed.), The future of affirmative action: New paths to higher education diversity after Fisher v. University of Texas, pp. 175–186. Washington, DC: Century Foundation.

Gaertner, M. N., & Hart, M. (2013). Considering class: College access and diversity. Harvard Law and Policy Review, 7, 367–403.

Gaertner, M. N., & Hart, M. (2015). From access to success: Affirmative action outcomes in a class-based system. University of Colorado Law Review, 86(2), 431–475.

Gándara, P. (2004). Equitable access and academic preparation for higher education: Lessons learned from college access programs. In R. Zwick (Ed.), Rethinking the SAT: The future of standardized testing in university admissions, pp. 167–187. New York: RoutledgeFalmer.

Gándara, P., Moran, R., & Garcia, E. (2004). Legacy of Brown: Lau and language policy in the United States. Review of Research in Education, 28, 27–46.

Geiser, S., & Santelices, M. V. (2007). Validity of high-school grades in predicting student success beyond the freshman year (Research and Occasional Paper Series: CSHE.6.07). Berkeley: University of California, Center for Studies in Higher Education.

Geiser, S., with Studley, R. (2001, March 12). Relative contribution of high school grades, SAT I and SAT II scores in predicting success at UC: Preliminary findings

(Internal report). Oakland, CA: University of California Office of the President.

Geiser, S., with Studley, R. E. (2004). UC and the SAT: Predictive validity and differential impact of the SAT I and SAT II at the University of California. In R. Zwick (Ed.), *Rethinking the SAT: The future of standardized testing in university admissions*, pp. 125–153. New York: RoutledgeFalmer.

Gewertz, C. (2016, March 22). State solidarity erodes on Common-Core tests. *Education Week*. Retrieved from http://www.edweek.org/ew/articles/2016/03/23/state-solidarity-erodes-on-common-core-tests.html.

Giancola, J., & Kahlenberg, R. D. (2016). *True merit: Ensuring our brightest students have access to our best colleges and universities* (Jack Kent Cooke Foundation Report). Retrieved from http://outreach.jkcf.org/TrueMerit/?utm_source=all&utm_medium=all&utm_campaign=True_Merit.

Gilbert, J. E. (2006). Applications Quest: Computing diversity. *Communications of the ACM, 49*(3), 99–104.

Gilbert, J. E. (2008). Applications Quest: A case study on holistic diversity in admission. *Journal of College Admission, 199*, 12–18.

Gilbert, J. E., & Johnson, A. E. (2013). A study of admissions software for achieving diversity. *PsychNology Journal, 11*(1), 67–90.

Gilbert, J. E., & Lewis, C. W. (2008). An investigation of computational holistic evaluation of admissions applications for a minority focused STEM research program. *Journal of STEM Education, 9*(1–2), 40–47.

Ginder, S. A., Kelly-Reid, J. E., & Mann, F. B (2015). *Postsecondary institutions and cost of attendance in 2014–15; Degrees and other awards conferred, 2013–14; and 12-month enrollment, 2013–14: First look (preliminary data)* (NCES 2015-097). U.S. Department of Education. Washington, DC: National Center for Education Statistics. Retrieved from http://nces.ed.gov/pubs2016/2016005.pdf.

Glenn, D. (2004, June 1). Admissions questionnaire used to measure noncognitive traits is said to be nearly invalid. *Chronicle of Higher Education*. Retrieved from http://chronicle.com/article/Admissions-Questionnaire-Used/102723/.

Godfrey, K. E. (2011). *Investigating grade inflation and non-equivalence* (Research Report 2011-2). New York: College Board.

Golden, D. (2003a, February 20). Many colleges bend rules to admit rich applicants. *Wall Street Journal*. Retrieved at online.wsj.com/public/resources/documents/golden2.htm.

Golden, D. (2003b, October 29). Bill would make colleges report legacies and early admissions. *Wall Street Journal*. Retrieved at online.wsj.com/public/resources/document/Polk_Legacies.htm.

Golden, D. (2006). *The price of admission*. New York: Crown.

Golden, D. (2012). The preferences of privilege. In J. A. Soares (Ed.), *SAT wars: The case for test-optional admissions*, pp. 13–22. New York: Teachers College Press.

Goldman, A. H. (1976). Affirmative action. *Philosophy and Public Affairs, 5*(2), 178–195.

Goldman, A. H. (1977). Justice and hiring by competence. *Philosophical Quarterly, 14*(1), 17–28.

Goodman, R. (2014). What if there was a college-admissions lottery? *The Atlantic.* Retrieved from http://www.theatlantic.com/education/archive/2014/05/the-case-for-a-college-admissions-lottery/361585/.

Goodwin, B. (2011). Justice and the lottery. In P. Stone (Ed.), *Lotteries in public life: A reader,* pp. 105–125. Luton: Andrews UK.

Gose, B. (1999). Colleges experiment with an alternative to standardized tests in admissions. *Chronicle of Higher Education.* Retrieved from http://chronicle.com/article/Colleges-Experiment-With-an/112005/.

Gottlieb, E. (2001). Using integer programming to guide college admissions decisions: A preliminary report. *Journal of Computing Sciences in Colleges, 17*(2), 271–279.

Gough, H. G. (1962). Clinical versus statistical prediction in psychology. In L. Postman (Ed.), *Psychology in the making: Histories of selected research problems,* pp. 526–584. New York: Alfred A. Knopf.

*Gratz v. Bollinger,* 539 U.S. 244 (2003).

Greely, H. (2011). The equality of allocation by lot. In P. Stone (Ed.), *Lotteries in public life: A reader,* pp. 49–89. Luton: Andrews UK.

Grofman, B., & Merrill, S. (2004). Anticipating likely consequences of lottery-based affirmative action. *Social Science Quarterly, 85,* 1447–1468.

Gross, A. L., & Su, W. (1975). Defining a "fair" or "unbiased" selection model: A question of utilities. *Journal of Applied Psychology, 60,* 345–351.

*Grutter v. Bollinger,* 539 U.S. 306 (2003).

Guinier, L. (1997, June 24). The real bias in higher education. *New York Times,* A1.

Guinier, L. (2000). Confirmative action. *Law and Social Inquiry, 25,* 565–583.

Guinier, L. (2001, December 14). Colleges should take "confirmative action" in admissions. *Chronicle of Higher Education.* Retrieved from http://chronicle.com/article/Colleges-Should-Take/22060/.

Guinier, L. (2015). *The tyranny of the meritocracy.* Boston: Beacon Press.

Harberson, S. (2015, June 9). The truth about "holistic" college admissions. *Los Angeles Times.* Retrieved from http://touch.latimes.com/#section/-1/article/p2p-83735748/.

Harvard bias complaint dismissed. (2015, July 8). *Los Angeles Times,* A13.

Haycock, K., Lynch, M., & Engle, J. (2010). *Opportunity adrift: Our flagship universities are straying from their public mission.* Washington, DC: Education Trust.

Heil, S., Reisel, L., & Attewell, P. (2014). College selectivity and degree completion. *American Educational Research Journal, 51,* 913–935.

Helms, J. E. (2006). Fairness is not validity or cultural bias in racial-group assessment: A quantitative perspective. *American Psychologist, 61,* 845–859.

Hensley-Clancy, M. (2015, March 25). After flood of requests, elite colleges begin destroying admissions records. *BuzzFeed.* Retrieved from http://www .buzzfeed.com/mollyhensleyclancy/elite-colleges-are-now-destroying -admissions-records#.bwKoP3z8M9.

Hernández, M. (1997). *"A" is for admission: The insider's guide to getting into the Ivy League and other top colleges.* New York: Warner Books.

Hiss, W. C., & Franks, V. W. (2014). *Defining promise: Optional standardized testing polices in American college and university admissions.* Retrieved from http://www .nacacnet.org/research/research-data/nacac-research/Documents /DefiningPromise.pdf.

Hofstee, W. K. B. (2011). Allocation by lot: A conceptual and empirical analysis. In P. Stone (Ed.), *Lotteries in public life: A reader,* pp. 246–267. Luton: Andrews UK.

Hoover, E. (2004, June 11). SAT scores "launder" backgrounds of students, study finds. *Chronicle of Higher Education.* Retrieved from http://chronicle.com/article /SAT-Scores-Launder/14296/.

Hoover, E. (2012, May 16). With choice of new leader, College Board hopes to extend its reach. *Chronicle of Higher Education.* Retrieved from http://chronicle .com/article/College-Boards-Next-President/131901/.

Hoover, E. (2013, January 14). "Noncognitive" measures: The next frontier in college admissions. *Chronicle of Higher Education.* Retrieved from http:// chronicle.com/article/Noncognitive-Measures-The/136621/.

Hoover, E. (2013, April 29). Creating software to enhance admissions diversity. *Chronicle of Higher Education.* Retrieved from http://chronicle.com/article /Software-to-Enhance-Diversity/138789/.

Hoover, E. (2014, June 6). ACT exam will include new writing scores and readiness indicators. *Chronicle of Higher Education.* Retrieved from http:// chronicle.com/blogs/headcount/act-exam-will-include-new-writing-scores -readiness-indicators/38473?cid=wb&utm_source=wb&utm_medium=en.

Hoover, E. (2014, June 18). Hampshire College will go "test blind." *Chronicle of Higher Education.* Retrieved from http://chronicle.com/blogs/headcount /hampshire-college-will-go-test-blind/38563.

Hoover, E. (2014, September 24). Applicants to Bennington College may now "curate" their applications. *Chronicle of Higher Education.* Retrieved from http://chronicle.com/blogs/headcount/applicants-to-bennington-college -may-now-curate-their-applications/39089.

Hoover, E. (2016, January 20). Wanted: High-character students. *Chronicle of Higher Education.* Retrieved from http://chronicle.com/article/Wanted-High -Character/234972.

Hoover, E. (2016, April 19). 7 questions about a new test-prep venture. *Chronicle of Higher Education*. Retrieved from http://chronicle.com/article/7-Questions -About-a-New/236157.

Hoover, E., & Supiano, B. (2008, May 27). Wake Forest U. joins the ranks of test-optional colleges. *Chronicle of Higher Education*. Retrieved from http:// chronicle.com/article/Wake-Forest-U-Joins-the-Ranks/834/.

Horn, C. (2012). Percent plan admissions: Their strengths and challenges in furthering an equity agenda. *Pensamiento Educativo: Revista de Investigacion Educacional Latinoamericana, 49*(2), 31–45.

Hossler, D., & Kalsbeek, D. (2009). Admissions testing & institutional admissions processes. *College & University, 84*(4), 2–11.

Hout, M. (2005, May). *Berkeley's comprehensive review method for making freshman admissions decisions: An assessment*. Retrieved from http://academic-senate .berkeley.edu/sites/default/files/committees/aepe/hout_report_0.pdf.

Huckabee, C. (2012, December 19). Analysis adds to data showing the economic benefits of a college degree. *Chronicle of Higher Education*. Retrieved from http://chronicle.com/blogs/ticker/new-analysis-adds-to-data-showing-the -economic-benefits-of-a-college-degree/53267.

Hughes, T. (1998, February 18). *Admissions criteria: Standardized testing* (California State Senate Bill 1807). Legislative Counsel's Digest. Retrieved from http://www.sen.ca.gov.

Humphreys, L. G. (1952). Individual differences. *Annual Review of Psychology, 3,* 131–150.

Ingels, S., Planty, M., & Bozick, R. (2005). *A profile of the American high school senior in 2004: A first look—Initial results from the first follow-up of the Education Longitudinal Study of 2002* (NCES 2006-348). Washington, DC: National Center for Education Statistics.

Ingels, S. J., Pratt, D. J., Alexander, C. P., Bryan, M., Jewell, D. M. Lauff, E., Mattox, T. L., & Wilson, D. (2015). *Education Longitudinal Study of 2002 (ELS:2002) Postsecondary Education Transcript Study data file documentation* (NCES 2015-033). Washington, DC: National Center for Education Statistics. Retrieved from http://nces.ed.gov/pubsearch.

Ingels, S. J., Pratt, D. J., Wilson, D., Burns, L. J., Currivan, D., Rogers, J. E., & Hubbard-Bednasz, S. (2007). *Education Longitudinal Study of 2002: Base-year to second follow-up data file documentation* (NCES 2008-347). Washington, DC: National Center for Education Statistics.

Inzlicht, M., & Schmader, T. (Eds.). (2012). *Stereotype threat: Theory, processes, and application*. Oxford: Oxford University Press.

Jaschik, S. (1990, October 17). U.S. finds Harvard did not exclude Asian Americans. *Chronicle of Higher Education*. Retrieved from http://chronicle.com/article /US-Finds-Harvard-Did-Not/86651/.

Jaschik, S. (2007, September 7). Who gets in: And why. *Inside Higher Ed.* Retrieved from www.insidehighered.com/news/2007/09/07/class.

Jaschik, S. (2013, February 27). A new SAT. *Inside Higher Ed.* Retrieved from www .insidehighered.com/news/2013/02/27/college-board-announces-plans -redesign-sat#ixzz2RDEqzNSN.

Jencks, C. (1989). If not tests, then what? In B. R. Gifford (Ed.), *Test policy and test performance: Education, language, and culture*, pp. 116–121. Boston: Kluwer Academic.

Johnson, V. E. (1997). An alternative to traditional GPA for evaluating student performance. *Statistical Science, 12* (4), 251–278.

Jones, S. (2013). "Ensure that you stand out from the crowd": A corpus-based analysis of personal statements according to applicants' school type. *Comparative Education Review, 57*(3), 397–423.

Jump, J. J. (1988, April 27). The only fair way for elite colleges to choose their freshman classes is by random selection. *Chronicle of Higher Education,* A52.

Kahlenberg, R. D. (1996). Class-based affirmative action. *California Law Review,* 84(4), 1037–1099.

Kahlenberg, R. D. (2012). *A better affirmative action.* New York: Century Foundation.

Kane, M. T. (2013). *The evaluation of admissions testing programs.* Unpublished manuscript, Educational Testing Service.

Kane, M. T., & Mroch, A. A. (2010). Modeling group differences in OLS and orthogonal regression: Implications for differential validity studies. *Applied Measurement in Education, 23,* 215–241.

Kane, T. J. (1998). Racial and ethnic preferences in college admissions. In C. Jencks & M. Phillips (Eds.), *The black-white test score gap,* pp. 431–456. Washington, DC: Brookings Institution Press.

Kaplan, J. (2005). The effectiveness of SAT coaching on math SAT scores. *Chance,* 18(2), 25–34.

Karabel, J. (2005). *The chosen.* Boston: Houghton Mifflin.

Karabel, J. (2007, September 24). The new college try. *New York Times.* Retrieved from http://www.nytimes.com/2007/09/24/opinion/24karabel .html?_r=1.

*Katzenbach v. Morgan,* 384 U.S. 641 (1966).

Kautz, T., Heckman, J. J., Diris, R., ter Weel, B., & Borghans, L. (n.d.). *Fostering and measuring skills: Improving cognitive and non-cognitive skills to promote lifetime success.* Paris: Organisation for Economic Co-operation and Development (OECD). Retrieved from http://www.oecd.org/edu/ceri/Fostering-and -Measuring-Skills-Improving-Cognitive-and-Non-Cognitive-Skills-to -Promote-Lifetime-Success.pdf.

Kidder, W. C., & Gándara, P. (2015). *Two decades after the affirmative action ban: Evaluating the University of California's race-neutral efforts.* Educational Testing Service Issue Brief. Retrieved from http://www.ets.org/Media/Research/pdf/kidder_paper.pdf.

Kidder, W. C., & Rosner, J. (2002). How the SAT creates built-in headwinds: An educational and legal analysis of disparate impact. *Santa Clara Law Review, 43*(1), 130–212.

Klitgaard, R. E. (1985). *Choosing elites.* New York: Basic Books.

Kobrin, J. L., Patterson, B. F., Shaw, E. J., Mattern, K. D., & Barbuti, S. M. (2008). *Validity of the SAT for predicting first-year college grade point average* (College Board Research Report No. 2008-5). New York: College Board.

Kohn, A. (2001, March 9). Two cheers for an end to the SAT. *Chronicle of Higher Education,* B12.

Krauthammer, C. (2001, July 16). Dissecting the convoluted state of affirmative action. *Chicago Tribune.* Retrieved from http://articles.chicagotribune.com/2001-07-16/news/0107160236_1_affirmative-action-hispanic-discrimination.

Kreiter, C. D. (2002). The use of constrained optimization to facilitate admission decisions. *Academic Medicine, 77*(2), 148–151.

Kreiter, C. D., & Solow, C. (2002). A statistical technique for the development of an alternate list when using constrained optimization to make admission decisions. *Teaching and Learning in Medicine: An International Journal, 14*(1), 29–33.

Kreiter, C. D., Stansfield, B., James, P. A., & Solow, C. (2003). A model for diversity in admissions: A review of issues and methods and an experimental approach. *Teaching and Learning in Medicine: An International Journal, 15*(2), 116–122.

Kuncel, N. R., Klieger, D. M., Connelly, B. S., & Ones, D. S. (2013). Mechanical versus clinical data combination in selection and admissions decisions: A meta-analysis. *Journal of Applied Psychology, 98*(6), 1060–1072.

Kutner, M. H., Nachtsheim, C., & Neter, J. (2004). *Applied linear regression models.* Boston: McGraw-Hill/Irwin.

Kyllonen, P. C. (2008). *The research behind the ETS Personal Potential Index (PPI).* Princeton, NJ: Educational Testing Service.

Kyllonen, P. C. (2012). The importance of higher education and the role of noncognitive attributes in college success. *Pensamiento Educativo: Revista de Investigación Educacional Latinoamericana, 49*(2), 84–100.

Laird, B. (2005a). *The case for affirmative action in university admissions.* Berkeley, CA: Bay Tree.

Laird, R. (2005b). What is it we think we are trying to fix and how should we fix it? A view from the admissions office. In W. J. Camara & E. W. Kimmel

(Eds.), *Choosing students: Higher education admissions tools for the 21st century*, pp. 13–32. Mahwah, NJ: Erlbaum.

Landy, D., & Sigall, H. (1974). Beauty is talent: Task evaluation as a function of the performer's physical attractiveness. *Journal of Personality and Social Psychology, 29*(3), 299–304.

*Lassiter v. Northampton Board of Education*, 360 U.S. 45 (1959).

Lauff, E., Ingels, S. J., & Christopher, E. (2014). *Education Longitudinal Study of 2002 (ELS:2002): A first look at 2002 high school sophomores 10 years later* (NCES 2014-363). Washington, DC: National Center for Education Statistics. Retrieved from http://nces.ed.gov/pubsearch.

Lawrence, I., Rigol, G., Van Essen, T., & Jackson, C. (2004). A historical perspective on the content of the SAT. In R. Zwick (Ed.), *Rethinking the SAT: The future of standardized testing in university admissions*, pp. 57–74. New York: RoutledgeFalmer.

Lawton, M. (1996, October 9). PSAT to add writing test to settle bias case. *Education Week*. Retrieved from http://www.edweek.org/ew/articles/1996/10/09/06psat.h16.html?qs=PSAT+to+add+writing+test.

Lee, V. E., & Burkam, D. T. (2002). *Inequality at the starting gate: Social background differences in achievement as children begin school*. Washington, DC: Economic Policy Institute.

Lemann, N. (1999). *The big test: The secret history of the American meritocracy*. New York: Farrar, Straus & Giroux.

Lewin, T. (2012, April 1). At the University of Texas, admissions as a mystery. *New York Times*. Retrieved from http://www.nytimes.com/2012/04/02/education/university-of-texas-mysterious-admissions-process.html?emc=eta1.

Lewin, T. (2014, July 15). Appeals panel upholds race in admissions for university. *New York Times*. Retrieved from http://www.nytimes.com/2014/07/16/us/appeals-panel-upholds-race-in-admissions-for-university.html?emc=eta1.

Linn, R. L. (2009). Comments on Atkinson and Geiser: Considerations for college admissions testing. *Educational Researcher, 38*(9), 677–679.

Linn, R. L., & Werts, C. E. (1971). Considerations for studies of test bias. *Journal of Educational Measurement, 8*, 1–4.

Lohman, D. F. (2004). Aptitude for college: The importance of reasoning tests for minority admissions. In R. Zwick (Ed.), *Rethinking the SAT: The future of standardized testing in university admissions*, pp. 41–55. New York: RoutledgeFalmer.

Long, M. C. (2015). *The promise and peril for universities using correlates of race in admissions in response to the Grutter and Fisher decisions* (Educational Testing Service issue brief). Retrieved from http://www.ets.org/Media/Research/pdf/long_white_paper.pdf.

Lorin, J. (2015, March 31). Harvard, Stanford reject 95 percent of applicants this year. *Bloomberg Business*. Retrieved from http://www.bloomberg.com/news /articles/2015-03-31/spurned-ivy-league-hopefuls-have-lots-of-company-in -their-misery.

Lorin, J. (2015, May 15). Harvard faces admissions bias complaint from Asian-Americans. *Bloomberg Business*. Retrieved from http://www.bloomberg .com/news/articles/2015-05-15/harvard-faces-admissions-bias-complaint -from-asian-americans.

Lucido, J. A. (2013, January). Lessons from the NFL for managing college enrollment. Center for American Progress. Retrieved from http://files.eric .ed.gov/fulltext/ED539755.pdf.

Lyall, S. (2014, April 27). Reporter digging into scandal hits a university's raw nerve. *New York Times*, Sports section, 1–2.

MacLaury, J. (2010). President Kennedy's E.O. 10925: Seedbed of affirmative action. In *Federal History 2010*. Retrieved from http://shfg.org/shfg/wp-content /uploads/2011/01/4-MacLaury-design4-new_Layout-1.pdf.

Malouff, J. (2008). Bias in grading. *College Teaching, 56*(3), 191–192.

Mank, B. C. (2008). Title VI. In M. B. Gerrard & S. R Foster (Eds.), *The law of environmental justice: Theories and procedures to address disproportionate risks* (2nd ed.), pp. 23–66. Chicago: American Bar Association.

Manning, W. H. (1977). The pursuit of fairness in admissions to higher education. In *Selective admissions in higher education* (Carnegie Council on Policy Studies in Higher Education report), pp. 19–64. San Francisco: Jossey-Bass.

Manski, C. F., & Wise, S. A. (1983). *College choice in America*. Cambridge, MA: Harvard University Press.

Mare, R. D. (2012). *Holistic review in freshman admissions at UCLA*. Retrieved from http://www.senate.ucla.edu/committees/.

Marin, P., & Lee, E. K. (2003). *Appearance and reality in the sunshine state: The Talented 20 program in Florida*. Cambridge, MA: Civil Rights Project at Harvard University.

Matloff, N. (1995, January 24). Why not a lottery to get into UC? *Los Angeles Times*, 7.

Mattern, K. D., Patterson, B. F., Shaw, E. J., Kobrin, J. L., & Barbuti, S. M. (2008). *Differential validity and prediction of the SAT* (College Board Research Report No. 2008-4). New York: College Board.

Mattern, K. D., Patterson, B. F., & Wyatt, J. N. (2013). *How useful are traditional admission measures in predicting graduation within four years?* (College Board Research Report No. 2013-1). New York: College Board.

Mattern, K. D., Shaw, E. J., & Marini, J. (2013). *Does college readiness translate to college completion?* (College Board Research Note No. 2013-9). New York: College Board.

Mattern, K. D., Shaw, E. J., & Williams, F. E. (2008). *Examining the relationship between the SAT, high school measures of academic performance, and socioeconomic status: Turning our attention to the unit of analysis* (College Board Research Note No. RN-36). New York: College Board.

McLoyd, V. C. (1998). Socioeconomic disadvantage and child development. *American Psychologist, 53*(2), 185–204.

McPherson, M. S., & Schapiro, M. O. (2006). *College access: Opportunity or privilege.* New York: College Board.

Mead, S. (2010, December 17). Admissions lotteries: Not just about fairness. *Education Week.* Retrieved from http://blogs.edweek.org/edweek/sarameads _policy_notebook/2010/12/admissions_lotteries_not_just_about_fairness .html?intc=es.

Meehl, P. E. (1954). *Clinical versus statistical prediction.* Minneapolis: University of Minnesota Press.

Meijler, F. L., & Vreeken, J. (1975, January 17). Lottery admissions system in the Netherlands [Letter to the editor]. *Science, 114.*

Messick, S. (1964). Personality measurement and college performance. In *Proceedings of the 1963 Invitational Conference on Testing Problems*, pp. 110–129. Princeton, NJ: Educational Testing Service.

Meyer, H.-D. (2013). Reasoning about fairness in access to higher education: Common sense, normative, and institutional perspectives. In H.-D. Meyer, E. P. St. John, M. Chankseliani, & L. Uribe (Eds.), *Fairness in access to a higher education in a global perspective*, pp. 15–40. Rotterdam: Sense Publishers.

Montgomery, P., & Lilly, J. (2012). Systematic reviews of the effects of preparatory courses on university entrance examinations in high school-age students. *International Journal of Social Welfare, 21*, 3–12.

Moores, J. (2003, October 23). *A preliminary report on the University of California, Berkeley admission process for 2002.* Regents of The University of California.

Moores, J. (2004, March 29). College capers. *Forbes.* Retrieved from www.forbes .com/forbes/2004/0329/040.html.

Moss, G. L., Chippendale, E. K., Mershon, C. W., & Carney, T. (2012). Effects of a coaching class on the ACT scores of students at a large Midwest high school. *Journal of College Admission, 217*, 16–23.

Nakanishi, D. T. (1989, Nov/Dec). A quota on excellence. *Change, 21*(6), 38–47.

National Association for College Admission Counseling. (2003). *Diversity and college admission in 2003: A survey report.* Arlington, VA: Author.

National Association for College Admission Counseling. (2008). *Report of the Commission on the Use of Standardized Tests in Undergraduate Admission.* Arlington, VA: Author.

National Center for Education Statistics. (2012). *The nation's report card: Science in action: Hands-on and interactive computer tasks from the 2009 science assessment*

(NCES 2012-468). Washington, D.C.: Institute of Education Sciences, U.S. Department of Education.

National Center for Education Statistics. (2014). *Digest of education statistics.* Retrieved from http://nces.ed.gov/programs/digest/2014menu_tables.asp.

National Center for Education Statistics. (2015a). *The condition of education 2015.* Retrieved from http://nces.ed.gov/pubs2015/2015144.pdf.

National Center for Education Statistics. (2015b). *Common core of data.* Retrieved from http://nces.ed.gov/ccd/tables/ACGR_RE_and_characteristics_2013-14 .asp.

New York reaches deal with Cooper Union, plaintiffs. (2015, September 2). *Diverse Issues in Higher Education.* Retrieved from http://diverseeducation .com/article/77609/.

Nieli, R. K. (2013, January 10). Asians as the new Jews, Jews as the new WASPs. *Minding the Campus.* Retrieved from http://www.mindingthecampus.org/2013 /01/asians_as_the_new_jewsjews_as_/.

Not educating the masses. (2014, January 4). *The Economist, 33.*

Office of Educational Research and Improvement of the U.S. Department of Education. (1994). *What do student grades mean? Differences across schools.* Retrieved from http://www2.ed.gov/pubs/OR/ResearchRpts/grades.html.

Office of Technology Assessment. (1992). *Testing in American schools: Asking the right questions.* Washington, DC: U.S. Government Printing Office.

*Oregon v. Mitchell,* 400 US 112 (1970).

Organisation for Economic Co-operation and Development. (2010). *PISA 2009 results: Overcoming social background—Equity in learning opportunities and outcomes* (Vol. 2). Retrieved from http://dx.doi.org/10.1787/9789264091504-en.

Owings, J., McMillen, M., & Burkett, J. (1995). *Making the cut: Who meets highly selective college entrance criteria?* (NCES 95-732). National Center for Education Statistics. Retrieved from http://nces.ed.gov/pubs95/95732.pdf.

Pashley, P. J., & Thornton, A. E. (1999). *Crafting an incoming law school class: Preliminary results* (Law School Admission Council Research Report 99-01). Newtown, PA: Law School Admission Council.

Pashley, P. J., Thornton, A. E., & Duffy, J. R. (2005). *Access and diversity in law school admissions.* In W. J. Camara & E. W. Kimmel (Eds.), *Choosing students: Higher education admissions tools for the 21st century,* pp. 231–249. Mahwah, NJ: Erlbaum.

Pennington, B. (2011, December 24). Before recruiting in Ivy League, applying some math. *New York Times.* Retrieved from http://www.nytimes.com/2011 /12/25/sports/before-athletic-recruiting-in-the-ivy-league-some-math.html ?pagewanted=all&_r=0.

Pérez-Peña, R. (2015, January 16). Students gain access to files on admission to Stanford. *New York Times.* Retrieved from http://www.nytimes.com/2015/01 /17/us/students-gain-access-to-files-on-admission-to-stanford.html?_r=0.

Perlmutter, D. D. (2004, December 10). Are we grading on the curves? *Chronicle Review, 51*(16), B13.

Perna, L., Li, C., Walsh, E., & Raible, S. (2010). The status of equity for Hispanics in public higher education in Florida and Texas. *Journal of Hispanic Higher Education, 9*(2), 145–166.

Pernell, B. D. (2015). Aligning "educational necessity" with Title VI: An enhanced regulatory role for executive agencies in Title VI disparate impact enforcement. *New York University Law Review, 90,* 1369–1408.

Perry, D. A., Brown, M. T., & Sawrey, B. A. (2004). Rethinking the use of undergraduate admissions tests: The case of the University of California. In R. Zwick (Ed.), *Rethinking the SAT: The future of standardized testing in university admissions,* pp. 103–124. New York: RoutledgeFalmer.

Petersen, N. S. (1976). An expected utility model for "optimal" selection. *Journal of Educational Statistics, 1,* 333–358.

Petersen, N. S., & Novick, M. R. (1976). An evaluation of some models for culture-fair selection. *Journal of Educational Measurement, 13,* 3–29.

Phillips, A. M. (2011, July 20). Bronx charter school disciplined over admissions methods. *New York Times.* Retrieved from http://www.nytimes.com/2011/07/21/nyregion/bronx-charter-school-disciplined-over-admissions.html.

Pinker, S. (2014, September 4). The trouble with Harvard. *New Republic.* Retrieved from http://www.newrepublic.com/article/119321/harvard-ivy-league-should-judge-students-standardized-tests.

Pitsch, M. (1990, October 10). College Board trustees postpone vote on S.A.T. revision. *Education Week.* Retrieved from http://www.edweek.org/ew/ew_printstory.cfm?slug=10370037.h10.

President emeritus talks about *The Big Test* and other timely subjects. (1999, October 14). *ETS Access, 10,* 2.

President Lyndon B. Johnson's commencement address at Howard University: "To fulfill these rights." (1965, June 4). LBJ Presidential Library. Retrieved from http://www.lbjlib.utexas.edu/johnson/archives.hom/speeches.hom/650604.asp.

Pulley, J. L. (2000, June 23). A $1-billion experiment seeks a new way to identify talented minority students. *Chronicle of Higher Education,* A42.

Powell, M. (2016, March 6). The tragedy of a Hall of Fame coach and his star recruit. *New York Times.* Retrieved from http://www.nytimes.com/2016/03/06/sports/ncaabasketball/smu-keith-frazier-larry-brown-corruption.html.

Quirk, M. (2005, November). The best class money can buy. *The Atlantic.* Retrieved from http://www.theatlantic.com/magazine/archive/2005/11/the-best-class-money-can-buy/304307/2/.

Radunzel, J., & Noble, J. (2012a). *Tracking 2003 ACT®-tested high school graduates: College readiness, enrollment, and long-term success.* ACT Research Report 2012(2). Iowa City: ACT, Inc.

Radunzel, J., & Noble, J. (2012b). *Predicting long-term college success through degree completion using ACT® composite score, ACT benchmarks, and high school grade point average.* ACT Research Report 2012(5). Iowa City: ACT, Inc.

Ramsey, J. (2008, August). *Noncognitive assessment and college success: The case of the Gates Millennium Scholars* (Issue brief). Washington, DC: Institute for Higher Education Policy.

Raudenbush, S. W., & Bryk, A. S. (2002). *Hierarchical linear models: Applications and data analysis methods.* (2nd ed.). Newbury Park, CA: Sage.

Rauschenberg, S. (2014). How consistent are course grades? An examination of differential grading. *Education Policy Analysis Archives, 22*(92). http://dx.doi.org /10.14507/epaa.v22n92.2014.

Rawls, J. (1999). *A theory of justice* (revision of 1971 edition). Cambridge, MA: Belknap Press of Harvard University Press.

Rebbapragada, S., Basu, A., & Semple, J. (2010). Data mining and revenue management methodologies in college admissions. *Communications of the ACM, 53*(4), 128–133.

Reinhold, R. (1970, March 13). College is prize in a hard game. *New York Times,* 41, 48.

Repairing the rungs on the ladder. (2013, February 9). *The Economist,* 12,14.

Reumer, C., & van der Wende, M. (2010). *Excellence and diversity: The emergence of selective admission policies in Dutch higher education: A case study on Amsterdam University College* (Research and Occasional Papers Series: CSHE 15.10). Berkeley, CA: Center for Studies in Higher Education, UC Berkeley.

Ricks College decides not to use lottery in admissions. (1996, October 4). *Chronicle of Higher Education.* Retrieved from http://chronicle.com/article /Ricks-College-Decides-Not-to/74871/.

Rigol, G. W. (2003). *Admissions decision-making models.* New York: College Entrance Examinations Board. Retrieved from http://research.collegeboard .org/publications/content/2012/05/admissions-decision-making-models -how-us-institutions-higher-education.

Robbins, S. B., Allen, J., Casillas, A., Peterson, C. H., & Le, H. (2006). Unraveling the differential effects of motivational and skills, social, and self-management measures from traditional predictors of college outcomes. *Journal of Educational Psychology, 98,* 598–616.

Robbins, S. B., Lauver, K., Le, H., Davis, D., Langley, R., & Carlstrom, A. (2004). Do psychosocial and study skill factors predict college outcomes? A meta-analysis. *Psychological Bulletin, 130*(2), 261–288.

Roberts, W. (1969, Nov.–Dec.). Federal City: Prospects for the common college. *Change in Higher Education, 1*(6), 44–47, 50–52.

Rooney, C., with Schaeffer, B. (1998). *Test scores do not equal merit: Enhancing equity & excellence in college admissions by deemphasizing SAT and ACT results.* Cambridge, MA: FairTest.

Rosen, A. (2013, August 20). Think outside the quad. *Los Angeles Times,* A13.

Rothstein, J. M. (2004). College performance and the SAT. *Journal of Econometrics, 121,* 297–317.

Sackett, P. R. (2005). The performance-diversity tradeoff in admission testing. In W. J. Camara & E. W. Kimmel (Eds.), *Choosing students: Higher education admissions tools for the 21st century,* pp. 109–125. Mahwah, NJ: Erlbaum.

Sackett, P. R., Kuncel, N. R., Arneson, J. J., Cooper, S. R., & Waters, S. D. (2009). Does socioeconomic status explain the relationship between admissions tests and post-secondary academic performance? *Psychological Bulletin, 135,* 1–22.

Sackett, P. R., Kuncel, N. R., Beatty, A. S., Rigdon, J. L., Shen, W., & Kiger, T. B. (2012). The role of socioeconomic status in SAT-grade relationships and in college admissions decisions. *Psychological Science, 23*(9), 1000–1007.

Sackett, P. R., & Wilk, S. L. (1994). Within-group norming and other forms of score adjustment in preemployment testing. *American Psychologist, 49,* 929–954.

Sacks, P. (n.d.). Class struggle. *The Nation.* Retrieved from www.thenation.com /authors/peter-sacks#axzz2YqTPrNTC.

Sacks, P. (1997). Standardized testing: Meritocracy's crooked yardstick. *Change, 29,* 25–31.

Sandel, M. J. (2009). *Justice: What's the right thing to do?* New York: Farrar, Straus & Giroux.

Sander, Richard (2012). The consideration of race in UCLA undergraduate admissions. Retrieved from http://www.seaphe.org/pdf/uclaadmissions .pdf.

Sarbin, T. R. (1943). A contribution to the study of actuarial and individual methods of prediction. *American Journal of Sociology, 48,* 593–602.

Saslow, L. (1989, May 7). Schools say inflated grades cut grants. *New York Times.* Retrieved from http://www.nytimes.com/1989/05/07/nyregion/schools-say -inflated-grades-cut-grants.html?src=pm.

Schaeffer, R. (2012). Test scores do not equal merit. In J. A. Soares (Ed.), *SAT wars: The case for test-optional admissions,* pp. 153–168. New York: Teachers College Press.

Schevitz, T. (2003, November 8). Regent ties dropout rate to admissions policy. *San Francisco Chronicle.* Retrieved from http://www.sfgate.com /education/article/Regent-ties-dropout-rate-to-admissions-policy-2549827 .php#page-1.

Schmidt, P. (2014, November 18). Lawsuits against Harvard and UNC-Chapel Hill urge an end to race-conscious admissions. *Chronicle of Higher Education.* Retrieved from http://chronicle.com/article/Lawsuits-Against-Harvard-and /150113/.

Schmitt, C. M. (2009). *Documentation for the restricted-use NCES-Barron's admissions competiveness index data files* (NCES 2010-330). Washington DC: National Center for Education Statistics.

Schmitt, N. (2012). Development of rationale and measures of noncognitive college student potential. *Educational Psychologist, 47*(1), 18–29.

Schmitt, N., Keeney, J., Oswald, F. L., Pleskac, T. J., Billington, A. Q., Sinha, R., & Zorzie, M. (2009). Prediction of 4-year college student performance using cognitive and noncognitive predictors and the impact on demographic status of admitted students. *Journal of Applied Psychology, 94*(6), 1479–1497.

*Schuette v. Coalition to Defend Affirmative Action,* 572 U.S. (2014), Docket No. 12-682.

Schwartz, B. (2005, February 25). Top colleges should select randomly from a pool of "good enough." *Chronicle of Higher Education.* Retrieved from http://www.chronicle.com/article/Top-Colleges-Should-Select/14215/.

Schwartz, B. (2012, July). Lotteries for college admissions. *The Atlantic.* Retrieved from http://www.theatlantic.com/magazine/archive/2012/07/lotteries-for -college-admissions/309026/.

Sedlacek, W. E. (1987). Black students on white campuses: 20 years of research. *Journal of College Student Personnel, 28,* 484–495.

Sedlacek, W. E. (1990). Noncognitive Questionnaire (revised 12/90). Retrieved from http://www.williamsedlacek.info/publications/surveys/universityof maryland.html.

Sedlacek, W. E. (1998, Winter). Multiple choices for standardized tests. *Priorities, 10,* 1–15.

Sedlacek, W. E. (2005). The case for noncognitive measures. In W. J. Camara & E. W. Kimmel (Eds.), *Choosing students: Higher education admissions tools for the 21st century,* pp. 177–193. Mahwah, NJ: Erlbaum.

Selingo, J. (2000, June 2). What states aren't saying about the "x-percent solu- tion." *Chronicle of Higher Education.* Retrieved from http://chronicle.com/article /What-States-Arent-Saying/33201/.

Shaw, E. J., Marini, J. P., Beard, J., Shmueli, D., Young, L., & Ng, H. (2016). *The redesigned SAT® pilot predictive validity study: A first look* (College Board Report 2016-1). New York: College Board.

Sherley, J. L. (2007, June 22). The utility of standardized tests [Letter to the editor]. *Science,* 1695–1696.

Shyong, F. (2015, February 22). Struggling with a new diversity. *Los Angeles Times,* B1, B6.

Silver, N. (2012). *The signal and the noise: Why so many predictions fail—But some don't.* New York: Penguin.

Sirin, S. R. (2005).Socioeconomic status and academic achievement: A meta-analytic review of research. *Review of Educational Research, 75,* 417–453.

Smith, D. G. (1997). *Diversity works: The emerging picture of how students benefit.* Washington, DC: Association of American Colleges and Universities.

Soares, J. A. (2009). Review of "Creating a class: College admissions and the education of elites," by Mitchell L. Stevens. *American Journal of Sociology, 114*(5), 1553–1555.

Soares, J. A. (2012). Introduction. In J. A. Soares (Ed.), *SAT wars: The case for test-optional admissions,* pp. 1–9. New York: Teachers College Press.

Sparks, S. D. (2015, June 2). "Nation's report card" to gather data on grit, mindset. *Education Week.* Retrieved from http://www.edweek.org/ew/articles/2015/06/03/nations-report-card-to-gather-data-on.html?tkn=RSTFbRArDwSbeDRVxoQODjZEnOJKxZSOxtak&print=1.

Starkman, R. (2013, August 1). Confessions of an application reader. *New York Times.* Retrieved from http://www.nytimes.com/2013/08/04/education/edlife/lifting-the-veil-on-the-holistic-process-at-the-university-of-california-berkeley.html?emc=eta1&_r=0.

Stasz, C., & van Stolk, C. (2007). *The use of lottery systems in school admissions.* Santa Monica, CA: RAND Europe.

Steele, C. M. (1999, August). Thin ice: Stereotype threat and black college students. *The Atlantic* [Online]. Retrieved from http://www.theatlantic.com/magazine/archive/1999/08/thin-ice-stereotype-threat-and-black-college-students/304663/.

Steele, S. (2001, February 7). X-percent plans: After preferences, more race games. *National Review, 22,* 24.

Stein, Morris I. (1963). *Personality measures in admissions.* Princeton, NJ: College Entrance Examination Board.

Steinberg, J. (2009, July 18). Before college, costly advice just on getting in. *New York Times.* Retrieved from http://www.nytimes.com/2009/07/19/education/19counselor.html?pagewanted=all.

Stemler, S. E. (2012). What should university admissions tests predict? *Educational Psychologist, 47*(1), 5–17.

Sternberg, R. J. (2005). Augmenting the SAT through assessment of analytical, practical, and creative skills. In W. J. Camara & E. W. Kimmel (Eds.), *Choosing students,* pp. 159–176. Mahwah, NJ: Erlbaum.

Sternberg, R. J. (2009). The Rainbow and Kaleidoscope projects: A new psychological approach to undergraduate admissions. *European Psychologist, 14*(4), 279–287.

Sternberg, R. J. (2010). *College admissions for the 21st century.* Cambridge, MA: Harvard University Press.

Sternberg, R. J., Bonney, C. R., Gabora, L, & Merrifield, M. (2012). WICS: A model for college and university admissions. *Educational Psychologist, 47*(1), 30–41.

Sternberg, R. J., & The Rainbow Project Collaborators. (2006). The Rainbow Project: Enhancing the SAT through assessments of analytical, practical, and creative skills. *Intelligence, 34*(4), 321–350.

Stevens, M. L. (2007). *Creating a class.* Cambridge, MA: Harvard University Press.

Stewart, J. B. (2013, May 10). How Cooper Union's endowment failed in its mission. *New York Times.* Retrieved from http://www.nytimes.com/2013/05/11/business/how-cooper-unions-endowment-failed-in-its-mission.html?_r=0.

Stone, P. (2011). Introduction. In P. Stone (Ed.), *Lotteries in public life: A reader,* pp. iii–xxxii. Luton: Andrews UK.

Stone, P. (2013). Higher education by the luck of the draw. *Comparative Education Review, 57*(3), 577–599.

Stricker, L. J., Rock, D. A., Burton, N. W., Muraki, E., & Jirele, T. J. (1994). Adjusting college grade point average criteria for variations in grading standards: A comparison of methods. *Journal of Applied Psychology, 79* (2), 178—183.

Studley, R. E. (2004). Inequality, student achievement, and college admissions: A remedy for underrepresentation. In R. Zwick (Ed.), *Rethinking the SAT: The future of standardized testing in university admissions,* pp. 321–343. New York: RoutledgeFalmer.

Sturm, S., & Guinier, L. (2000). The future of affirmative action. *Boston Review.* Retrieved from http://bostonreview.net/forum/susan-sturm-lani-guinier-future-affirmative-action.

Taylor, H. C., & Russell, J. T. (1939). The relationship of validity coefficients to the practical effectiveness of tests in selection: Discussion and tables. *Journal of Applied Psychology, 23,* 565–578.

Terenzini, P. T., Cabrera, A. F., Colbeck, C. L., Stefani, A. B., & Parente, J. M. (2001). Racial and ethnic diversity in the classroom: Does it promote student learning? *Journal of Higher Education, 72,* 509–531.

Terris, W. (1997). The traditional regression model for measuring test bias is incorrect and biased against minorities. *Journal of Business and Psychology, 12,* 25–37.

Thomas, L. L., Kuncel, N. R., & Credé, M. (2007). Noncognitive variables in college admissions: The case of the Non-Cognitive Questionnaire. *Educational and Psychological Measurement, 67*(4), 635–657.

Thresher, B. A. (1989). *College admissions and the public interest.* New York: College Entrance Examination Board. [reissue of a 1966 monograph]

Toutkoushian, R. K., & Paulsen, M. B. (2016). *The economics of higher education: Background, concepts & applications.* Dordrecht, The Netherlands: Springer.

Tracey, T. J., & Sedlacek, W. E. (1984). Noncognitive variables in predicting academic success by race. *Measurement and Evaluation in Guidance, 16* (4), 171–178.

Tracey, T. J., & Sedlacek, W. E. (1985). The relationship of noncognitive variables to academic success: A longitudinal comparison by race. *Journal of College Student Personnel, 26,* 405–410.

Trounson, R. (2003, October 17). UC Berkeley admissions dispute becomes heated. *Los Angeles Times.* Retrieved from articles.latimes.com/2003/oct/17/local/me-ucletter17.

Underwood, B. D. (1979). Law and the crystal ball: Predicting behavior with statistical inference and individualized judgment. *Yale Law Journal, 88,* 1408–1448.

University of California. (2001). *Comprehensive review.* Retrieved from www.ucop.edu/news/factsheets/2001/comprev.pdf.

University of California Office of the President. (2013). *The University of California statistical summary of students and staff: Fall 2013.* Retrieved from http://legacy-its.ucop.edu/uwnews/stat/statsum/fall2013/statsumm2013.pdf.

University of California Office of the Vice President, Student Affairs & Office of the General Counsel. (2008, May). *Race, sex and disparate impact: Legal and policy considerations regarding University of California admissions and scholarships* (Briefing report for the Committee on Educational Policy). Retrieved from http://regents.universityofcalifornia.edu/regmeet/may08/e2attach.pdf.

*University of California Regents v. Bakke,* 438 U.S. 265 (1978). FindLaw. Retrieved from http://laws.findlaw.com/us/438/265.html.

U. of I. opens doors for 839 barred by admissions lottery. (1969, December 13). *Chicago Tribune.* Retrieved from http://archives.chicagotribune.com/1969/12/13/page/1/article/u-of-i-opens-doors-for-839-barred-by-admissions-lottery.

U.S. Government Publishing Office. (2005). *Code of federal regulations,* Title 34, Subtitle B, Chapter 1, Section 100.3: Discrimination prohibited (7-1-05 edition). Retrieved from https://www.gpo.gov/fdsys/pkg/CFR-2005-title34-vol1/pdf/CFR-2005-title34-vol1-sec100-3.pdf.

Van Buskirk, P. (2006, October 6). A call for transparency in college admission. *Inside Higher Ed.* Retrieved from http://www.insidehighered.com/views/2006/10/06/vanbuskirk#ixzz30VIyuE5P.

Wainer, H., & Brown, L. M. (2007). Three statistical paradoxes in the interpretation of group differences: Illustrated with medical school admission and licensing data. In C. R. Rao & S. Sinharay (Eds.), *Handbook of statistics,* vol. 26, *Psychometrics,* pp. 893–918. Amsterdam: Elsevier / North-Holland.

Wald, A. (1950). *Statistical decision functions.* New York: Wiley.

Waldman, P. (2014, September 3). How to get into an Ivy League college—guaranteed. *Bloomberg Businessweek.* Retrieved from http://www.bloomberg.com/news/articles/2014-09-04/how-to-get-into-an-ivy-league-college-guaranteed.

Walker, C., Tilley, D. S., Lockwood, S., & Walker, M. B. (2008). An innovative approach to accelerated baccalaureate education. *Nursing Education Perspectives, 29,* 347–352.

Warburton, E. C., Bugarin, R., Nuñez, A-M., & Carroll, C. D. (2001, May). *Bridging the gap: Academic preparation and postsecondary success of first-generation students* (NCES 2001-153). Washington, DC: National Center for Education Statistics.

Wechsler, H. S. (1977). *The qualified student: A history of selective college admission in America.* New York: Wiley.

Weissbourd, R. (n.d.). *Turning the tide: Inspiring concern for others and the common good through college admissions.* Harvard Graduate School of Education. Retrieved from http://mcc.gse.harvard.edu/files/gse-mcc/files/20160120_mcc_ttt _report_interactive.pdf?m=1453303517.

Weissglass, J. (1998, April 15). The SAT: Public-spirited or preserving privilege? *Education Week.* Retrieved from http://www.edweek.org/ew/articles/1998/04 /15/31weiss.h17.html.

Westrick, P. A., Le, H., Robbins, S. B., Radunzel, J. M. R., & Schmidt, F. L. (2015). College performance and retention: A meta-analysis of the predictive validities of ACT® scores, high school grades, and SES. *Educational Assessment, 20*(1), 23–45.

White, K. R. (1982).The relation between socioeconomic status and academic achievement. *Psychological Bulletin, 91,* 461–481.

Why the "4 percent solution" won't restore racial diversity at selective California campuses [Editorial]. (1999, Summer). *Journal of Blacks in Higher Education, 24,* 25–26.

Wiggins, N., & Kohen, E. S. (1971). Man vs. model of man revisited: The forecasting of graduate school success. *Journal of Personality and Social Psychology, 19,* 100–106.

Wildavsky, B. (2015, July 16). Can a Dear Cal letter get you into Berkeley? *Los Angeles Times,* A21.

Willingham, W. W. (1974). Predicting success in graduate education. *Science, 183,* 273–278.

Willingham, W. W. (1985). *Success in college: The role of personal qualities and academic ability.* New York: College Entrance Examination Board.

Willingham, W. W. (2005). Prospects for improving grades for use in admissions. In W. J. Camara & E. W. Kimmel (Eds.), *Choosing students,* pp. 127–139. Mahwah, NJ: Erlbaum.

Willingham, W. W., Pollack, J. M., & Lewis, C. (2002). Grades and test scores: Accounting for observed differences. *Journal of Educational Measurement, 39,* 1–37.

Winerip, M. (1994, February 16). Merit scholarship program faces sex bias complaint. *New York Times.* Retrieved from http://www.nytimes

.com\1994\02\16\merit-scholarship-program-faces-sex-bias-complaint .html.

Wolf, C. (2014, July 25). Op-ed: Rise of test-optional college admissions will backfire. *Digital Journal*. Retrieved from http://www.digitaljournal.com/news /politics/op-ed-rise-of-test-optional-college-admissions-will-backfire/article /392519.

Wolfle, D. (2011). Chance, or human judgment? In P. Stone (Ed.), *Lotteries in public life: A reader*, pp. 31–32. Luton: Andrews UK.

Wollan, M. (2011, September 26). A "diversity bake sale" backfires on campus. *New York Times*. Retrieved from http://www.nytimes.com/2011/09/27/us/campus -diversity-bake-sale-is-priced-by-race-and-sex.html?emc=eta1&_r=0.

Woodhouse, K. (2015, June 11). Cooper Union upheaval. *Inside Higher Ed*. Retrieved from https://www.insidehighered.com/news/2015/06/11/president -and-five-trustees-quit-amid-bitter-unrest-cooper-union.

Worland, J. C. (2011, May 11). Legacy admit rate at 30 percent. *Harvard Crimson*. Retrieved from http://www.thecrimson.com/article/2011/5/11/admissions -fitzsimmons-legacy-legacies/.

Yablon, M. (2000, October 30). Test flight: The real reason colleges are abandoning the SAT. *New Republic*, 24–25.

Young, J. W. (1993). Grade adjustment methods. *Review of Educational Research, 63*(2), 151–165.

Young, J. W. (2004). Differential validity and prediction: Race and sex differences in college admissions testing. In R. Zwick (Ed.), *Rethinking the SAT: The future of standardized testing in university admissions*, pp. 289–301. New York: RoutledgeFalmer.

Young, M. (1994). *The rise of the meritocracy*. New Brunswick, NJ: Transaction.

Zimdars, A. M. (2016). *Meritocracy and the university: Selective admission in England and the United States*. London: Bloomsbury.

Zimmerman, J. (2012, April 29). Asian-Americans, the new Jews on campus. *Chronicle of Higher Education*. Retrieved from http://chronicle.com/article /Asian-Americans-the-New-Jews/131729/.

Zumbrun, J. (2014, October 9). SAT scores and income inequality: How wealthier kids rank higher. *Wall Street Journal*. Retrieved from http://blogs .wsj.com/economics/2014/10/07/sat-scores-and-income-inequality-how -wealthier-kids-rank-higher/.

Zwick, R. (1999, December). Eliminating standardized tests in college admissions: The new affirmative action? *Phi Delta Kappan*, 320–324.

Zwick, R. (2002a). *Fair game? The use of standardized admissions tests in higher education*. New York: RoutledgeFalmer.

Zwick, R. (2002b, Winter). Picking the perfect freshman class: Balancing the academic and nonacademic goals of admissions policy. *National CrossTalk*, 13.

Zwick, R. (2002c, December). Is the SAT a "wealth test"? *Phi Delta Kappan,* 307–311.

Zwick, R. (2004). Is the SAT a "wealth test"? The link between educational achievement and socioeconomic status. In R. Zwick (Ed.), *Rethinking the SAT: The future of standardized testing in university admissions,* pp. 203–216. New York: RoutledgeFalmer.

Zwick, R. (2007a, December). Casting lots for college. Online *Education Week* commentary. Retrieved from www.edweek.org/go/zwick.

Zwick, R. (2007b). College admissions in 21st century America: The role of grades, tests, and games of chance. *Harvard Educational Review, 77,* 419–428.

Zwick, R. (2012, October). The role of admissions test scores, socioeconomic status, and high school grades in predicting college achievement. *Pensamiento Educativo: Revista de Investigación Educacional Latinoamericana,* www.pel.cl.

Zwick, R. (2013). *Disentangling the role of high school grades, SAT scores, and SES in predicting college achievement* (ETS Research Report 13-09). Princeton, NJ: Educational Testing Service.

Zwick, R. (2016, January 17). Transparency in college admissions is key to a fair policy on race. *Chronicle of Higher Education.* Retrieved from http://chronicle.com/article/Transparency-in-College/234949.

Zwick, R., & Bridgeman, B. (2014). Evaluating validity, fairness, and differential item functioning in multistage testing. In D. Yan, A. von Davier, & C. Lewis (Eds.), *Computerized multistage testing: Theory and applications,* pp. 271–284. Boca Raton, FL: CRC Press.

Zwick, R., Brown, T., & Sklar, J. C. (2004). *California and the SAT: A reanalysis of University of California admissions data.* Center for Studies in Higher Education, UC Berkeley, Research and Occasional Papers Series. Retrieved from http://repositories.cdlib.org/cshe/CSHE-8-04.

Zwick, R., & Dorans, N. J. (2016). Philosophical perspectives on fairness in educational assessment. In N. J. Dorans & L. Cook (Eds.), *Fairness in educational assessment and measurement,* pp. 267–281. New York: Routledge.

Zwick, R., & Green, J. G. (2007). New perspectives on the correlation of SAT scores, high school grades, and socioeconomic factors. *Journal of Educational Measurement, 44,* 23–45.

Zwick, R., & Himelfarb, I. (2011). The effect of high school socioeconomic status on the predictive validity of SAT scores and high school grade-point average. *Journal of Educational Measurement, 48,* 101–121.

# Acknowledgments

It is truly a challenge to thank all those who made this book possible. I appreciate the generous support of Educational Testing Service, which allowed me to conduct research for the book during my workday. I am also grateful for the contributions of many ETS staff members. In particular, my thanks go to John Mazzeo and Ida Lawrence for their backing of the project, to Lei Ye, Steven Isham, and Zhumei Guo, data analysts *par excellence*, and to the terrific ETS library staff, who helped out with innumerable reference requests. I'm also thankful to other ETSers who provided reviews or supplied needed information: James Carlson, Neil Dorans, Shelby Haberman, Michael Kane, David Klieger, Donald Powers, Amy Schmidt, Elizabeth Stone, Peter van Rijn, and especially Michael Zieky. I am indebted to my editors at Harvard University Press, Elizabeth Knoll and Andrew Kinney, for their guidance and support, and to Elizabeth for proposing the name "Who Gets In?" I'm also appreciative of all the other members of the HUP team—copyeditors, proofreaders, designers, and publicists—who have contributed to this project, and to the two reviewers commissioned by the publisher, who provided significant and helpful recommendations—Patricia Gándara of the Civil Rights Project at UCLA and an anonymous individual. I am grateful to the many others who responded to requests for information, including Kenneth Bozer, Wayne Camara, Elise Christopher, Matthew Gaertner, Deborah Harris, Robert Mare, Peter Pashley, Christine Phillips, Rassan Salandy, Neal Schmitt, Emily Shaw, Jeffrey Strohl, and Robert Toutkoushian. I thank them, as well as any others I may have inadvertently omitted. Finally, I reserve my deepest appreciation for my two most dedicated readers—my husband, Gregg Zachritz, and my friend Bella DePaulo—who offered perceptive reviews of every chapter, sage advice, and much-needed encouragement throughout the project.

# Index

Academic indexes for use in admissions, 79–81, 98–99, 110–112, 131, 191. *See also* Composite of high school grades and test scores

ACT (test), 3, 5–6, 13, 50, 52, 54, 55–56, 73; association with college performance, 37–38, 42, 81, 89, 96–98, 151; ethnic and socioeconomic score disparities, 8, 35–36, 61, 89, 140; test preparation, 66, 67, 68. *See also* Admissions test scores

ACT, Inc. (company), 54, 55–56, 68, 74, 196

Admissions test content, 3, 9–10, 53, 54–55, 61–63, 73, 196

Admissions test scores: as predictors of college performance (*see* ACT [test]: association with college performance; SAT: association with college performance); in ELS (*see* ELS:2002 analysis of admissions); misuse of, 73–74, 195–196; properties of, 8, 9–10, 35–36, 54, 55, 59–66, 73–74, 87–89; role in the admissions process, 6, 7, 8–10, 21–23, 25, 47, 50, 66–68, 128–129, 140–142, 195–196

Affirmative action: in ELS analyses, 112–115, 121–125, 189–192; race-based, 1, 8, 87, 100–108, 193–195; race-neutral alternatives, 10–11, 46–47, 112, 126–128, 136, 138–139, 153, 181–182; socioeconomic-status-based, 86, 109–112

African Americans, 5, 24, 29, 35, 36, 51, 105–106, 132; in ELS analyses, 13, 14, 19, 113, 115, 155, 169, 187–188, 190, 192; in previous research, 92–93, 109, 116, 129–130, 134, 136, 148, 149–151, 154, 167. *See also* Underrepresented minorities

American Indians. *See* Native Americans

Applications Quest, 181–182

Asian Americans. *See* Asians

Asians, 5, 10, 22, 35, 36, 45–46, 102, 119, 152; in ELS analyses, 13, 14, 19–20, 69, 76, 121, 155, 160, 168, 171, 184, 190; in previous research, 35, 86, 93, 116, 130, 132, 134, 136, 151

Astin, Alexander, 162–163, 170

Athletes, 11, 115–116, 117–120, 145, 193, 195

Atkinson, Richard, 9, 10, 21, 52–53, 88

*Bakke* case. See *University of California Regents v. Bakke*

Belasco, Andrew, 136–137, 141

Bias: in grades, 42, 58–60; in prediction of college GPA, 39–40, 91–94, 94–96; in tests, 2, 23, 35–36, 39–40, 59–60, 92

Binet, Alfred, 53

Blacks. *See* African Americans

Bok, Derek, 10, 31, 92, 109

Bowen, William, 31, 42, 71, 92, 97–98, 109, 110–111, 114, 116, 118, 188, 197

Breland, Hunter, 40–41

Brennan, Robert T., 59

Brigham, Carl, 51–53, 56, 57, 78–79

Buchmann, Claudia, 67

Carnevale, Anthony P., 129–130, 167–168, 217n26, 218n29